Black Identity Viewed from a Barber's Chair

WILLIAM E. CROSS JR.

Black Identity Viewed from a Barber's Chair

Nigrescence and Eudaimonia

TEMPLE UNIVERSITY PRESS
Philadelphia / Rome / Tokyo

TEMPLE UNIVERSITY PRESS
Philadelphia, Pennsylvania 19122
tupress.temple.edu

Copyright © 2021 by Temple University—Of The Commonwealth System of Higher Education
All rights reserved
Published 2021

Library of Congress Cataloging-in-Publication Data

Names: Cross, William E., 1940– author.
Title: Black identity viewed from a barber's chair : nigrescence and eudaimonia / William E. Cross Jr.
Description: Philadelphia : Temple University Press, [2021] | Includes bibliographical references and index. | Summary: "This book examines the pathway leading to black consciousness, details how black identity is transacted and performed, offers a critique of the deficit perspective on black life, and sheds new light on the way slaves raised children to explain the psychological strengths many ex-slaves exhibited as adults following slavery's end"—Provided by publisher.
Identifiers: LCCN 2020029895 (print) | LCCN 2020029896 (ebook) | ISBN 9781439921050 (cloth) | ISBN 9781439921067 (paperback) | ISBN 9781439921074 (pdf)
Subjects: LCSH: African Americans—Race identity. | African Americans—Psychology. | Blacks—Race identity. | Blacks—Psychology.
Classification: LCC E185.625 .C758 2021 (print) | LCC E185.625 (ebook) | DDC 305.896/073—dc23
LC record available at https://lccn.loc.gov/2020029895
LC ebook record available at https://lccn.loc.gov/2020029896

9 8 7 6 5 4 3 2 1

To Tuere Binta Cross, my daughter;

also, my two favorite girlfriends, Michelle Fine and Helen Neville;

my late brother, "Chuckie";

and my late friend who I miss everyday—Badi G. Foster

Contents

	Preface and Acknowledgments	ix
1	The Barbershop Bias	1
2	Nigrescence Revisited: The Models	19
3	Nigrescence, Part 2: Issues	43
4	Double-Consciousness and the Performance of Identity	77
5	Interrogating the Deficit Perspective	105
6	Slavery, Trauma, and Resilience	137
	References	157
	Index	171

Preface and Acknowledgments

Inclusion of the word "barbershop" in the title of this book emerged during discussions with my mentee of three years, Jessica Reinhardt, and an advanced graduate student from the University of Denver Counseling Psychology Program, Mackenzie Jessen. At the time we interacted, practically the entire faculty in Counseling Psychology concluded Mackenzie is brilliant and likely to become an exceptional counselor. I invited her to lunch to convey my observations about her potential, and the next thing I knew I dumped half of my life's history in her lap. She quietly created a warm, accepting, nonjudgmental atmosphere, and I guess I needed to talk! Writing this book was on my mind, and I shared a childhood experience regarding a barbershop on the South Side of Chicago. The barbers and the men passing in and out seemed so normal, yet, in graduate studies, the readings and lectures presumed the men to be self-hating and pathological. This memory was part of a larger discussion dealing with the drive to research and construct a counternarrative to the deficit orientation propagated by Mamie and Kenneth Clark (1939) and E. Franklin Frazier (1939). Their conclusions about black self-hatred and culturally backward black families did not sit well with my black consciousness, which erupted in the aftermath of Martin Luther King Jr.'s assassination. Thereafter, no matter what portion of the draft of this book that she read, Mackenzie never failed to nudge me about putting in a statement capturing the barbershop memory.

Jessica and I took dinner to celebrate her new appointment at Temple University and to clink our water glasses for what we both agreed was a fulfilling mentor-mentee relationship. After ordering wine, she began to give me feedback on one of the chapters of this book. The conversation began to focus on the barbershop memory, and she blurted out—"Oh, your barbershop bias." Hearing her say the phrase out loud struck me like a bolt of lightning, and the next day I changed the title to include "The Barbershop Bias." One of the external reviewers for Temple University Press suggested that the word "bias" had too negative a connotation, thus the title was changed to read: *Black Identity Viewed from a Barber's Chair*.

The weekend following the dinner with Jessica, the annual Denver Cherry Creek Art Festival was held, and, for the third year in a row, the works of the Chicago-based artist-photographer Clifton Henri were on display. Stepping inside his booth, I was immediately drawn to a photo of three elderly black men holding forth at a black barbershop, and, as Chicago is his home, it was taken on the South Side. He titled the work *The Teacher's Lounge*.

I purchased two copies of the barbershop scene as gifts for Jessica and Mackenzie, attaching a note about my decision to include "barbershop" in the title. Mackenzie, her husband, and I performed a private mini ceremony in hanging the artwork on a featured wall in their recently purchased home.

After reading an early version of the chapter on Nigrescence, Kahlea Hunt-Khabir, an M.A. candidate in higher education, suggested the manuscript could benefit from additional observations on black identity made by black feminists. Coincidentally, this was the focus of the last three brunch conversations I had had with the phenomenal Reiland Rabaka, a black scholar who, at forty-five years of age, has authored eleven books and counting, most on W.E.B. Du Bois. In prepping for his new graduate seminar on Black Lives Matter (BLM), Rabaka found himself engaging, with renewed appreciation, black feminist literature. Over brunch we compared notes on how the messages contained in the writings of bell hooks, Patricia Hill Collins, Maya Angelou, and Shani Jamila and the sisters spearheading the BLM movement helped us both see, feel, hear, and interpret with greater precision, understanding, and depth of knowledge. Consequently, Kahlea's feedback to me was readily received and incorporated in the next draft, about which she expressed approval. Thank you, Kahlea.

One of the departments in the School of Education at the University of Denver is Library Science. The ubiquity of ProQuest aside, there is nothing like the support of a competent library scientist! Some searches covering 1880–1930 constituted a *Columbo*-like mystery, and my partner in crime was Bridget Farrell, whose dogged, tenacious attitude, combined with highly refined search skills, helped me chase down references with cryptic location markers.

I am a hunt-and-peck typist, which means every now and then I "hit" the wrong keys, causing the computer to insert a line, jump multiple spaces, or some other "stuff" for which I have no knowledge on how to correct or delete. No problem—Gabrielle Reimer was always there to ease my anxiety and cause me to smile, while deleting whatever mistake I had unintentionally created. Gabrielle also proofread the entire manuscript and constructed the two figures found in Chapters 2 and 3. This warm, engaging, thoroughly competent, and mild-mannered assistant is a jewel, period. Family became involved in proofreading the revised manuscript, and warm thanks are extended to my niece, Nikka Cooper, and Tuere Binta Cross, my daughter.

I cannot work at home and Dean Karen Riley made it possible to write the book on campus in an office shared with Kathy Green. While not a neat freak, Kathy nonetheless showed amazing patience when my stuff spilled over onto her section of the shared space. Sorry, Kathy! One of the nice things about writing on campus is that from time to time I could wander from my desk and go visit, annoy, and interrupt Maria Riva, Jesse Owen, or Tara Raines. Most of the time I used our exchanges to practice the wording of a sentence I was having trouble bringing to life on paper.

I shared a chapter with James Jones and Michelle Fine and am deeply grateful for their feedback. I am trained in social psychology, but early on I explored clinical psychology at Roosevelt University—just enough to make me overconfident in offering clinically related interpretations. I tried to right myself by auditing a course on infant and early child development taught by the amazing Jeanine Coleman. Her lectures and required readings helped me better comprehend all that goes into the attachment experience between infant and mother, as discussed in Chapter 6.

I am profoundly indebted to my daughter, Tuere Binta Cross, whose studies in social work at NYU and years of clinical practice have resulted in exposure to all manner of human worry, anxiety, stress, pain, and redemption, resulting in a depth of knowledge about the human condition that is extraordinary. Binta pulled me from several intellectual sinkholes and helped me reshape simplistic notions into revised statements that are now textured, compelling, sensitive, complex, honest, and authentic. Truth be told, her contributions to my thinking on slavery, trauma, and resilience should have made her the coauthor of Chapter 6, a credit she fought hard against, claiming it would distract from my contributions! I was determined to write a book offering a counternarrative to both the Clarks, and their racial preference doll studies, and Frazier, and his book on broken black families. This meant taking positions likely to arouse the guardians of the deficit perspective. Binta and I worried about being labeled romantics, yet we pushed forward, having in mind the goal of deliberately annoying, disrupting, and overturning the status quo to show that the biggest nemesis to black uplift has always been socioeconomic oppression combined with systemic racism, and not some mysterious lingering effects of slavery.

Finally, while not directly related to the production of this work, I want to thank those who over the years helped me become a better scholar and human being. This list is long: James Turner and the Cornell University Africana Studies Program, Mon Cochran, Gerald Jackson, Michelle Fine and the students and faculty of the CUNY Critical Psychology Program, Yasser Payne, Hollie Jones, Peony Fhagen, Michelle Donovan, Frank Worrell, Beverly Vandiver, Thomas

Parham, the late Joe White, Maria Riva, Little Margaret Sponsler, the late Badi Foster, Robert Harris, Bailey Jackson, Linda James Myers, Wade Boykin, James Jones, AJ Anderson, Linda Clark, Dean Karen Riley, Helen Neville, the late Urie Bronfenbrenner plus his wife and daughter Katherine, Margaret B. Spencer, Nikki Carrier, Jessica Reinhardt, Mackenzie Jessen, Ted and Reggie Short, Sam Blair, Roger Kritz, Barry and Jill Golden, my late brother Charles Cross, Mary Pat Cross, Ashleigh and Leigh Cross, my sisters Charlene Cross and Judy Cross, Janet Bennett and all associated with the Summer Institute for Intercultural Communication (SIIC), Rameri Moukam and the staff of the Pattigift Therapy Center (Birmingham, UK), Rita Hardiman, Charmaine Wijeyesinghe, William Hall, students and faculty in the Counseling Psychology and Higher Education Departments at the University of Denver, Leon Spencer and the Georgia Southern Annual Cross Cultural Conference, Robert Sellers and the MMRI Research Group out of the University of Michigan, and everyone associated with APA-Division 45. I cannot fail to mention Misty Monroe and her unapologetically black proclamation. Without the love and support of my daughter, Tuere Binta Cross, and my former wife, Dawn Cross, nothing about me would be positive.

A Final Expression of Thanks

For this last statement I have struggled mightily to find the right words. In the early days of black studies, there was a messianic dimension. Scholars and students alike felt a moral obligation to the black community to, first, disrupt ongoing dehumanizing narratives and, second, produce new works speaking truth to power. My time on earth is fading fast, thus I want to say out loud how grateful I am for being allowed to be an advocate of black studies. I am not a spiritual person; nonetheless, I feel blessed and thank the community from the bottom of my heart for its guidance, support, and patience. I hope this work rewards your faith in me. It probably falls short of expectations, but it represents the best I can do. I have lived a wonderful life made possible by the joy of first advocating and then living Africana.

Black Identity Viewed from a Barber's Chair

1

The Barbershop Bias

Preference and Distorting Black Humanity

I park my car in Lot L, the parking structure nestled alongside the School of Law at the University of Denver. Closing the car door, first thoughts concern whether to purchase coffee and a scone from the law school café, or the one managed by Sister Kim and Brother Donald in the student center. The coffee is the same; however, Donald bathes the air with jazz and an occasional hip-hop tune, and the combination of their brown faces and smooth jazz turns the taste of regular medium roast into something special. The walk between Lot L and the entrance to the Morgridge College of Education is periodically interrupted by my new friend and her mother, as they walk toward the Ricks Center for Gifted Children, where she is a student. Margaret, a white preschooler, shares the first name of my late mother—Margaret Carter Cross. Little Margaret has found a special place in my heart by stirring up memories of play time with Binta, my daughter, when my wife, Dawn, Binta, and I lived in Ithaca, New York, and I was a faculty member at the Cornell University African Studies and Research Center, then headed by the cultural visionary James Turner.

Turner and I met in the summer of 1969, while he was a graduate student and leader of the black student uprising at Northwestern University. At the time, I was the director of a local community center—Evanston West Side Service Center—for which I designed and instituted projects and activities meant to inject blackness into the consciousness of key leaders of Evanston's black community. In many ways, I was only a few steps ahead of the people I was trying to convert. The weekends found me admiring the *Wall of Respect* mural on the South Side of Chicago (Alkalimat, Crawford, & Zorach, 2017) and attending open meetings sponsored by the Organization of Black American Culture (OBAC), during which Phil Cochran played an African thumb piano, while various speakers mesmerized those in attendance with messages of consciousness and commitment. It was like an advanced seminar in blackness taught by the OBAC leadership, which included the poet Don L. Lee (Haki R. Madhubuti); the editor of the monthly periodical *Black World*, Hoyt Fuller; and Jeff Donaldson, the future head of the Department of Art at Howard University; to mention a few (Alkalimat, Crawford, & Zorach, 2017). With inspiration garnered from the images of black heroes enshrined in the *Wall of Respect* mural and my notes taken at the OBAC meeting, the following Monday found me formulating activities and programs to be carried out by the center staff. The OBAC leadership stressed love and patience, as those who have yet to commit themselves to blackness will be afraid and extremely hesitant. Subsequently, our strategy was to start small and nurture consciousness here and there, with the hope that unity would follow soon thereafter. Included was the short-lived House of Blackness, which sold black books, African statues, and trinkets—all "imported" from the South Side of Chicago.

When James Turner and his crew from Northwestern got wind of my activities, they made it a point to visit the center and check out what was going on. By the time Turner took over the directorship of the Africana Center at Cornell, my article "The Negro-to-Black-Conversion Experience" had appeared in the July 1971 issue of *Black World* (formerly *Negro Digest*). When I hit the job market, Turner *forever* changed my intellectual future by granting me an academic appointment in black studies rather than my other choice of joining a white-dominated mainstream psychology department. My years at Africana made the imagination and production of *Shades of Black* possible (Cross, 1991), a work synthesizing material from Africana studies and mainstream psychology.

Turner, along with A. Wade Boykin—at the time a member of the Cornell Psychology Department—helped paint my consciousness black. Before moving on to Howard University, Boykin, Anderson Franklin, and Frank Yates—all black psychologists—organized a series of conferences on empirical research in black psychology (Boykin, Franklin, & Yates, 1980). The empirical conferences represented a counternarrative, of sorts, to the clinical-praxis emphasis of the newly organized Association of Black Psychologists, which was dominated by practitioners, many of whom held clinical positions that made it difficult to impossible to conduct research, given the time required of practice and interventions. Persons attending the empirical conferences left with a highly technical appreciation of the benefits of taking the black experience seriously; we saw ourselves fusing mainstream methodologies with theories grounded in a black perspective. Unlike the evolving Afrocentric movement, which rejected conclusions about the black experience derived from studies based on mainstream psychological approaches, our "empirical" clan saw ourselves not unlike jazz artists. Just as jazz is premised on the basic melodic chord structure of European music theory—this being true for even the most dissonant of jazz artists such as Thelonious Monk or Cecil Taylor—likewise black scholars could discover truths about blackness using methodologies commonplace to Western psychology. Compared to Miles, Monk, Ella, or Coltrane, we had faith in our ability—through imaginative *research designs* and culture-infused *interpretation of results*—to confirm and validate psychological truths about the black experience. One could say we were applying what today is called a critical race perspective in our application of mainstream methodologies to research about black people. As an aside, this tradition of empirical black psychology continues through the advocacy of Kevin Cokley and Germine Awad (2013), despite their association with African Psychology, many advocates for which argue against the value of empiricism.

Returning to Little Margaret, she was on my mind as I strolled through the arts and crafts kiosks set up during the holiday season at Grand Central Station in New York City. In one, the craftsperson displayed small cloth dolls and accompanying dresses that could be wrapped in a knapsack configuration, enveloping both the doll and the dresses. When I returned to Denver, I placed one of the dolls as a gift in the mailbox, addressed to Margaret's mom, with a note indicating that the doll's name was Binta, because her brown facial color and beautiful dresses reminded me of my daughter. A few days later, Margaret's mom reported back that, in preparing for sleep, Margaret now arranged her two favorite friends so that her doll Claire was on the far left of the bed, the Binta doll was in the middle, and Margaret slept right of center. A few weeks passed, and Margaret's mom—now several months pregnant and showing—popped into my office to relate a wonderful story—the kind Art Linkletter used to pull from the untarnished minds of little ones on his television show. Tests showed that cooking in her mom's tummy was a little boy, and, the night before, Margaret approached her mom to ask an incredible question: "Can we have a black baby? Can my brother be a black baby?"

Little Margaret's situation reminds one of the choices children grappled with while participating in racial preference doll studies conducted in the 1930s by the famous husband-and-wife psychologist team, Kenneth B. and Mamie Clark (Clark & Clark, 1939). The Clarks were among those who believed racial segregation resulted in psychological damage, such as a tendency for Negro children—Margaret's age—to evidence a preference for white in addition to using pejorative language ("ugly") to describe brown dolls meant to represent black infants—that is, meant to represent themselves! Going further and within the same historical period (circa the late 1940s to early 1960s), two psychiatrists conducted in-depth psychoanalytic interviews with a cluster of working-class and middle-class black adults and concluded that what begins in youth as racial preference ends in adulthood as low self-esteem and damage to one's self-concept (see Kardiner & Ovesey, 1951). In their book *The Mark of Oppression*, Kardiner and Ovesey presented this state as the point of departure for understanding the *average* black person, with low self-esteem being the norm for Negroes living anywhere in the United States, regardless of social class. Negro psychopathology as the "norm" was recently revisited and defended in an exhaustive and erudite summary by Joe L. Rempson (2016).

Critique of the Clarks' racial preference study, which had been conducted in 1939, was delayed in large measure because findings from the study became part of the legal rationale used by the Supreme Court in the construction of its 1954 decision declaring school segregation unconstitutional. To scrutinize the racial preference research was therefore considered the same as challenging the Court's decision. While the scientific method depends on the interrogation of ongoing research, where findings from study X are then challenged or given added credence by follow-up research and so on and so on, linkage of the Clark studies to the elimination of legal segregation resulted in their work becoming untouchable and thus sacrosanct. "Recognizing that the eyes of history were on them, the National Association for the Advancement of Colored People (NAACP) trial team explored innovative ways to prove their case. . . . Robert Carter devoted considerable personal time developing the testimony of a young unheralded psychology professor at the City College of New York, Dr. Kenneth Clark, who had conducted cutting-edge psychological studies on the impact of racial segregation on black children" (Gergel, 2019, p. 225).

Black Studies and the Search for Something More

Many of the scholars who were instrumental in founding black studies were the progeny of black working-class families, and we took it as a personal affront that the extant literature depicted black people in general and the black working class in particular as self-loathing and pathological. Our mindset was not to summarily dismiss previous findings; rather, we thought new research would show that the racial self-hatred, mark of oppression, and deficit tropes went too far, resulting in caricatures rather than three-dimensional depictions of black individuals and black families. Which is to say, our own family members and friends.

Personally, I was driven by my "barbershop bias." After I was born at Provident Hospital, the first African American–owned-and-operated hospital in America, Mom and I were transported to the family's apartment in a cab, as Dad never learned to drive and thus there was never a family car. Originally, the first male child was to be named Charles Frank Cross, but after three daughters—the third named Charlene as a replacement for Charles Frank—Dad took no chances, and I was named William E. Cross Jr. Our address was 6601 South St. Lawrence, part of the Englewood/Woodlawn neighborhood on Chicago's South Side, and three blocks from Emmett Till's home at 6427 South St. Lawrence. As I grew older, my sisters took me to a barbershop on Sixty-Seventh Street for my haircuts. In the following recollection, my image of the decor may be off, but the interactional issues are accurate. The shop was long and narrow, with rectangular black-and-white floor tiles connecting to five-sided parquet wall tiles of the same colors that extended halfway up the wall, ending at the base of panoramic mirrors. The mirrors and lights obviously helped the barbers monitor the progress of each customer's haircut, and in addition somehow made the entrance of each customer a special event. At least one of the barbers knew the nickname of every entering customer, and, after its elocution, there followed banter full of rhymes and signifying centered on the customer's identity and reputation. I sometimes fantasized my entrance when I became an adult, and with what nickname the shop would christen me.

Because of my small size, a child's seat was set atop the adult chair, and this lift gave me a dramatic, unobtrusive view of everyone's movement, customers and barbers alike. My experiences at the barbershop in the presence of ordinary black men caused me to develop a "barbershop bias," and adding to this bias were the normal black men who showed up at our front door, calling out the names of my older sisters whom they sought to court and charm. When I was a sophomore and junior in high school, my black role models drove buses for the Chicago Transit Authority (CTA), worked at the post office, rode the back of garbage trucks, and what few professionals there were seemed beyond my reach. Only years later, following blackenization of my consciousness through Nigrescence, did I venture toward becoming an academic. Consequently, as an adolescent I had my sights on becoming a steady Eddie worker, like the working-class men who dated my older sisters, such as Sam Adams. My sister Dee married Sam, a bus driver for the CTA, and they had a small, clean, one-story house, and a cool car. It was Sam who taught me how to lovingly extract an LP record from its cover case by first inserting the index finger over the hole in the middle of the record while simultaneously gripping the outer edge with my thump, a maneuver keeping the natural oils from one's skin from ever contacting and gumming-up the record grooves. I "blame" Sam for my very expensive audiophile hobby. When Sam and Dee ventured to see Ramsey Lewis at the SRO Club on Clark Street or arranged a barbecue outing for the black football players from the Chicago Cardinals professional football team, Sam would go into his bedroom still wearing his CTA uniform and then reappear, as a handsome brother, dressed to the nines. Of course, I could say the same about the many black women to whom I was exposed through my sisters and my mom. Two of my sisters were part of the army of women making up the support staff for a renowned black law firm based in downtown Chicago, who, like the other normal women of their day, spent an inordinate amount of time keeping the paws of the male bosses at bay. Truth be told, my mindset, as an adolescent, was highly gendered, so my recollections are slanted toward the world of males, with women in the background.

The Search for Something Missed or Overlooked

As a new faculty member at Cornell's Africana Center, I was charged by Director James Turner with developing the outline for the Africana course on black families, and I planned to cover the established works of E. Franklin Frazier and the Clarks. However, as their analysis did not capture the men in the barbershop, the Cardinal football players, nor those who courted my sisters, in addition to the women at the law offices, I had to reach beyond the social scientific literature and embrace the voices of Zora Neale Hurston, Amos Wilson, and Lorraine Hansberry. In the process I also rediscovered W.E.B. Du

Bois. Truth be told, had Du Bois's depiction of black people been adopted more so than Frazier's problematic and distorting tropes, our current understanding of the actual legacy of slavery would be more advanced and accurate. Du Bois and black literary figures, more so than Frazier or the Clarks, depicted black men and women with integrity and wholesomeness. Such is the origin of my barbershop bias and the motivation it triggered for what I came to call "the search for something missed or overlooked."

As a black psychologist, I joined with others in trying to determine how the Clark doll racial preference studies (they conducted more than one) distorted and oversimplified, because we knew from personal experience that many black people were normal, thus our motivation to modify the deficit perspective. Ironically, the process was kicked off by a research publication appearing in one of the top mainstream academic journals sponsored by the American Psychological Association (APA). In 1976, W. Curtis Banks startled the research community with a reanalysis of a cluster of racial preference studies, showing that, statistically speaking, black children's doll choices fit a pattern of randomness or "chance" behavior, as in an "Eeny, meeny, miny, moe" orientation (Banks, 1976). However, rather than random behavior, another interpretation for the "split" choice pattern is a performance of biculturalism, wherein the children are wanting to display favorable attitudes toward *both* preferences (Cross, 1983). That black children are socialized to become biculturally oriented and white children more monoculturally focused was explored in a study of black, white, and white ethnic families guided by the theoretical writings of Urie Bronfenbrenner (1979) on the ecology of human development. The study of black and white families incorporated an identity component designed to reveal the racial-cultural messaging embedded in the ecology of everyday mother-child interactions and activities. An identity interview recorded the TV shows watched with the child and/or programs playing in the background, types of music listened to, types of human figures found among the child's playthings, the history of the child's name or nickname, stories read to the child, the books the child was allowed to play with, and much more. The scoring categories were black culture, white culture, and general American culture, and, all told, an identity score from 0 to as high as 22 was possible. The results showed white mothers presenting the world in *monoracial* terms, and, using this information to predict racial preference, white children would be expected to evidence a monoracial white doll preference pattern.

Turning to the results for black families, 21 percent of the activities described by the black mothers had, on average, a black culture emphasis, and 79 percent a white-general American undertone. This "split" cultural pattern was all the more evident with the doll-human figure count. Typically, 40 percent of the dolls found in black homes were black and 60 percent were white. Regardless of the activity in question, the *person or persons* participating in the activity with the child were black 90-95 percent of the time. Thus, some variant of a *black perspective* was operating in the ecological presentation of the "world" to the child, whether the cultural messaging concerned black, white, or general American activities, places, or things. *Black children raised in such a fashion can be expected to display an attraction to both black and white dolls in the context of a racial preference study.* The resulting "split" is better understood as an evolving bicultural frame rather than confused or random behavior, as suggested by Banks (1976). Long ago Du Bois spoke of the African American need to develop "double consciousness," and, rather than pathology, racial preference findings may tap into a child's evolving understanding that in being black in America, one must come to terms with the power and, yes, beauty of things white.

In addition, those "ugly" doll comments expressed during the doll study are transformed—over the course of a black child's exposure to black culture—into a *capacity to play the dozens of elocutions of signifying monkey rhymes before an audience of one's peers on the school playground.* Through play, humor, and intense communal jesting, black people prepare themselves for the hatred and disdain spewing from the white psyche. Signifying involves games—serious interactional games—where, on the one hand, an audience helps a person feel the type of intense, heated, stressful pressure linked to encounters with racism, and, on the other hand, the same audience offers criticism and feedback for the way the person *proposes* to act, respond, and survive encounters with racism. Practice at staying cool when under pressure is a theme embedded in many hip-hop lyrics (Majors & Billson, 1993). Today, equating racial preference with deep structure personality constitutes a *simplistic* psychological model for explicating black behavior. The research reviewed above clearly shows that in the search for blackness, there is something beyond racial preference. Racial preference and psychoanalytic studies such as the *The Mark of Oppression* are pillars of the more comprehensive theory known as the deficit perspective on black culture, the origin of which can be traced to the 1939 publication of E. Franklin Frazier's seminal work on the black family.

E. Franklin Frazier and the Deficit Perspective

Between 1919 and 1930, the second wave of the Ku Klux Klan was successful in spreading the doctrine of residential and school segregation throughout the United States (Pegram, 2011). President Woodrow Wilson did his part by embracing the logic of the vile racist film *The Birth of a Nation* and instituting racial segregation within federal offices, modeling the policy eventually enacted across all facets of everyday American life—North and South (Wolgemuth, 1959). Writing in the late 1930s, E. Franklin Frazier documented what, at the time, appeared to be a dramatic rise in black juvenile delinquency to make two points: first, that blacks were adjusting poorly to life in northern urban centers; and, second, that "damaged" black family structures were churning out poorly socialized youth, and "ineffective" socialization processes were understood to be a negative legacy of slavery. Frazier completed his doctoral studies at the University of Chicago, and his adviser was considered the leading expert on experiences of white ethnic migrants—for example, Italians, Jews, and the Irish. At the time Frazier was conducting his research in Chicago, the city was literally under siege from the activities of Irish and Italian gangs, culminating in the horrific Saint Valentine's Day Massacre on February 14, 1929. Despite the fact that white ethnic crime and white ethnic social disorganization was rampant, Frazier and the black community in general were up against the commonplace social perceptions that black people were biologically inferior. Anthony M. Platt notes that:

> When Frazier began his research on Afro-American families, most of the available studies presented a gloomy picture of widespread family disorganization and sexual immorality. The prevailing literature assumed that Afro-Americans were either inherently or culturally incapable of being assimilated into "Western civilization." . . . Frazier explicitly set out to repudiate these racist interpretations and to demolish stereotypes about the monolithic nature of the black family. (A.M. Platt, 1971, p. 137)

In point of fact, Frazier's analysis covers intact as well as broken families, families of the *lumpenproletariat* as well as the middle class; however, it was his description and analysis of black urban-based poor families for which he is remembered. Foundational to his interpretations was the role of socioeconomic factors and forces—not race and eugenics. However, even though he was a dedicated socialist who lost academic positions because he was considered too radical (T. Platt, 1991), he is "blamed" for having constructed an *essentialist* explanation of black "difference" that over time became as damning in its social implications as genetic suppositions.

The "Must Be" Hypothesis

Frazier constructed a deficit perspective based on the "must be" hypothesis. Frazier's frame of reference about black people was heavily influenced by none other than Robert Ezra Park, who for nine years was secretary to Booker T. Washington at the Tuskegee Institute. Park thought Africans were biologically inferior and that whatever human capacity they possessed when in Africa was forever destroyed during capture, transport, and enslavement. Subsequently, exiting slavery, the ex-slaves were illiterate, destitute, and poor but also "damaged" in ways hard to define. This added factor was theorized by Park's most famous graduate student, E. Franklin Frazier, as the "legacy of slavery," and its analogue was the *deficit perspective* on black culture and family life. In effect, he argued that "cultural distortions" *must be* accounted for in addition to any damage to blacks linked to social class. Thus, in studying black people, whether poor or middle class, one might be able to isolate socioeconomic dynamics; however, in the final analysis, the negative effects of slavery *must be* added to the equation. From this perspective, black poverty, as an example, can never be equated with white poverty, because black poverty incorporates not only behavior, social attitudes, and ideas shared with other poor people, but, in addition, dynamics above and beyond that are explained by socioeconomic status (SES). This added factor—unique to black people—this *legacy of slavery*, if you will, made black poverty different, intractable, and resistant to intervention. This presumed added factor helped to *essentialize the discourse on blackness* in ways that made it possible to put black inferiority back on the table, while, at the same time, allowing one to declare oneself not a racist when pointing out this legacy. Frazier would say as much about black elites in *The Black Bourgeoisie* (Frazier, 1957). Inevitably, such an emphasis eventually led to a distorted victim-blame analysis and a tendency to underplay, if not make invisible, the role of systemic racism that, in point of fact, made black poverty seem as though it was something self-inflicted. Blacks were seen as their own worst enemy.

Over time, this added feature came to be known as the *deficit perspective on black life*. This assumption that slavery left an indelible mark on the soul of black people is a pillar of Frazier's work on the black poor, as well as foundational to the Moynihan Report on black families; clearly embedded in *The Mark of Oppression* by Kardiner and Ovesey (1951) as well as the logic behind racial preference studies; reinvigorated in Joe L. Rempson's narrative on problems facing black urban youth in 2019; and the cornerstone of Joy DeGruy's narrative on post traumatic slave syndrome (DeGruy Leary, 2005). I have lost track of the number of times black graduate students have formulated research proposals where the point of departure was presumed psychological damage traceable to slavery. That is, there "must be" something wrong with black people.

A major objective of black studies was and remains the disruption and contestation of the deficit model, in some cases by constructing counternarratives—an example being the earlier discussion of racial preference as biculturalism. Searching for counternarratives, one is immediately confronted with the 100 percent evil trope. It is generally assumed slavery was 100 percent evil to the point that even a slight adjustment to this trope puts one at risk of being accused of romanticism. Yet, none other than W.E.B. Du Bois put the spotlight on ex-slaves who, while born and raised in slavery, recorded personal achievements as ex-slaves that defy the logic of the 100 percent evil trope. Human beings who, as adults, recorded uplift within a modest time period after exiting slavery force us to consider that in the midst of an otherwise evil system, the slave community fashioned a positive ecology of human development that made it possible for mothers and infants to accomplish the fundamental foundation for humanization—infant-mother attachment followed by a protracted period of positive child development resulting in slave youth and young adults who exhibited positive personality traits and high levels of interpersonal competence. While these psychological strengths were first put to use in completing/fulfilling the demands/instructions made by their owners, such strengths were *portable* in the sense that, once emancipated, the ex-slaves were free to employ these same psychological assets in the enactment of their wishes and dreams after exiting slavery. Such a figure is part of my family tree—Hamilton Hatter (Caldwell, 1923). He spent his first nine years as a child in slavery, and the only way one can explain the magnitude of his accomplishments in his adult life as an educator and community leader is to backtrack and pinpoint his early socialization as a slave child by his mother, male and female fictive kin, and the slave community.

We take for granted that Frederick Douglass and Booker T. Washington exhibited any number of positive psychological assets, but they are generally viewed as exceptional cases, with limited generalizability to the experiences of most ex-slaves. Hamilton Hatter and others like him call into question the exceptionalism thesis. The deficit perspective distorts our ability to comprehend that an unknown percentage of ex-slaves walked out of slavery with psychological assets. The slave community fashioned child socialization practices, despite the otherwise horrific dynamics of the slave enterprise, and the effectiveness of these practices is revealed in the many positive and accomplished ex-slaves who burst on the scene during the first twelve years of Reconstruction (Gates, 2019). Furthermore, ex-slaves who were themselves illiterate, poor, with communication skills centered on Ebonics rather than standard English, nevertheless raised children who became highly successful within mainstream society (Du Bois, 1924/2007). This volume deconstructs the deficit perspective and ends by offering a counternarrative showing that the slaves and slave community did more to forge and then protect black humanity than it is generally given credit for. A summary of the chapters follows.

Summary of Chapters 2–5

Although the Internet had yet to be invented, radio and television reportage of the assassination of Martin Luther King Jr. was received by black people with amazing simultaneity, regardless of where they lived. Chapter 2 opens with a review of four identity-change models crafted by four different observers positioned at four different cities across the United States. I present material showing that black consciousness, triggered by King's murder, unfolded in stages, and the four authors, without collaboration, described the same process, despite the fact that their observations were made in four different corners of the nation: Los Angeles, Boston, Chicago, and Pittsburgh. In addition, although the four observers received their doctorates in psychology at different institutions, the curriculum at each included comprehensive exposure to transpersonal psychology, stressing how higher consciousness unfolds in multiple stages. I argue that Nigrescence models are, in effect, extensions of existential psychology, albeit an important extension. Chapter 2 compares and contrasts each of the four models. The models were written by males, and Chapter 3 adds a feminist dimension to show how female observers inserted corrections for the gender bias endemic to the original models. I also examine in Chapter 3 a counternarrative presented by Afrocentric psychologists as well as a discussion of the way the effects of *deindustrialization* have slowed the spread of black consciousness. Initially, black consciousness, black power, and affirmative action advocated and energized black social mobility, as evidenced by the fact that black studies programs were created and staffed by scholars, most of whom were born to working-class families. I point out that *deindustrialization* practically brought to a halt programs promoting large-scale uplift for members of the working class. Although Nigrescence incorporated a strong commitment to the folk, it would take the evolution of hip-hop culture to complete an imperfect and spotty dissemination of blackness across class lines. I take up all of these issues in Chapter 3.

Social identity, more crudely referenced as group identity, turns on the unique human capacity for self-consciousness, self-reflection, and meaning making. Erik Erikson (1968) has achieved international recognition for this theory that maps the unfolding of self-consciousness, meaning making, and one's attachment to a particular social group. Chapter 4 closes the gap revealed in Erikson's inability to account for the phenomenon called *double-consciousness* that is paramount to social identity development and general adjustment for human beings stigmatized by mainstream society. The focus here is on the way twoness is foundational to black identity. I present a handful of theories offered as "addendums" to Erikson that (1) describe the environments triggering one sense of self versus another, (2) describe the performance features of twoness, and (3) highlight the human feature too often overlooked in discourses on social identity: *individuality*. I level a critique at the depiction of racial identity within a binary framework, as if the only healthy social identity to be found among black people gives high salience to race and black culture. I point out the capacity for "some" black people to construct a social sense of self on factors other than race as a bridge for the better understanding of a *range of social identity stances* found in a large sample of *black people*, and this is probably true for any stigmatized group.

Chapter 5 presents research captured by the phrase "The Barbershop Bias" in that my evolving understanding of black people being more "normal" than described in the research literature has its origin in the men encountered at my barbershop. I expand upon my discussion in this introductory chapter and trace the origins of the deficit perspective on black life to scholarship produced in the 1930s by the faculty and students at the University of Chicago Department of Sociology. It was based primarily on black family research conducted by the department's heralded first black doctoral student, E. Franklin Frazier. I provide a close reading of Frazier's work, along with a critique based solely on information readily available to Frazier when he conducted his research and wrote his results. Many will be surprised that such important information readily available to Frazier was nonetheless not incorporated into his analysis. I assert that Frazier's influence should have been short-lived, as it failed to predict black family trends, reflected in census reports following publication of his text. Had he studied the experiences of black sharecroppers who migrated to California rather than cities in the North and Midwest, he would have been forced to write a different book altogether. Overlooked data and the California track are discussed in Chapter 5. This chapter ends with an analysis of the effects of deindustrialization on black and white communities and how the spatial separation between the two communities led observers to interpret the economic crisis in the black community with racial rather than economic tropes, while applying an SES analysis to explain the negative social effects of deindustrialization on white communities. Although white people were never slaves, research is presented showing that in the face of deindustrialization, whites began to evidence the type of individual and family dysfunctionality Moynihan and others once thought unique to blacks because of the legacy of slavery. I cover material showing that, in effect, deindustrialization revealed the way SES factors and not "race" provide a better platform upon which to explicate the twists and turns in the history of the black community, from slavery to the present. Revealed in the chapter is the way Frazier's racial tropes and myths helped to blind observers to the power of racism and SES factors in understanding impediments to black progress, despite the fact that he was a sociologist. In showing that the deficit perspective was a deeply flawed analysis to begin with, the door is open for scholars to apply our imagination in interpreting the psychology, motivation, and behavior of slaves as they exited slavery, and this new perspective is the focus of the final chapter—Chapter 6. This book sets out to annoy, disrupt, and agitate, because we can do better in capturing the humanity of black people.

2

Nigrescence Revisited

The Models

Overview

Given my age, this might be my last opportunity to revisit the model that over time has provided me with recognition and notoriety. Updating Nigrescence Theory is covered in two chapters, and this first chapter begins on a historical note, when, in the aftermath of the murder of Martin Luther King Jr., the spontaneous eruption of *black consciousness* was recorded by not one but four black psychologists. Each constructed a model depicting the evolution of black consciousness in four stages—amazingly similar in content and dynamics—despite being based on observations recorded in four different urban centers: Los Angeles, Boston, Chicago, and Pittsburgh. Central to the chapter is a clear, detailed description of the models authored by Charles Thomas, Bailey Jackson, Jake Milliones, and William Cross, and the contributions of Thomas Parham and Janet Helms are highlighted as well. The Nigrescence lifespan model tracking three types of identity trajectories—high salience, low salience, and internalized racism—is summarized. Also presented is the way the theory was transformed into an identity measure—the CRIS, or Cross Racial Identity Scale, for use in the empirical study of black identity. Important ancillary issues not related to the description of the models are covered in the next chapter.

Nigrescence and History

Nigrescence addresses the process of becoming black in one's thinking and consciousness, resulting in a state of being "woke," or awareness of racism; although Nigrescence adds a second dimension—awareness of one's attachment to black people and black culture. While a concept associated with the 1960s and 1970s, the phenomenon of a black person suddenly changing consciousness dates back to slavery. Josiah Henson became such a trusted slave that when his owner experienced economic distress and had to sell a group of slaves to a new owner whose plantation was downstream, Henson was given the task of transporting the group. At one point in the journey, the raft was positioned between one riverbank that marked slavery territory across from the other, where a slave could be free. Henson knew this, but having given his word to his owner, he pushed on and delivered his community members to their new owner. He and his family subsequently escaped slavery and settled in Canada, where he came to understand, long after the fact, that his mindset made him blind to reality. He literally could not "imagine" taking an action to free the group of slaves, so dedicated was he to his sense of honor, trust, and obligation. Reliance on a mindset that minimizes the ability to make decisions in line with one's best self-interests defines the orientation targeted for change during consciousness-raising (Henson, 1852).

Fast-forwarding, we arrive at the life and times of the phenomenal cycling champion Major Taylor (Kranish, 2019). He rose to prominence at the turn of the twentieth century during what is called the nadir of black history, when African Americans were treated as a caste. In the face of white competitors trying to make him crash as well as hostile acts by fans, Taylor toyed with using skin-bleaching products to lighten his skin in hopes of making himself more "acceptable." His biographer, Michael Kranish, says that when enough was enough, Taylor had an *epiphany* in April of 1898 and thereafter stated,

"My color is my fortune" (Kranish, 2019, p. 107). The Harlem Renaissance and the New Negro Movement of the 1920s produced literature, poems, essays, and musical lyrics pregnant with messages of "woke." The very phrase "New Negro" signals a rise in consciousness. In the early 1960s, Malcolm X's identity change foreshadowed identity conversions of the 1970s. Which brings us full circle to the psychological eruption following the murder of Martin Luther King Jr.

The Aftermath of King's Death

News of King's murder traveled across the nation through televised reporting, nearly as fast as today's Internet. Black folks in Oakland, Boston, Atlanta, Chicago, Miami, Montgomery, Salt Lake, and Denver seemed to react in unison—"Jesus Christ, what the fuck?!"—followed by a thunderous cry for "black power!" King was the black "hope" for bringing white people to their senses, and, with his death, many blacks turned inward and focused on the development of black consciousness. The term "Nigrescence" emerged from discussions held between French West African writers—Aimé Césaire, Léon Damas, and Léopold Sédar Senghor—whose Negritude social movement affirmed the social, political, and literary validity of an African aesthetic and worldview (Rabaka, 2015). Based on his observations of Africans in the context of the African independence movements that followed the end of World War II, the French psychiatrist Frantz Fanon anticipated the American-based Nigrescence experience by nearly twenty years with the "woke" trope incorporated in his 1952 treatise, *Black Skins, White Masks* (Fanon, 1952), and expanded upon in *Wretched of the Earth* (Fanon, 1961). As I documented in *Shades of Black* (Cross, 1991), several white social scientists constructed similar models from their observations of the black social movement, the most famous being Albert Memmi in *The Colonizer and the Colonized* (1957/1991).

In the United States, documenting the phases, or "stages," of black consciousness development became the preoccupation of four black American scholars. That four independent black scholars could simultaneously construct overlapping, if not nearly identical, stage models explicating the evolution of black consciousness strikes many as odd, if not extremely improbable. However, in an essay appearing in the May 12, 2008, issue of *The New Yorker* magazine, Malcolm Gladwell (2008) pointed out that simultaneous or multiple "discoveries" of the same inventions, theories, and perspectives are not uncommon in the history of science, especially when ideas about a subject are in the air, so to speak, and can be deduced by independent thinkers familiar with the topic at hand.

Certainly, black power and black consciousness *were* in the air, as from 1960 onward the oratory of Malcolm X asked black people to stop looking for "hope" in the beliefs and actions of white people, and, a few years before King's assassination, Stokely Carmichael agitated King to no end, when, during a protest march, Carmichael began to shout "black power!" as if to undermine King's agenda of seeking the support and cooperation of whites. However, Gladwell's historical analysis aside, insight into the way the four scholars composed models that incorporated similar descriptors, images, and tropes, despite not knowing each other and separated by hundreds of miles, is better explained by the role *transpersonal psychology* played in their doctoral training.

Transpersonal and existential psychology emerged at the turn of the twentieth century and, following World War II, re-emerged as an important framework, as people, such as Viktor Frankl, wrestled with the existential implications of the Holocaust. All four of the scholars I discuss were trained in psychology involving curriculums—at four different institutions—that included heavy exposure to Simone de Beauvoir, Abraham Marlow, Jean-Paul Sartre, Kurt Lewin, Viktor Frankl, Hannah Arendt, and other transpersonal-existential thinkers. The influence of existentialism seemed to function at the subliminal level, as only one of these scholars—Charles Thomas—made explicit reference to existentialists in his writings and speeches: "We all owe a debt to Abe Maslow, . . . , Erik Erikson and others for giving a time dimension by pointing out ways in which the demands of history affect personality" (Gardner & Thomas, 1970, p. 53). As we will see, the other three scholars, like Thomas, envisioned the achievement of black consciousness and awareness using shapes, images, colors, and dynamics drawn from transpersonal designs such as Maslow's hierarchy of needs (Maslow, 1970). There is much irony that models meant to describe the evolving *psychological independence* of black people were framed with metatheories commonplace to Western psychology. This is true even of the Afrocentric models, as they borrow and make heavy use of tropes readily traced to both white nationalism and the early twentieth-century [white] pseudoscience known as eugenics.

In any case, history shows that (1) Charles Thomas, working in the Oakland–Los Angeles area of California; (2) Bailey Jackson, situated in the Amherst–Boston areas of Massachusetts; (3) Jake Milliones, a doctoral student at the University of Pittsburgh; and (4) myself in Chicago and Evanston, Illinois, each observed and recorded the attitudinal and behavioral changes being exhibited by black folks across the United States in the aftermath of King's assassination. Jake Milliones was working under the amazing and frequently overlooked black psychologist Jerome Taylor. Reading his dissertation can create the false impression that Milliones did not construct his own model independently of others; however, I traveled to Pittsburgh and had the honor of speaking with both him and Taylor, and I can attest to the fact that Milliones's observations were as original as the other three scholars'. Milliones was the first person to develop an identity measure based on the identity-change model: Developmental Inventory of Black Consciousness (DIBC) (Milliones, 1980).

In some quarters Charles Thomas is the sentimental favorite for being recognized as "the" originator of the consciousness-development thesis. He was the first president of the Association of Black Psychologists, and before he could take his bow, he was viciously murdered in an apparent robbery (Monroe, 1990). In point of fact, Thomas *never published his model*; rather, he referred to his ideas about identity change while being interviewed for an article in *Psychology Today* (Gardner & Thomas, 1970). Nevertheless, even a cursory examination of the words and key phrases he incorporated in several essays appearing in his book *Boys No More* (Thomas, 1971) demonstrates that identity change was a major focus of his thinking. For example, "increased awareness" (p. 1); "awareness of new perspective" (p. 2); "a change in perspective" (p. 2); "reconstruct our lives" (p. 6); "understand the transformation taking place" (p. 101); and in particular these two phrases: "the identity change in Afro-Americans, with the advent of becoming black" (p. 103); and, finally, "the Afro-American, who has become black" (p. 123). While Thomas should be given his due, the fact of the matter is, the phenomenon of black identity change and the unfolding of black consciousness within the black community that was ignited after Martin Luther King Jr.'s murder was recorded—simultaneously—by four people, not one person.

The Four Models

Each of these scholars' models depicts the unfolding of black consciousnesses in four to five stages/levels/phases. To differentiate revelatory identity change from a slight shift in opinion or belief, terms and phrases like "conversion," "epiphany," "moment of truth," or "apocalyptic insight" are used to describe Nigrescence. The four authors saw themselves presenting a descriptive picture of the different phases people experienced on their way to embracing black consciousness.

Stage 1 Summary: As shown in Table 2.1, Stage 1 represents the point of departure and a description of the identity to be abandoned. The descriptions depict both personality distortions, if not outright psychopathology, along with a literal "craving" for white acceptance. The identity label capturing this stage was "Negro," as used by Malcolm X in his speeches. Thomas invented the term "Negromachy" (Thomas, 1971).

Stage 2 Summary: Stage 2 is the experience triggering the conversion. At the time, the specific experience was understood to be King's murder, but in the abstract, Stage 2 is the "Encounter," referencing whatever event triggers the drive for identity change. In the transcendental literature, this is the "aha!" moment, when the flaws of the old identity, operating at the subconscious level, become like a flashing billboard in the person's head. The old and new self are juxtaposed, with the new fast becoming dominant, captivating, mesmerizing, compelling, and addictive, thus the shared descriptors

TABLE 2.1. STAGE 1 EXCERPTS	
Charles Thomas	*Negromachy:* "It is only when Afro-Americans conquer *Negromachy* [that which is ruled by confusion of self-worth and dependency upon white society] that, as black people, we become capable of being human. This process will succeed only when the uniqueness of self is not fixated on [need for] white approval; escaping from self; guilty feelings over exemptions from social responsibilities; receptivity to fears of growth; obeying self-defeating impulses.... [Need for] white approval is the most pathological factor in the denial of fulfillment in Afro-Americans" (Thomas, 1971, pp. 103–104). He continues by noting that "the *white is right* behavior is used in maintaining, protecting, and enhancing the quality of life" (Thomas, 1971, p. 104).
Bailey Jackson	*Stage 1—Passive Acceptance:* "[Seeking] to gain resources [approval, sense of worth, goods, power, money, etc.] by accepting and conforming to white social, cultural, and institutional standards" (Jackson, 1976, p. 28).
Jake Milliones	*Pre-conscious Stage:* "They exhibit a high degree of *Nadanolitization*, the internalization of white racial stereotypes in relation to blacks" (Milliones, 1980, p. 175).
William Cross	*Pre-encounter Stage:* "In the pre-encounter stage a person is programmed to view and think of the world as being non-Black, anti-Black or the opposite of Black.... The person's worldview is dominated by Euro-American determinants.... [H]istorical perspective distorts Black history" (Cross, 1971, pp. 14–15).

in Table 2.2. The need for change is unquestioned. Neville and Cross (2017) report that "Encounter," when understood as a consciousness trigger or epiphany, is a common element in narratives dealing with racial identity for people of color living in Australia, Bermuda, South Africa, and the United States. In Birmingham, England, therapists associated with the Pattigift Therapy Center report that for clients in therapy involving questions of existence and meaning making, the Encounter experience is a major step forward in a client's quest for personal healing (McInnis & Moukam, 2013).

If a transcendental perspective, such as Maslow's hierarchy of needs, helped guide the thinking of all four theorists, in hindsight a second theory drawn from the mainstream literature explicates the most dramatic elements of Stages 2 and 3—Festinger's dissonance theory (Brehm, 2007). As I explore in greater detail shortly, disso-

TABLE 2.2.	STAGE 2 EXCERPTS
Charles Thomas	While one can infer that Thomas incorporated a "turning point" in his analysis, the fact of the matter is there is no documentation of how he conceived of the second stage.
Bailey Jackson	*Active Resistance:* "Stage Two begins with the total rejection of all that is white. There is a strong need for a thorough cleansing of the person's system" (Jackson, 1976, pp. 32–33).
Jake Milliones	*Confrontation Stage:* "[This stage] characterizes individuals who have begun the conversion to black process and who display strong anti-white sentiments. Characteristically, there is an extreme dichotomization of black-white attitudes such that black is seen as positive and good, whereas white is perceived as negative and evil. These individuals also espouse militant rhetoric and are generally emotional" (Milliones, 1980, p. 175).
William Cross	*Encounter:* "Some experience that manages to slip by or even shatter the person's current feelings about himself and his interpretation of the condition of Black people.... Encounter entails two steps: first, experiencing the encounter; and, second, beginning to reinterpret the world as a consequence of the encounter" (Cross, 1971, pp. 17–18).

nance theory helps explain that, when fundamental elements of a person's frame of reference are challenged, resulting in *intense dissonance*—as happens with the Encounter stage and acted out during the Immersion-Emersion stage—subsequent actions taken to reduce dissonance may find the person performing in dramatic fashion the new frame of reference. This can create the illusion that being "woke" results in both personality and worldview change, when, in fact, change is primarily in one's social cognitions that inform perception, interpretation, sense of commitment, and actions taken in line with one's new beliefs. This is captured in Table 2.2.

Stage 3 Summary: This is a state of "in-betweenness," where the person is attempting to loosen, if not destroy, the grip of the identity to be abandoned, at the same time that exploration of the new identity has begun in earnest. The person throws caution to the wind and, in an experience akin to being taken over by a strange but wonderful force, immerses her or his mind, heart, and soul in the mesmerizing world of blackness. Neither being completely free of the old, while a neophyte to the new, the person is subject to extreme acts that demonstrate total commitment to the new. This *blacker-than-thou* mindset makes the person appear an extremist to onlookers, giving rise to the stereotype of the white-hating, close-minded black militant, a major theme in Table 2.3.

When a person is under its spell, the new is romanticized, glorified, and placed on a pedestal. As a positive motivating force, this stage lets people feel they cannot consume enough information and history about their group, and, as a negative force, it promotes simple-minded, black-white, categorical, "either/or" forms of thinking. Transition, the yin-yang quality of being in-between, is a constant theme in the comments included in Table 2.3.

The palpable sense of rage and anger captured in these models deserves commentary, as later in this analysis we discuss the pushback by black feminists, who link this rage to a male-centric understanding of Nigrescence (Msimang, 2017). The four authors were haunted by memories of outlandish lynchings. Milliones, Cross, and Jackson were adolescents when, under the guidance and approval of Emmett Till's mother, *Jet Magazine* published the horrific pictures of his pulverized face in the September 15, 1955, issue. His death was said to be justified because, as his killers stated, he violated some cryptic protocol for how black males should behave when in the presence of white women. In most black homes, they still had memories of World War II and the way returning black GIs were greeted when, still dressed in their uniforms, they stepped off buses and trains, only to be treated in America the way Jews had been treated in Europe.

> On February 12, 1946, Sergeant Isaac Woodard, a decorated African American soldier, was beaten and blinded in Batesburg, South Carolina, by the town's police chief on the same day of his discharge from the U. S. Army, while still in uniform. . . . [And, in another case, t]he four were taken into the woods and shot sixty-six times. The victims were virtually unrecognizable, and Roger Malcolm was castrated. One of the ringleaders later explained that the execution of George Dorsey was necessary because "until George went into

the Army, he was a good nigger. But when he came out, they thought they were as good as any white people." (Gergel, 2019, pp. 4, 35–37)

Jones was forced to endure a horrible death. Both of his hands were chopped off with a meat cleaver; then, as the mob held him down, his face and body were seared with the flame of a blowtorch. "The excessive heat and beating caused his eyes to pop out from their sockets," according to an NAACP account. "Jones was light yellow complexion, but when his body was found his face was charred black." (Dray, 2007, p. 375)

Of the over four thousand lynchings in the United States between late 1882 up to Till's lynching in 1954, the vast majority were of black males, and more than a few involved their being castrated plus burned at the stake *while still alive*. Nigrescence fueled male memories, and they responded with rage (Grier & Cobbs, 1968). Steven Best and Douglas Kellner describe how hip-hop culture narrates contemporary black male rage (Best & Kellner, 1999). Whether the rage embedded in the models is unique to black males is a point of debate; however, given their historical and contemporary treatment by the social order, it should come as no surprise that rage and perhaps fantasies of revenge fueled the black male depiction of awakening.

Stage 4 Summary: The dynamics of the in-between stage cannot be sustained, and the person either continues toward Internalization, or, if somehow the thrust toward further growth is thwarted, the person may go in reverse and return to the old identity. The four models focus primarily on continued growth, where resolution of the struggle between the old and new identities is achieved such that the person is said to internalize the new identity. The person is described as feeling resolute and devoid of anxiety about "not feeling black enough." As captured across the depictions in Table 2.4, the models tend to suggest that, beyond Internalization, as a personal quality, the person gravitates toward actions and activities to better and strengthen community. Dedication to community may be

TABLE 2.3. STAGE 3 EXCERPTS	
Charles Thomas	In an essay, Thomas appears to be discussing a person new to her or his blackness and the state of in-betweenness. "'Rappin on Whitey' is beneficial in an initial phase in becoming black.... These expressions are quite important because they become the decisive factor in later impressions, feelings, and ideas of social reality.... The next phase requires a 'testifying' about the struggle to become black.... These activities will erect the new framework of the new identity and consequent expected behavior.... These concepts of self-determination and self-surrender have definite mystical and transcendental quality. As a matter of fact, Blackness can be regarded as a return to the mystical roots of mother Africa" (Thomas, 1971, pp. 113–114).
Bailey Jackson	*Redirection Stage:* "Describes the black person who seeks to define his/her blackness in positive terms, independent of perceived good or evil of white people" (Jackson, 1976, pp. 36–37).
Jake Milliones	*Internalization Stage:* At this point, "individuals... have begun to incorporate positive values that relate to the black experience while there is diminution of anti-white sentiments" (Milliones, 1980, p. 177).
William Cross	*Immersion-Emersion:* "The experience is an immersion into blackness and a liberation from whiteness. The immersion is a strong, powerful, dominating sensation constantly energized by Black rage, guilt, and a third and new fuel, a developing sense of pride. The white world, white culture and white persons are dehumanized and become biologically inferior, as the Black person and black world are deified. Everything that is black is good and romantic" (Cross, 1971, pp. 19–20).

a point made within the description of Internalization, or it may be described as a separate fifth stage. While Nigrescence models depict the struggle to "withdraw" from all things white (rage) as well as ritual-like activities meant to show one is no longer a "Negro" (feelings of guilt), the narratives shown in Table 2.4 tend to suggest that resolution of rage, hatred, and guilt make possible a *rapprochement with whites* and mainstream society.

Stages 4 and 5 Summary: Amazingly, a process beginning with withdrawal, separation, and negation of all things white ends with an ability to re-engage white society on terms suggesting relative—not absolute—independence of thought and action. As Thomas noted,

TABLE 2.4. STAGES 4 AND 5 EXCERPTS	
Charles Thomas	"The fifth stage is transcendental—through your unique blackness you lose your hang-ups about race, age, sex and social class and see yourself as part of humanity in all its favors" (Thomas, 1971, p. 78).
Bailey Jackson	*Internalization:* "Synthesis . . . to integrate his/her sense of Blackness with other aspects of the person's identity, e.g., sexual identity, role identities, spiritual identity, etc. . . . [The person] is able to interact with any white person or group without feeling compromised or violated[,] . . . seeks to synergistically make sense of the bi-cultural nature of his/her experience in American society[, is] . . . able to separate those oppressive aspects of the [white] society from those neuter or supportive. . . . [Has an] awareness used in battle against oppression. . . . The focus is to seek out and engage other Black people [in the middle] of transformation" (Jackson, 1976, pp. 40–41).
Jake Milliones	*Internalization-Integration Stage:* After depicting internalization, Milliones addressed "integration," where persons "are committed to a plan of action aimed at the eradication of oppression and dehumanization. . . . They possess tolerant and empathic attitudes toward those who are functioning in a less adaptive manner in relation to racism and oppression. These individuals appear to have integrated the emotional and cognitive components of their experiences in such a way that they can genuinely assert their energies toward the continued growth and liberation of themselves and others" (Milliones, 1980, p. 177).
William Cross	*Internalization:* "As internalization and incorporation increase, attitudes toward white people become less hostile, or at least realistically contained. Weusi Anxiety diminishes [anxiety over whether one is black enough], and pro-black attitudes become expansive, open and less defensive. The person [moving forward] is committed to a plan. . . . He is going beyond rhetoric and into action and defines change in terms of the masses of Black people" (Cross, 1971, pp. 22–23).

this transcendental capacity, while not minimizing racism, stimulates an awareness of the connection between racism and other forms of oppression, as in Critical Race Theory. "Race" as a simplistic, essentialist, catchall category loses its analytic power and is replaced by discourses on power, privilege, and dominance. Consequently, the person reaching Internalization may engage and even identify with members of other groups whose oppression is not directly linked to racism but rather to sexism, homophobia, anti-Semitism, and so on. Jackson notes that "race" is but one cell in a person's overall *identity matrix*, and Internalization allows the person to take stock of her or his "other" selves, as in a person being black, female, gay, overweight, and middle class—that is, a person's "intersectionality," or interlocking identities (see Harris, 2009).

Transcendence led Jackson to progress from a race-specific to *generic* model of identity conversion, applicable to the consciousness-raising experience of many groups. In moving from the production of his dissertation, where the focus was race specific, his initial publication was coauthored with a straight white woman and a lesbian white woman, and, in the analysis presented in the journal article, the Internalization stage takes on an unmistakable transcendental quality (Hardiman, Jackson, & Griffin, 2007). Still, none of the model builders anticipated the critique made by black feminists that the original narratives were far too male-centric, a criticism explored in Chapter 3. As is pointed out later, the founders of the Black Lives Matter organization stress a vision of the self that is matrix-like, as did Bailey Jackson, and their identity complexity model is, in point of fact, another way to express humanism (Garza, 2016).

While the discourse on black identity change was originally guided by four independent observers—Thomas, Milliones, Cross, and Jackson—over time several voices dropped out and the literature centered on the Cross Nigrescence Model. My attempt to fuse the Thomas and Cross models (Cross, 1978) was cut short by the untimely death of Charles Thomas. Milliones shifted his focus from scholarship to local politics and was elected president of the school board for the city of Pittsburgh; with the exception of one publication, he never returned to research and theory. He also died at an early age. Jackson incorporated his model into a graduate-level seminar at the University of Massachusetts–Amherst. In addition, he created a consulting firm, which functioned mostly on the East Coast, to conduct diversity training for educational and industrial clients. Within academic circles, the identity-change narratives proffered by me and Janet Helms became dominant.

Janet Helms and Thomas Parham

Helms: As much as anyone, Janet Helms almost singlehandedly established racial identity as a key element of the modern discourse in the field of counseling psychology. Several of Helms's former students—Robert Carter of Columbia University (Helms & Carter, 1991) and Thomas Parham of California State University, Dominguez Hills (Parham & Helms, 1981)—produced seminal studies demonstrating the way the racial identity construct was readily subject to empirical analysis. More importantly, Helms's work marked the shift in the discourse on racial identity to one of a narrow "within-group" focus solely stressing the identity development experiences of black people to a more *interactional and conversational perspective* wherein both black and white people examine how their respective socialization experiences—from childhood to early adulthood—included being *racialized*. In this perspective, the state of being "woke" was required of both black and white people and consciousness-raising became the object of *everyone in the room*.

Going a step further, Helms, along with Bailey Jackson, who also stressed generic notions of identity development, helped to awaken counseling psychology, if not all of psychology, to the reality that each and every affinity group has, as part of their intimate self-narrative, a unique "model" of how consciousness-raising is experienced within one's respective community. Thus, the fourth edition of *The Handbook of Multicultural Counseling* (Casas et al., 2016) incorporates a plethora of identity models covering just about every important cultural affinity group found in the United States.

One of the most important consequences of the work and perspective sparked by Helms's theory making was the emergence of Division 45 (the Society for the Psychological Study of Culture, Ethnicity and Race) within the American Psychological Association, along with the creation of the new APA journal *Cultural Diversity and Ethnic Minority Psychology*. In her work with APA Division 35 (Psychology of Women), Helms played no small part in incorporating an *intersectional perceptive*, such that the status of being woke covers not only one's specific cultural moorings but an awareness of the multiple categories that are included in one's personal identity matrix, as in being male, biracial, gay, left-handed, or white female, stout, right-handed, blind, and a victim of abuse. In the summer of 2019, Helms was awarded the gold medal for lifetime achievement in psychology and the public interest by the APA.

Parham: Thomas Parham (Parham, 1989) extended Nigrescence Theory by noting how a person may continue to experience moments of advanced thinking in light of a new experience or, for lack of a better term, a new mini-encounter that, while not as dramatic and powerful as the original, nonetheless can reshape aspects of a person's thinking about race and culture. He calls this "recycling." History has provided two dramatic exemplars of recycling that grew into social movements: Black Lives Matter and Me Too. In both instances, persons drawn into these movements were not neophytes but informed feminists and experienced black leaders and thinkers.

Nigrescence and a Lifespan Perspective

One of the major contributors to the development of a scale designed to measure Nigrescence dynamics (the CRIS) was Peony Fhagen-Smith, at the time a graduate student in developmental psychology. Aside from our work on scale construction, Peony and I held intense discussions on the challenge of merging Nigrescence Theory with a more traditional narration of identity development. Our collaborations resulted in the production of a descriptive model on ego identity and Nigrescence from a lifespan perspective (Cross & Fhagen-Smith, 1996), covering six developmental sectors, depicted in Figure 2.1.

Sectors 1 and 2: Taking as the point of departure Beverly Tatum's analysis of the *range of black viewpoints about race and culture held by black caregivers* (Tatum, 1997/2003), lines linking the child in Sector 1 connect to Sector 2 as Pre-adolescent frames, which are heavily influenced by the frames inculcated by parents and can actually be considered parental identity frames. These are: High Race Salience (HRS); Low Race Salience (LRS); and Internalized Racism (IR)—incorporating negative attitudes toward blackness. Thus, in Sector 2, early messages help the child absorb and assimilate the content of

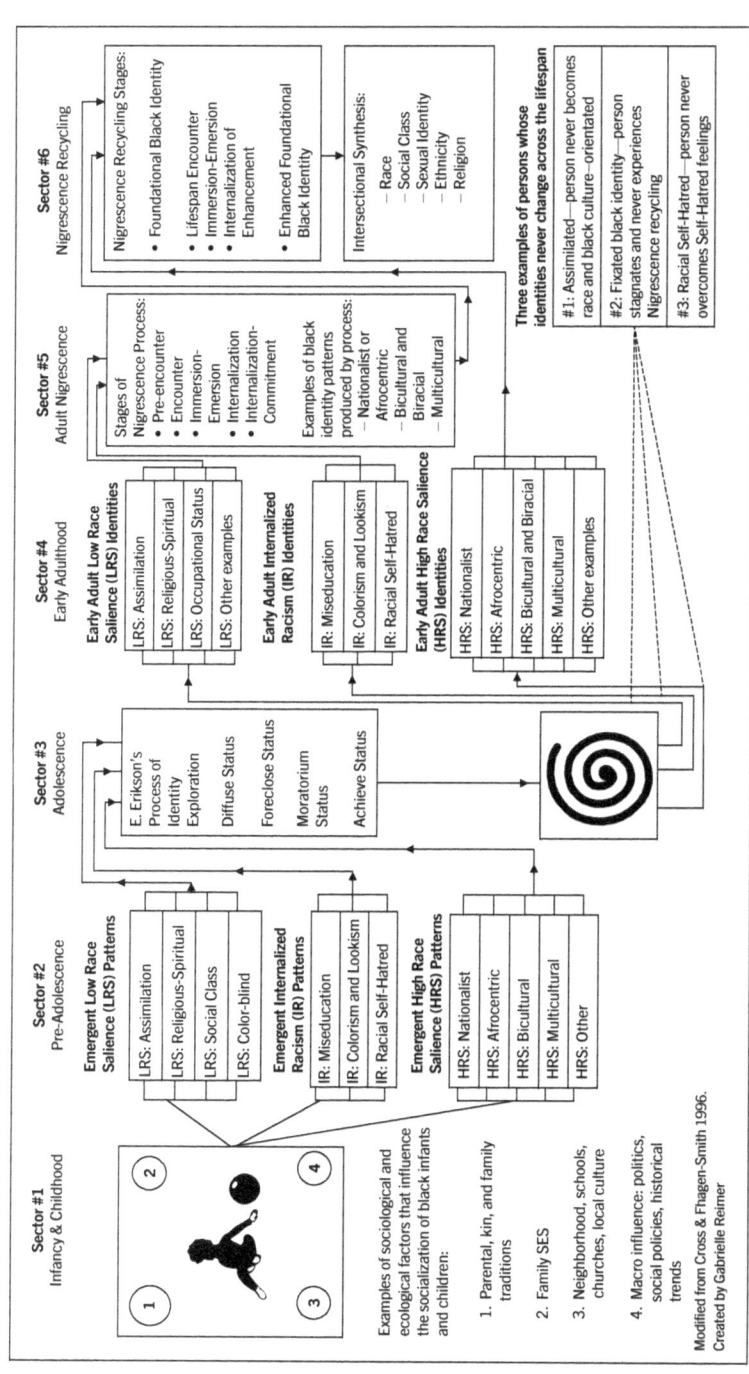

Figure 2.1 Descriptive model of the relationship between ego identity and Nigrescence: A lifespan perspective. Modified from Cross & Fhagan-Smith 1996. Created by Gabrielle Reimer.

one's surroundings, by naming, touching, categorizing, using/handling, and, of course, playing/interacting with objects, people, places, and things, with a broad overlay. Note that each category has multiple entries as a way of messaging about race, culture, or, as the case may be, about cultural schemes for which race and culture *are not* stressed. In unfortunate circumstances, the racial messaging may be negative, reflective of *Internalized Racism*.

Each identity category is linked to more than one expression, as a way of communicating the multidimensionality of each frame and reflective of a key assumption for Nigrescence Theory that *there is no one way to be black*. The figure shows there is no one way to express High Race Salience, Low Race Salience, or even Internalized Racism. Black identity is a complex topic because black people are human and human beings are complicated.

If the size of the clusters depicted in Sector 2 reflect the proportion of blacks falling into each, the size of the High Race Salience cluster would be the largest by far, as most black families inculcate a positive black-oriented frame of reference. Those gravitating toward identity structures for which something other than race and black culture are stressed would, by comparison, be modest in size. The middle cluster, representing miseducation, colorism, and racial self-hatred, would be *extremely small, if not tiny*, as only a miniscule percentage socialize black children to be racially self-hating. That said, and as an important aside, "miseducation" might be applied across the board to every identity framework depicted in Sector 2, as it is difficult for blacks to totally avoid falling victim to ideas about black people that prove to be forms of propaganda, lies, or stereotypes.

Sector 3: All the beliefs systems represented in Sector 2 are linked (by lines) to Sector 3, because between adolescence and early adulthood, the individual's capacity to think critically emerges, as made possible by the increasing maturation of one's prefrontal cortex. During childhood, a black youth's affirmation of identity and beliefs has an *imitative, declarative, and unexamined* quality, but from adolescence forward, beliefs and identity affirmations take on the texture of that which has been tested and examined, as the person's capacity for existential thinking expands exponentially. The curlicue design at the base of Sector 3 symbolizes unpredictability, because the unique life experiences of human beings make it difficult to impossible to accurately predict life trajectories from late adolescence onward, as circumstances insert more twists and turns than already reflected in Figure 2.1.

Sectors 4 and 5: For those who continue to evolve an identity greatly informed by their earlier socialization, the range of identity categories, first explored in Sector 2, reappear in Sector 4. However, now the social cognitions reflect having been existentially processed: examined, authenticated, personalized, and internalized. Lines extending from both the LRS and IR clusters connect to Sector 5, as black adults socialized to accord limited or negative salience to race and black culture are vulnerable (and in need of) conversion leading to a state of "woke," because a successful Nigrescence experience will change LRS attitudes and beliefs into beliefs that accord high salience to race, blackness, and black culture. Cross and Fhagen-Smith stress that for black people who enter Nigrescence with low self-esteem traceable to their socialization between infancy and early adolescence, Nigrescence will not eliminate such self-negativity; however, the identity conversion may help a person gain insight into the actual origins of her or his negativity, and this insight may help them accept the need for counseling.

Sector 6: At the base of Sector 4, a line bypasses Sector 5 and connects to Sector 6, reflecting the experience for black people who evolved a black identity as a result of the way they were socialized by their parents and community across infancy, childhood, adolescence, and early adulthood. As such, they *do not require* a Nigrescence Encounter, because, in effect, they already embrace a positive, well-developed sense of blackness. On the other hand, such persons may experience "recycling" when a previously unexamined issue comes to their attention. A similar line/connection is found at the base of Sector 5 to show that persons who have successfully navigated Nigrescence may, later in life, recycle when an overlooked issue finally comes into focus. Recycling may be triggered by issues that take on considerable importance, leading even to a new social movement, as in the Black Lives Matter movement and the Me Too movement, both of which are populated by rather sophisticated participants. Such sophistication belies the fact that the person enters recycling having already attained a high level of consciousness, from which the new insight may very well have evolved.

Bottom of Sector 6: Nigrescence spotlights "race" above and beyond all other social categories. However, especially as influenced by black feminism and voices from the LGBTQIA communities, an intersectional perspective now permeates the discourse on blackness. Thus, at the base of the rectangle representing Recycling (Sector 6) is another box labeled Intersectional Synthesis to symbolize that beyond Nigrescence and a step further than Recycling is the phenomenon of *intersectionality.* Just below the intersectionality box is another section that links back to the base of Sector 3 through a set of dashed lines. This represents black people who, after progressing to adolescence and early adulthood, never seem to change across the remainder of their development. Such persons will be called steady Eddies: old, reliable, stuck-in-the-mud, or simply persons who have an aversion to change. Explicating the cause of their rigidity is beyond the scope of the current discussion.

The lifespan figure presents a multidimensional and complex depiction of blackness across the lifespan, and its complexity is a reminder that black people are first and foremost human beings, and humans by their very nature *resist linearity and oversimplification.* When examined at the level of the individual black person, we are in awe of the way things work out for figures such as Maya Angelou, Malcolm X, Frederick Douglass, Harriet Tubman, Miles Davis, Michelle and Barack Obama, and my daughter, Tuere Binta Cross. One can make the case that their ability to go off course, to resist what was expected of them, explicates their ultimate success.

Scales That Measure Nigrescence

During my brief tenure at Penn State University, I was surrounded by an amazing crew of Africana scholars and a black multiracial graduate student close to completing her degree. This Penn State team consisted of Frank Worrell, Beverly Vandiver, Peony Fhagen-Smith, and me. Linda Clark Strauss was not on the scale construction team; however, our joint study (Strauss & Cross, 2005) on the everyday enactments of identity helped me, personally, think more deeply about the various factors imbedded in the Nigrescence Model that would be transformed into subscales for the CRIS. In addition, the erudite Kevin Cokley offered advice and critique at different turns in the scale construction process. Our meetings were like an advanced seminar on the history of scale construction and psychometrics. Vandiver presented a checklist of factors that result in poor scale construction, by which she meant scales evidencing poor reliability and validity. In light of her historical perspective, she outlined a process that required replication after replication along with intense scrutiny of every scale and individual scale item. For example, Pre-encounter eventually morphed into not one but three subscales: Assimilation, Miseducation, and Racial Self-Hatred. Vandiver's process resulted in the CRIS (Vandiver et al., 2002), which, after over twenty years of use in the field now, represents one of the most valid and reliable scales ever constructed for use in the study of psychological blackness (Worrell, 2012). The original CRIS was validated on late-adolescent and young-adult respondents; the CRIS-A on adult populations (Worrell et al., 2016). For the newly constructed Cross Ethnic-Racial Identity Scale (CERIS) (Worrell, Mendoza-Denton, & Wang, 2019), all the items are written with neutral language for application with any adult population to test whether the dimensions incorporated in Nigrescence Theory are generalizable to populations across contexts and cultures.

While the original application of the CRIS stressed a respondent's highest scale score, reflecting an *identity status perspective*, more recent scoring has shifted to a profile analysis. Here the thinking is that most black people are exposed to and absorb, to some degree, elements from each of the scale factors. Such theorizing has produced at least one spectacular finding. The profile representing a "multicultural" stance is clearly in evidence in studies where black students are attending a predominantly white college/university. However, this profile literally disappears when the CRIS is employed with black students attending a historically black college (Worrell et al., 2006).

All of the scales generated by Nigrescence Theory are premised on the perspective that *group identity is a multidimensional construct*, and, in that sense, we share a viewpoint with Robert Sellers. Sellers was trained as a social psychologist, and his theory applies a trait analysis to black identity, as reflected in his Multidimensional Model of Racial Identity (MMRI) (Sellers et al., 1998), which proved foundational to the development of a scale carrying a similar name: Multidimensional Inventory of Black Identity (MIBI) (Sellers et al., 1998). Rather than focus on identity in transition, as captured in the Nigrescence discourse, Sellers focuses on identity in a stabilized steady state. In effect, he argues that whatever one's explanation for how identity evolves, the internalized or steady-state identity reveals four dimensions: Salience, Regard, Centrality, and Ideology. *Salience* depicts the degree to which race is important to the person; *Centrality* speaks to whether race plays a primary role in the construction of the self; *Regard* taps the person's conception of how one "thinks" others view one's group (others-exterior), and a second component taps the person's personal view of the group (self-interior); and, finally, *Ideology* taps the four dominant ways black people accord philosophical meaning to race: as a nationalist, an oppressed minority, a humanist, or an assimilationist.

Sellers's work represents perhaps the most elegant, well-informed, and compelling theory synthesizing mainstream psychology and black psychology. In doing so, he shows himself to favor a humanist stance on race and ethnicity, where variables capable of interrogating the humanity of whites can also be applied in the explication of feelings, thoughts, and behaviors linked to *any* group of human beings, regardless of the nominal identity forced upon them by the larger society.

The Paradox of Group Compared to Self-Identity Research

In Nigrescence Theory, Salience and Ideology are baked into the identity statuses, while issues of Regard are incorporated into the Miseducation and Racial Self-Hatred CRIS subscales. Nigrescence Theory places the greatest emphasis on the reference group implications of Ideology. Ideology, when understood as an existential point of departure, helps a person comprehend how to find meaning in life, is foundational to personal values and preferences, and explains behavior when the person is interacting with the larger society. Most importantly, Ideology provides insight into what it means to be *racialized and objectified* by the larger society, as differentiated from one's private, interior understanding of oneself, captured in the phrase "The quiet self" by Kevin Quashie in his text *The Sovereignty of Quiet: Beyond Resistance in Black Culture* (2012). Quashie makes the argument that the black aesthetic is based on resistance and protest, while contemporary black artists are more attuned to one's interior psychology: "The right to be one's self—this is the right that black people, and black women specifically, don't get to inhabit. And yet, this notion of being for self is essential to experiencing and living through one's humanity" (Quashie, 2012, p. 70).

As an aside, Tommy Curry (2017) would argue that this applies as much to black men as women. From one angle, Quashie appears to be advocating narcissism, but as an artist, he simply means to say that art can and should be inspired more by one's felt humanity and not entirely by the psychological dynamics linked to one's social ascription. To use a phrase I prefer, "something other than race" can inspire a black artist's creativity. Ultimately, Quashie's proposition is an oversimplification because, since the publication of *The Souls of Black Folk* by Du Bois (1903), black artists have explored both the veil, or mask, as well as the private or quiet self hidden behind it. That said, the argument can be made that, from the 1970s onward, as well-documented by Quashie, increasingly black artists have been driven more by their interior psychology than by their ascriptions. In effect, one measure of the success attributed to the black social movement of the 1970s—clearly a group identity phenomenon—has been the creation of expanded "personal" space within which black artists can create and produce.

Group identity is an important part of a person's self-concept, and while it is accorded disproportionate importance, given the psychological stress generated by everyday experiences with discrimination, we need to be more cognizant that psychological measures such as the MIBI, CRIS, and Multigroup Ethnic Identity Measure (MEIM) do not measure the private or quiet self. *That the history of the psychological study of the black self-concept has been constructed on an overreliance of group identity research, which by definition taps only a "portion" of the more complex and multidimensional aspects of a person's self-concept, reveals how distorted our understanding of black humanity is. Time and again, and contrary to Quashie's assertion otherwise, it is the black poet, black novelist, black movie producer, and black playwright who has better presented an expansive picture of our whole self than does psychology.*

Unapologetically and Unabashedly Black

Finally, it is noted that, although Nigrescence and black consciousness originated in events dating back to the early 1970s, the model and analysis of consciousness remain a central element in black psychology and multicultural education. However, the two concepts have morphed into the popular trope "woke"—said to have application in understanding the phenomenon of rising consciousness among a broad range of individuals belonging to social groups subject to stigmatization by the larger society. Woke is a strand braided into the narratives of Jews, LGBTQIA individuals, Muslims, Native Americans, and so on, and is the ultimate counternarrative to miseducation. In effect, Nigrescence has broken free of its historical and cultural constraints, providing a platform for interrogating contemporary consciousness-raising experiences, an example of which is educator/actress Misty Monroe's theatrical depiction of her personal awakening performed at the Groundlings Theatre in Los Angeles on September 11, 2016. Monroe used the stages of Nigrescence to structure the telling of her epiphany. She made a video recording of the performance, which can be accessed online by searching for the title *Misty Monroe: Unapologetically Black*. It is a startling example of how Nigrescence continues to find favor, usefulness, and application some fifty years after its original publication.

Across the globe, most black people (and people of color everywhere) receive a formal education fraught with *miseducation* that manages to explain the lack of progress through cultural and personological faults of the group itself, while minimizing societal and systemic causes. Miseducation can be understood as a series of psychological "clamps" holding the person down, even though the person feels "normal." One clamp replaces clarity of thinking with an opaque vision, another produces ambiguity leading to adventures without purpose, and still another mystifies the connections between past and present events and circumstances. Most devastatingly, it dampens the human spirit, resulting in constraints on what can be thought, imagined, felt, or actualized. During Encounter, the constraints break loose and one is thrust to the surreal outer edges of what is possible for self and community. When youth of color encounter *their authentic story*—narrated from the bottom up—something that typically does not happen until reaching college, their true story is so at odds with the earlier understanding of facts that the truth is experienced as an out-of-body, mind-blowing event—an epiphany, if you will. *The truth and its transcendent mysticism and spirituality make it possible to be, perhaps for the first time ever, unapologetically and unabashedly black, gay, trans, Jewish, Muslim, Native American, or female, and so on, and various combinations thereof.*

3

Nigrescence, Part 2

Issues

Overview

Chapter 2 focused solely on Nigrescence Theory and measurement, but since its inception in the late 1960s, a number of issues have arisen that require exploration. The four models were created by men; thus, a discussion of gender is warranted. Here I provide a critical analysis of African-centered psychology, as its adherents offer an important critique of Nigrescence Theory. The negative portraiture of Pre-encounter is contested to show that, rather than psychopathology, the "Negro" identity reflects a different point of view about the meaning of blackness. In another section I discuss how Nigrescence became braided with social mobility, as "woke" blacks forged their way into every nook and cranny of the American economy and society, and likewise, the forces of deindustrialization are shown to have curtailed social mobility. I present an extended discussion on personality, social identity, and eudaimonia (Ryff & Keyes, 1995). The chapter ends by interrogating why a consensus for defining blackness and black identity is problematic.

Gender and Nigrescence

The original Nigrescence models privileged male voices. True, Bailey Jackson incorporated multiple voices in his model, but there is a complete and conspicuous absence of alternative voices in the models by Milliones and myself. Charles Thomas found himself openly critical of women and the feminist movement. In the September 1970 issue of *Psychology Today*, there appeared a debate between Charles Thomas and J. Ann E. Gardner, a white feminist. Thomas opened with this shot across the bow:

> I would be less than candid, Jo Ann, if I did not say the women's movement is a diversion. Like the environmental thing that college kids are flocking into, feminism appears to middle class whites in part because it is an activist way to ignore racism. It is avoidance behavior. . . . As a black man I feel my family, my wife and children must sacrifice for me. There is an interesting kind of dynamic here. My family realizes that if I don't make it they won't make it either. (Gardner & Thomas, 1970, p. 51)

Although in his writing (Thomas, 1971) Thomas inserts here and there comments about black women's issues and perceptions, nowhere does he give the slightest hint of understanding that Nigrescence and awakening are not the same for black women as for black men. If anything, he expresses contempt for feminism while suggesting that black liberation is about freedom for black males who "head" black households. Women's perception and critique of this bias can be found in many places, but a more recent expression has been penned by Sisonke Msimang, in *Always Another Country*:

> I am full of judgment and righteousness. I throw myself into more Malcolm X. I go back to Steve Biko, whom I read in high school and did not really understand until I was in America. I read Stokely Carmichael. I read about the Black Panthers. The poetry we perform is mainly by women, but the politics—the

words that animate our conversations and push us to act in the real world—these belong to men. It takes a while before I understand the effects this has on my own political sensibilities.... It is years before I understand bell hooks' ideas about radical love and discover Audre Lorde. The words of these particular men—the way they express anger—is so seductive. I ignore the way in which their blackness seems to have little space for my woman-ness. (Msimang, 2017, pp. 190–191)

The black feminist artist Shani Jamila describes a pathway to consciousness very similar to that of Msimang (Jamila, 2019). Before entering Spellman, her thoughts were anchored by the works of Martin Luther King Jr. and Malcolm X; however, from the very beginning of her undergraduate studies at Spellman, she became deeply grounded in the writings, poetry, and narratives of black women writers, leaders, and artists. From there she never looked back.

As discussed in Chapter 2, Janet Helms became a central contributor to the Nigrescence discourse; otherwise, women have been in the vanguard of *refining* Nigrescence, especially in moving from the notion of awakening and its emphasis on race, as a monotonic construct, to a consideration of race as but one element in a *matrix of interlocking identities*. Black women came into their own not by offering still another and thus redundant model but by revealing the limitations of male-defined blackness and its tendency to center oppression solely on black males, with perhaps passing reference, if at all, to issues unique to black females. Instead, black women outlined a vision of interlocking identities inclusive not only of women's voices and experiences but of those of the LGBTQIA community. Inclusion of the LGBTQIA community was deliberate and meant as a forceful counternarrative to black men's homophobic attitudes. Part of the Combahee River Collective Statement reads:

> The most general statement of our politics at the present time would be that we are actively committed to struggling against racial, sexual, heterosexual and class oppression and see as our particular task the development of integrated analysis and

practice based upon the fact that the major systems of oppression are interlocking.... It was our experience and disillusionment within these [male dominated] liberation movements, as well as experience on the periphery of the white male left, that led to the need to develop a politics that was antiracist, unlike those of white women, and antisexist, unlike those of black and white men. (Combahee River Collective, 1977)

Black women do not take issue with a model that depicts change taking place in stages, but given that a person has reached Internalization, the writings of black women raise questions about how the person defines blackness, what the person's priorities are, what actions the person will undertake, and what the anticipated results are (Collins, 2002).

While Nigrescence and the 1977 statement of the Combahee River Collective cannot be directly connected, there is historical evidence that shows the ongoing Social Justice Education Program at UMass Amherst, Bailey Jackson's 1976 dissertation, and the black feminist statement all evolved within the same geographic location, as Amherst is a short distance (less than nine miles) from South Hadley, Massachusetts. In the early 1970s, UMass Amherst was brimming with academic visionaries who helped to establish one of the first programs in black studies in the year 1970, and in 1973 they hired Maurianne Adams as director of a residential college program known as Project 10 (Adams, 2020). Adams developed a special curriculum that focused on racism, sexism, heterosexism, classism, and ableism. In effect, she integrated the series of identity politics discourses percolating across academe. She later brought together like-minded scholars to create the Social Justice Education Program and its primary text—coauthored with two white feminists—titled *Teaching for Diversity and Social Justice* (Adams, Bell, & Griffin, 1997). In effect, Adams and her faculty were teaching a Combahee-like philosophy to UMass undergraduates several years before the Combahee statement was published, and Bailey Jackson's dissertation was completed while he was immersed in the Social Justice Education activities, as a graduate student and instructor. He would later become dean of the college. As previously noted, Jackson's last stage was more explicitly transcendental and multicultural than any of the four models, and, as it was completed in 1976, his thinking anticipated the Combahee philosophy by at least a year, if not longer, since his dissertation proposal was accepted several years earlier. Recall, as well, that aside from his negative and thus paradoxical statements about feminism, Charles Thomas spoke of identity politics ending in a transcendental state of mind, where the woke person is able to comprehend the connection between race, social class, and so on. Finally, the Cross Racial Identity Scale (CRIS) includes the subscale Multicultural Inclusive, and its transcendent qualities are obvious. Thus, while any connection between UMass and the Combahee Collective is speculative, Malcolm Gladwell's (2008) observation that when research and experience point to a certain conclusion that is "in the air," so to speak, multiple actors familiar with the direction to which "facts" are pointing will almost simultaneously articulate the same "finding" or conclusion. In this case, actors only nine miles apart, inclusive of white feminists, can be credited with independently arriving at the same concept that today is credited, rightfully so, to the Combahee Collective.

The identity matrix concept advocated by the UMass Social Justice Education Program, Jackson's notion of multiple selves, and black feminists' concept of intersectionality all incorporate an "inclusive" messaging that, in the case of the Black Lives Matter (BLM) social movement, has helped to attract white participation across the United States and, surprisingly, across the globe. Is there any wonder that many observers were capturing the moment in the aftermath of George Floyd's murder with phrases along these lines: "It's different this time"? Seventeen days following Floyd's murder, the *New York Times* published a map of the United States with red dots indicating the location of villages, small towns, and large urban centers where protest marches were organized and carried out (Burch et al., 2020). Soon thereafter, the national *PBS NewsHour* included a special segment (Schifrin, 2020) devoted to the spread of the protest across international borders. In point of fact, the scope of the protest following Floyd's murder has been documented as the largest in the history of the United States (Buchanan, Bui, & Patel, 2020).

While observers within the United States spoke of the legacy of slavery, protesters in other countries unearthed their countries' role in the transatlantic slave trade, and, going a step further, the systemic racism in the *contemporary* politics and economy of their countries. Consequently, as U.S. protesters struggled to destroy statues of bygone Southern elites from the Confederacy and the era of Reconstruction, Europeans were toppling statues of historical figures whose actions and policies facilitated the slave trade and/or the ruthless inhumane folly known as European colonization. On July 3, 2020, King Philippe of Belgium apologized for the actions of King Leopold II of Belgium and his demonic treatment of Africans in the Congo Free State between 1885 and 1908 (Pronczuk & Specia, 2020).

One of the reasons for the spread of the protests was their link to the BLM organization (Buchanan, Bui, & Patel, 2020), which, while not directing/dictating each protest, nevertheless provided material, guidance, and a framework for new activists—a framework fundamentally intersectional in nature and thus welcoming of broad participation. Stated more starkly, *white participation was welcomed from the get-go.* From the vantage point of the BLM movement, this is not solely a George Floyd moment, where the emphasis centers exclusively on black males; rather, when appropriate, the BLM organization is quick to list a number of people killed by the police as a reminder that the police killings have involved both black men and black women and that harsh treatment has also been meted out to black gays and lesbians in addition to black trans individuals, especially black trans women. Some have offered a critique of the BLM movement using the phrase "All lives matter." My daughter recently purchased a T-shirt for me incorporating a statement appropriate to end this section on Nigrescence and gender: "All lives matter when black lives matter."

Nigrescence, Social Mobility, and Deindustrialization

As black people experienced black consciousness, they immediately put pressure on society to change business as usual, resulting in access to previously racially restricted opportunities across many, if not every, sector of the American economy. Within the academy, the push to identify, train, and graduate new black scholars was stressed, and many of these new graduates, upon receipt of their doctorates, turned the tables and, with support from black undergraduate students, demanded the creation of black studies centers and programs. Those scholars who helped shape and establish black studies were often the *progeny of working-class families.* These include the likes of Henry Louis Gates Jr., Anne Adams, James Turner, Helen Neville, Reiland Rabaka, Brendesha Tynes, retired Cornell historian Robert Harris, and myself, to mention a few. Thus, at a personal level, black consciousness facilitated one's social mobility from working class to middle class. The linkage among black power, black consciousness, and social mobility was cut short by a powerful economic trend known as *deindustrialization* and its handmaiden, *globalization.* Recognition of this reality was postponed by the fiasco of then assistant secretary of labor Daniel Patrick Moynihan's report, *The Negro Family: The Case for National Action* (the "Moynihan Report") (Ryan, 1965; Moynihan, 1965/1997), which blamed black people for their own unemployment. An unstated "fact" about the black power movement and black identity change is that it met its match in the nearly invisible force of deindustrialization, which I discuss more extensively in Chapter 5.

Nigrescence funneled folks into colleges; graduate schools of law, medicine, and engineering; entertainment; and the armed forces. Today, there is some degree of "blackness and color representation"—male and female—in every nook and cranny of everyday American life. However, for every black person lifted into the middle class or above, others fell (or were pushed backward) into the depths of a rapidly expanding black "underclass." The adults "passed over" by deindustrialization, and beyond the reach of Nigrescence, gave birth, first, to street life and a reinvigorated drug culture and, second, to the hip-hop generation, which, through music and dance, put the spotlight on street life. All was not lost: blackness, black beauty, Africa, and love of community are common themes of hip-hop lyrics and general culture. Also, it is commonplace for figures like LeBron James, Steph

Curry, Maya Moore, Tim Duncan, Liz Cambage, the late Kobe Bryant, and others to make "giving back" a major personal mission, as do scores of hip-hop artists (Stapleton, 1998). Thus, while the influence of black consciousness was and remains ubiquitous across all levels of the black community, its power was curtailed. One of the last things imagined by participants in the black movement who, coincidently, experienced social mobility is that their status change would result in a splitting of the black community into the haves and have-nots. History has a way of repeating itself. During the Harlem Renaissance of the 1920s, Langston Hughes reminded his fellow artists that their achievements did not increase the wages of the common black man (Singleton, 1982). Nigrescence and black consciousness led to social mobility, but many were passed over.

The Challenge of Afrocentricity: Essentializing Race

The eclectic, cosmopolitan, and racially progressive stance underscored by the four models was met by a vigorous critique from a small but influential cluster of black psychologists, who established the African-centered school of thought, with its academic base at the Department of African Psychology, Florida Agriculture and Mechanical University. The department held its ninth annual conference on African psychology in November of 2018. Shortly thereafter it lost one of its primary advocates—Kobi Kazembe Kambon (a.k.a., Joseph A. Baldwin)—who died suddenly on December 31, 2018, at the age of seventy-five. The most comprehensive summary of the tenets of African psychology can be found in the text edited by Daudi Azibo titled, *African Psychology in Historical Perspective and Related Commentary* (Azibo, 1996).

African Psychology (AP)

In African psychology, the notion of identity variation is rejected, and, in its place, the detailed outlines of "the" African identity are prescribed; this doctrinaire approach is evident throughout the AP analysis. The AP theorists studied ancient texts, more specifically the Egyptian Mystery System—a system said to provide directives on how to view the world and live one's life that are timeless and thus as helpful in guiding one's life in the present as in the past. AP theory is an extension of black nationalism; consequently, a major theme is the connection between the individual and the group, whereby the individual is indecipherable from the group and the group defines the individual. The occult quality of this assertion can be traced to the philosophy of the Nation of Islam, where wayward persons are asked to fully submit to an ideology that, if followed, will rid the person of the temptations that led to his or her imprisonment in the first place. AP theory offers a worldview that proclaims a holistic orientation, where the spiritual and material are inseparable.

The materialism and science of the West are said to fundamentally taint the humanity of white people, making them crave control and domination over others. Mass murder, genocide, and slavery are seen as "natural" outcomes of a worldview primarily driven by materialism, as is unrestrained greed. This part of AP theory points to the possibility that whites display a greater tendency toward sociopathy, and blacks toward empathy. Here the theory takes on the qualities of *emergent fascism* with its need to find motivation through devaluing "others" such as whites and/or members of the LGBTQIA community. Having first denigrated science and materialism, AP theory then does an about-face and embraces one of the most discredited forms of Western science (some would say pseudoscience): *eugenics, or the so-called science of racial differences*. Rather than turning to IQ tests, AP theory turns to studies on the role of melanin in human biology and human behavior. Melanin is said to be linked to empathy, and the absence of melanin to sociopathy. The white propensity toward greed, dominance, and murder is thought to be hardwired, as is the African orientation toward humanism.

From the mid-1970s onward, the leadership of the Association of Black Psychologists (ABPsi) was dominated by AP theorists and advocates. Nevertheless, several factors prevented AP theory from gaining widespread acceptance within black academic circles, although it has influenced ABPsi in particular. First, as most AP theorists were black men who embraced a particular mindset, homophobia became an issue, and openly gay persons were not welcomed as members of ABPsi. Second, the resurrection of racial essentialism in AP's reliance on eugenics—the "science and biology of race"—gave it the status of an occult theory, with "truth" derived from necromantic, supernatural, mystical, paranormal, and esoteric forces. In his erudite discussion of Afrocentricity and psychology, Kevin Cokley wrote: "Some of the more sensational media depictions of Afrocentricity are a result of this racialized rhetoric. An example is the rhetoric of [name deleted], who has publicly stated that Whites are biologically inferior because of their lack of melanin and because their genes were malformed by the Ice Age. Statements such as this made by 'Afrocentric scholars' make the Afrocentric enterprise fodder for scholarly and public ridicule" (Cokley, 2015, p. 144).

In presenting dichotomized, either/or thinking, prescriptive interpretations of blackness, and romantic interpretations of ancient philosophy, while enveloping a hatred for whites in a biogenetic trope, the eugenics-oriented AP camp displays traits linked with the Immersion-Emersion stage of Nigrescence. *It should be added that ABPsi has changed, as members of the LGBTQIA community now join and serve openly in the organization.*

Afrocentrism as a Cultural Phenomenon

Not every advocate of African psychology makes melanin central to their analysis, relying, instead, on a more cultural than biogenetic approach. As exemplars, the works and writings of Thomas Parham and Rosyln M. Caldwell-Gunes, Kevin Cokley, and Linda James Myers come to mind.

Thomas Parham and Roslyn M. Caldwell-Gunes and the Bakari Project: Thomas Parham, recently appointed president of California State University, Dominguez Hills, and Roslyn M. Caldwell-Gunes, professor of psychology at Prairie View College, recently wrote a thirty-nine-page unpublished manuscript titled *The Bakari Project:*

A Lifeline for African American Adolescent Development and Success (Caldwell-Gunes & Parham, 2019). The project is a program intervention designed for at-risk African American youth. The Arabic term *bakari* means "promising" and in Egyptian Arabic means "noble oath." The beginning of the manuscript presents a detailed analysis of educational, socioeconomic, and family-related challenges all American youth face, with particular emphasis on the experiences and "situation" encountered by black adolescent males. The authors start with a Critical Race Theory orientation and fade into an African-centered analysis. However, their emphasis is on worldview, mindset, culture, and values, with no mention of any biogenetic trope. Their intervention targets the youth's existential self.

Kevin Cokley: Cokley, professor of psychology and African American and African diaspora studies and educational psychology at the University of Texas at Austin, is the author of an extremely important critical analysis titled "Afrocentricity and African Psychology," which appears in the edited volume by James Conyers titled *Afrocentricity and the Academy* (Conyers, 2015). Among the important points he makes is the differentiation between Afrocentrists who embrace the biogenetic-melanin hypothesis, which he subjects to harsh criticism, and scholars voicing a primarily culture-based Afrocentricity, devoid of any eugenics emphasis. Cokley points out that the biogenetic-melanin camp presents arguments that are the mirror image of white racist tropes developed by J. Philippe Rushton (Cokley, 2015, p. 154). Elsewhere, Cokley presents what is essentially his culture-based orientation and interpretation of African psychology and African identity (Cokley, 2005). Cokley is one of a select few Afrocentrists to openly support making empirical research a component of African psychology. In an important article written with his wife, Germine Awad, titled "In Defense of Quantitative Methods: Using the 'Master's tools' to Promote Social Justice" (Cokley & Awad, 2013), it is argued that despite the history of the use of findings from research in stereotyping and stigmatizing minority groups, one should nonetheless strive to separate value-neutral methodologies from an interpretation bias that supports social hierarchies.

Optimal Psychology

Linda James Myers: In what may be the most compelling, concise, engaging, and well-informed cultural-based statement on African psychology, Linda James Myers, professor in the Department of African American and African studies at The Ohio State University, developed Optimal Psychology as an attempt to articulate, from start to finish, a comprehensive understanding of African psychology without reference to biogenetic tropes (Myers, 1993). It is not that she avoids dichotomizing between the worldview characteristic of Western thinking versus what she calls an African worldview. All Afrocentrists ponder the question of why so much human destruction and tragedy falls at the feet of the West, whether it be the colonization and genocide heaped upon American Indians, two calamitous world wars, the Holocaust, or slavery in the Americas. This understanding of human tragedy is myopic, as seldom are instances of African genocide integrated in the analysis, including the role of continental Africans in the slave trade (Foster, 1976; Richardson & Eltis, 2015). Myers tries to argue that, in placing so much faith in science and materialism, the West has lost its soul, so to speak, and thus does not hesitate to commit horrific acts when the objective is to dominate and create wealth. Thus, in her system, a sociopathic "gene" is replaced by a materialistic orientation that can result in philosophical estrangement. In effect, she links science, technology, and empiricism to the West, compared to omnipotent and omnipresent spiritualism in Africa. As such, Myers (1993) can be credited with constructing a modern form of shamanism (Harvey, 2003; Hoppál, 1996).

Shamanic practices and beliefs look to ancient beliefs that stress a connection to an all-powerful essence and the steps required to become both self-aware and at peace with nature. Myers's (1993) system does not engage exorcistic practices. However, she does require absolutism and true-believer attitudes in that one must follow to the letter the steps in her belief system (absolutism) and submit, personally, to a belief that her vision of the optimal is not subject to falsification and/or a counternarrative (true-believer attitudes).

While it is possible to trace elements of Optimal Psychology to prescriptions for life found within the Egyptian Mystery System, the fact of the matter is that, long before Myers constructed her system, numerous Western "white" gurus advocated transpersonal psychology, shamanistic in character, dating back to the turn of the twentieth century, with a resurgence following World War II and the search for meaning in the aftermath of the Holocaust. In the 1920s, thus over one hundred years ago, George Ivanovitch Gurdjieff (1866–1949), after studying ancient knowledge from Greece, Egypt, and the Middle East, created a system of higher awareness, with its apogee being "the fourth way"—very similar to Myers's Optimal level. Gurdjieff claimed that his interventions and teachings, if followed, made possible the highest level of awareness and eudaimonia—that is, well-being—as explicated in his text *In Search of Being: The Fourth Way of Consciousness* (De Salzmann, 2011). His work remains a mainstay of the Shambhala organization's website, which features transcendentalism-related books, videos, online courses, and events celebrating the spiritual and esoteric.

Transpersonal psychology positions itself as a remedy to trauma. In the aftermath of a traumatic experience, the person/client often experiences *psychological fragmentation*, where emotions and cognition become scrambled and dissociated. From transpersonal orientations such as Optimal Psychology have sprung therapeutic interventions designed to help a person reintegrate and achieve psychological wholeness. Myers is correct in linking this perspective to the thinking of philosophers from the ancient Egyptian dynasties. However, Egyptians also advocated and provided some of the original thinking about "science," which is to say, one should not confuse Egyptian prescriptions focusing on personal psychology with their separate and distinct thinking and actions that reveal an emerging *philosophy of science*. In addition, it is simply not true that science and materialism necessarily lead to fragmented perceptions and actions. *For example, cutting-edge ecological research shows the circular and holistic connection between layers of the earth's atmosphere and surface with the everyday behavior of human beings.* In point of fact, Egyptian science made advances in agriculture, construction, medicine, astronomy, literature, and measurement (that each rock cube used in constructing the pyramids had nearly the same dimensions continues to amaze scientists). The pyramids were not built on spirituality but on scientific thinking involving measurement; plans for construction; problem solving, such as how to transport rocks from the quarries and position them at different levels of the structure; geometry, as the structures were obviously pyramidal in shape; and labor considerations. As painful as it is to say it, the pyramids were a precursor to capitalism in that the society required that the masses dedicate their lives for the benefit of 1 percent of the population. Thus, the anti-science bias of African psychology represents a profound misrepresentation of Egyptian thinking.

Optimal Psychology is not a philosophy of science. Science reflects a fundamental human tendency to be *curious* about how plants grow, how rocks can be shaped, what human needs can be satisfied using what things, what the utility of this versus that is, and what the relationship should be between humans and various objects, vegetation, and things found in the natural environment. That aspects of the Mystery System should appear to be contradictory is no surprise. Almost all ancient philosophies start with the proposition that *everything is everything,* leading to a long history of tension between humans who want to be free to let their curiosity run its course and resistance within a society alarmed that such humans are acting in defiance of God's will to accept things as they are, without the necessity of human inquiry. The Egyptian Mystery System presents holistic statements about the meaning of life, and it also reveals the emergent thinking at that early time about a philosophy of science. The contradictions, diunitalism, and tension between the two kinds of statements anticipate by centuries future arguments between the Catholic Church and the counternarrative by Galileo.

Afrocentricity and Blacker-Than-Thou Attitudes

Afrocentric psychology attempts to attract people of African descent into a way of thinking that both empowers them and reduces their susceptibility to cultural miseducation (King, 2015; Shockley

& Hilliard, 2008). Its emphasis on ritual and total immersion in African culture is demonstrated by the fact that every ABPsi convention ends with a dinner banquet scripted by Afrocentrists. Attendees come dressed in Africana attire, ranging from the understated to the outrageous, with the beat of African rhythms floating in the background, and speakers whose every turn of sentence is flowered with words and phrases borrowed from Africa and enunciated by an otherwise English-speaking person.

On the other hand, one is reminded of the observation made by black feminists that black rage distorts and constricts the societal and self-perceptions held by black men more so than those held by black women (Msimang, 2017). At practically every gathering of Afrocentrists, one or more speakers find a way to insert a white presence, even if in fact no white people are in the audience, by reminding the audience of black-white "differences." What begins as a statement about Africanity turns into a series of bipolar assertions—we are this way, they are that way; we display empathy, they evidence sociopathy; our philosophy is pure, theirs is tainted. Suppressed anger and hatred of white people infects African psychology. At the fifty-first annual convention of ABPsi held in Orlando, Florida, in the summer of 2019, a central authority on Afrocentricity suggested to the audience that he no longer classified himself as human, for that might link him to whites. In effect, "humanism" has no standing within Afrocentric psychology. This speaker stressed being of African descent with the clear implication that being African and human was categorically different from being European and human. There is no surprise that, from a people that has collectively been the object of much pain and sorrow traced to the actions of the larger white society, several of its highly educated elites construct theories fueled in part by hostility toward whites.

At the same conference in 2019, another important member of ABPsi noted that some newly minted graduates declined to seek membership because they perceived themselves as *not black enough*, given the Afrocentric identity espoused by the organization's leadership and key figures linked to Afrocentric psychology. In addition, the organization's anti-science bias does not help matters, a bias that contradicts AP advocates' claim to have mastered Egyptian philosophy and history. Graduate students are required to embrace the scientific method, and master's students produce final projects, doctoral students dissertation projects. *This is true whether they are enrolled in a Historically Black College or University (HBCU) or a mainstream white institution.* Ironically, while adult members of ABPsi were pontificating about the need to turn away from empiricism, in the poster-presentation gallery, where projects by tomorrow's black psychologists were on display, practically all represented empirical studies.

It is unlikely students will turn around and embrace the admonition of arm-chair philosophers to reject and discard all the thinking that went into the attainment of their advanced degrees. Most alarming is the fact that key African American scholars who play a *disproportionate role in the production of new black doctoral recipients in psychology*, such as Margaret B. Spencer at the University of Chicago, A. Wade Boykin at Howard University, Robert Sellers at the University of Michigan, and Kevin Cokley at the University of Texas–Austin, are by implication not welcomed by ABPsi because they are empiricists! Cokley has offered a forceful and convincing defense of the role empirical research can play in the search for social justice (Cokley & Awad, 2013). As long as a philosophy designed to shed light on how to bring relief to humans who in the aftermath of trauma experience psychological fragmentation is misperceived as a philosophy of science, the organization will lose membership. *Fostering black psychological curiosity and thinking should be the motto of the organization moving forward.*

Nigrescence and the Existential Self

I discussed above how the theory of dissonance is very useful in helping to understand what aspect of the self-concept is most likely to be changed when a person undergoes a sudden, jarring identity shift, as happens with Nigrescence, or becoming woke. Recall the self-concept is multidimensional, consisting of personal identity (PI) and a second layer represented as social identity (SI), or reference group orientation (RGO). Another way to grasp social identity and RGO is to envision what gives direction and meaning to one's life, because the cognitions that construct SI/RGO address existential questions. The *existential self* encompasses a person's *ideas and beliefs* (social cognitions) about life, as captured by the list below and Figure 3.1.

1. Value system
2. Meaning-making system
3. Purpose in life
4. Cultural orientation
5. Sex-role identity
6. Ideas about the importance of relationships
7. Sense of community
8. Religious-spiritual ideas
9. Racial-cultural preferences

Social identity, reference group, and existential self are important because in affirming oneself to be Jewish or black, and so on, a person relies heavily on what she or he *perceives to be* the thoughts, opinions, writings, or actions associated with the group. How a person comes to find *meaning in life* will depend on the group to which the person refers. In the case of religious beliefs, systems of thought are codified in texts such as the Koran, Bible, Egyptian Mystery System, Mormon Text, Talmud, and so on. The importance of ideas as pillars to a person's mindset is depicted by Figure 3.1.

Nigrescence is akin to starting out as an atheist and becoming a believer or vice versa. Originally, Nigrescence Theory narrated the sojourn of *reference group change*, symbolized as the *Negro-to-black conversion experience*; however, Nigrescence continues to be relevant in present-day black psychology, as it has taken on a more generic meaning of struggling to become woke. Nigrescence-related epiphanies do not target a person's entire existential frame; rather, the focus is on changing the relationship between the person's sense of self and her or his relationship with community. To borrow traits from Sellers's theory, *the relationship becomes salient and central as organizing principles for living one's life.*

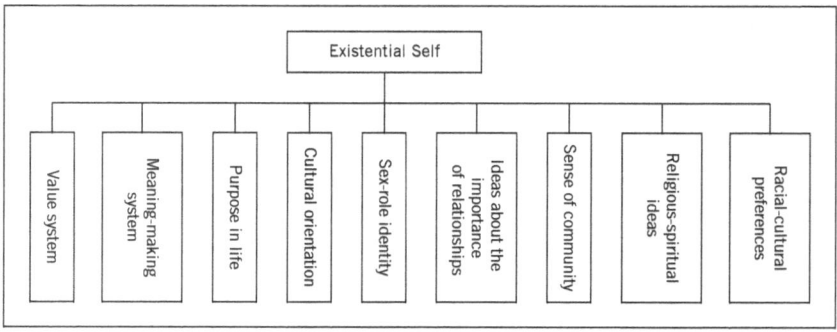

Figure 3.1 Designed by Gabrielle Reimer.

The four models discussed in Chapter 2 present a positive but critical analysis of the transformation process as depicted in Stages 2, 3, 4, and 5. However, each depicts the Negro identity—Stage 1—in pejorative language that reveals bias; consequently, a revision is needed that removes the concept of Negro from the realm of pathology. In effect, the judgments and choices of those who were not black power-oriented were pathologized, and Msimang has suggested that dismissive attitudes may be related to the way men more so than women treat divergent viewpoints:

> It takes time for me to discover it is possible to embrace radicalism that looks and feels different from the radical ideas of men. And it takes me longer than I would have liked to see that there are ways of being tough and angry and confrontational without being judgmental about the choices of others. It takes me even longer to realize that those with more moderate politics than mine were making choices that weren't necessarily based on being compromised or constrained. [My parents] Mummy and Baa weren't ignorant of Biko. They had considered his point of view and differed—not on the basis of weakness, but on the legitimate basis of intellectual and strategic disagreement. I couldn't see that then, though it is plain now. (Msimang, 2017, p. 191)

Msimang's insight is important, because in the United States divergent thinking within stigmatized groups has a history of being viewed as *psychopathology* rather than ideology. For a black person "not" to embrace a black identity was seen as *abnormal*. While never the intent, theorists left a very important factor out of the equation. When the meaning-making systems of a large number of people are sampled, an amazing variety of systems are revealed, because human beings are wont to find meaning in life through a broad range of beliefs. As cases in point, within the Jewish community one can find both devout ultra-orthodox Jews as well as atheists, and, among blacks, some are conservative Republicans who voted for Donald Trump. Thus, although the study of black identity may show blackness is "normative" in the sense that the majority of black people hold a black identity—normative in a statistical sense—it should be expected that *some blacks* will evidence forms of social identity for which *something other than race* plays an important role.

This emphasis on identity dissimilarity led to the affirmation found in my book *Shades of Black* that blackness is about identity variation, as there *is no one way to be black* (Cross, 1991). This put Nigrescence Theory in conflict with an African-centered perspective, which asserted black identity can be defined by specific standards derived from the Egyptian Mystery System, as discussed above. In addition, Nigrescence Theory seemed to go against a finding in the mainstream literature showing that it is the "norm" for members of ethnic-racial groups to identify with their group and that such identification is linked to positive mental health, typically measured as level of self-esteem or level of well-being.

Phinney, Erikson, and Marcia

One line of theorizing and research supporting the normative perspective can be found in the work of Jean Phinney (1989). First, it needs to be noted that Phinney's intent has been to interrogate *ethnic identity* and not necessarily racial identity. However, her theory and research are worth mentioning, because a study group focusing on Ethnic Racial Identity (ERI) in the twenty-first century (Umaña-Taylor et al., 2014) noted that the majority of the research from the two areas overlap in four ways:

1. Most of the measures do not measure race or ethnicity exclusively.
2. The foundational psychological processes for each overlap more than diverge.
3. Racial identity is often activated by ethnic triggers and vice versa.
4. Racial identity attitudes can be linked to strong cultural antecedents.

Phinney starts with the developmental theory constructed by Erikson (1968) and its truncated version expressed as ego identity statuses by James Marcia (1993). While both Erikson and Marcia narrate identity dynamics applicable to all human beings, Phinney goes a step further to suggest that, if one's nominal identity is ethnic (or racial), the identity to which the person aspires should, therefore, be grounded in a sense of ethnicity or race. The "should be" phrase makes this a prescriptive assumption. In other words, Phinney does not suggest or explore the possibility that persons nominally associated with an ethnic group may become attached—*in a healthy and psychologically positive way*—to an identity for which ethnicity and race are not salient.

Phinney and her students developed the Multigroup Ethnic Identity Measure (MEIM) (Phinney & Ong, 2007), and, during instrument construction, Phinney considered the need for a subscale measuring other-group orientation, but this effort was dropped. In effect, Phinney briefly envisioned a multidimensional scale but subsequently decided on a bivariate measure to operationalize the concept of ethnicity. Consequently, that "something other than ethnicity" may drive a person's identity is not accounted for by her theory or measure. This means that if, in fact, ethnicity is truly a multidimensional variable, her scale subsumes these other sources of variance as error.

Evidence has accumulated showing a strong positive correlation between the MEIM (ethnicity) and self-esteem (Smith & Silva, 2011). Low scores on the MEIM correlate with lower self-esteem, and it is typically assumed that a low score on the MEIM reflects that the respondent's perceptions of ethnic identity are negatively skewed. However, my recent study, authored with a number of colleagues (Cross et al., 2020), shows that low scores on the MEIM can reflect *two different mindsets*:

- First, the respondent is trying to communicate that she or he has a low opinion of the group, and these negative perceptions seem to carry over to perceptions of the self that are negative as well.
- Second, it acts as an expression that ethnicity is *not important* to the respondent (low salience). If some respondents ground their social identity in something other than their nominal ethnic identity, then they should score low on the MEIM but high to average on self-esteem, given that *something other than race or ethnicity* sustains and gives meaning to their lives.

My colleagues and I (Cross et al., 2020) gained access to two data sets, both consisting of MEIM scores and scores on a measure of well-being. When data from the first study (Schmidt et al., 2014) were subjected to cluster analysis, this revealed a significant subset of people, who, while nominally associated with an ethnic group, nevertheless produced low scores on the MEIM and high-to-average scores on self-esteem. The analysis was repeated with scores from a second data set, revealing the same pattern. To be clear, two clusters stood out in support of Phinney's theory, as one showed positive ethnicity correlated with positive well-being, and another the reverse trend; however, a third cluster showed subjects with adequate well-being even though their ethnicity score was low. Thus, *all three patterns are true*, but, more to the point, a significant number of persons seemed to be achieving a sense of well-bring through something other than ethnicity or race. The analysis revealed that the MEIM, a bivariate measure of ethnicity/race, actually *distorts* the relationship between ethnicity and self-esteem, as respondents holding a social sense of self for which ethnicity-race is not salient are "hidden" in variance linked to persons who identify as ethnic but hold negative perceptions of the self and one's group. When this variance is accounted for, as done in our study, something other than ethnicity/race is shown to be as capable of sustaining one's sense of well-being as holding an ethnicity-race based identity. In short, racial-ethnic identity is not prescriptive.

In line with John Berry's (1976) four-category thesis that incorporates alternate identity options—where alternate signifies something other than race or ethnicity—Yip and Cross (2004) sorted four identity classifications from a sample of one hundred youth of Chinese descent. During the fourteen-day diary study, research participants recorded daily ethnic identity salience, American identity salience, ethnic behaviors, and psychological well-being. The results showed that forty-four participants stressed Chinese salience and were Chinese-identified, nineteen showed a balanced or bicultural pattern, twenty-nine emphasized American salience and American identification, and nine did not fit any category. As part of their participation, each respondent completed a battery of measures at the beginning of their participation, including the MEIM, a self-esteem scale, and a measure of collective self-esteem. The Chinese-identified and bicultural groups recorded the highest MEIM scores; however, the three groups could not be differentiated on collective self-esteem, individual self-esteem, or scores on well-being. Thus, the American-identified—the alternate identity category—evidenced the same psychological strengths as respondents making ethnicity more salient to their sense of self.

Human beings who are nominally associated with an ethnic label or category are not hardwired to find meaning in life solely through ethnic identification. Rather than being prescriptive, ethnic identity is constructed, and, in some instances, members of the group will find meaning in life through frames of reference for which ethnicity-race is not inscribed. In other words, for a significant number of study participants, *something other than a sense of ethnicity or race* was driving their state of well-being. This pattern is consistent with Erikson's thinking, as he predicted that when one finds meaning in life—whatever the "content" of one's meaning making—there is a good chance the person will experience psychological well-being—that is, eudaimonia. These results are consistent with the position stated above—that depending upon the person's life story, ethnicity *may or may not* be salient to the way the person constructs her or his existential self, even if at birth, the larger society pins a nominal stigmatized identity on one's forehead.

The psychological relevance of racial-ethnic identity must be revised and even makes possible a major revision in theory on the relationship of PI and SI, or RGO. One overlooked possibility suggests that positive people make positive reference group choices, independent of their nominal membership in an oppressed group. *I hypothesize that*, when a youth reaches the developmental stage, when the outlines of personality have taken on predictable characteristics—ages ten–eleven–twelve—and given the person exhibits reasonably *positive* personality traits and assuming the person's personality traits are accompanied by positive and trustful attitudes toward life in general, the combination of personality strengths and positive attitudes will position the person to make positive decisions concerning reference group and philosophy of life, assuming no trauma or tragedy is experienced that alters the person's frame of reference.

In this case, positive self-esteem does not result from existential choices, rather, humans who are inclined to see the positive in life, as a function of their youthful development, are drawn toward positive social identities, positive reference groups, and evidence a positive valance enveloping their existential contemplations. This presumes that the larger society makes positive choices accessible. In his study of black men living the street life, Yasser Payne (2006) reveals that when paths to employment or educational opportunities are made scarce, as happens during deindustrialization and globalization, otherwise "normal" humans—in this case black males and females—turn to the streets and various underground economic ventures. In Chapter 5 I review information showing that whites—who were never slaves—evidenced the same pattern of turning to drugs and crime when deindustrialization blanketed their communities. *In effect, positive choices by positive people require the presence of positive opportunities created by the larger society.*

In the specific case of persons holding a nominal identity subject to historical denigration by the larger society, the majority may make their racial identity salient, and their majoritarian pattern tends to obscure the fact that those whose system of meaning makes salient something other than race also achieve eudaimonia. Adding to the confusion is that those who evidence actual negative attitudes about their racial-ethnic status do, in fact, evidence lower levels of eudaimonia. Thus, while identity choices within or outside the group are linked to eudaimonia, there is, in fact, a cost for holding *demonstrative negative attitudes* about one's group. When these dynamics are assessed with a *binary measure* such as the MEIM, evidence of those expressing actual self-hatred is conflated with evidence of persons scoring low on the MEIM, as an expression that *something other than race-ethnicity* is behind their positive social identity. In point of fact, the correlation between social identity and personality is probably *spurious* because, as the average person evidences positive (or good enough) personality development at around age twelve, the average person subsequently will make positive social identity choices down the line. Positive self-esteem is more a function of early development and may be sustained but not "caused" by choice of social identity, which takes place in early adolescence or early adulthood.

This complicated pattern of identity dynamics played itself out during the construction of the CRIS. The final version of the scale determined that three dimensions are best represented by "separate" subscales: Assimilation, Miseducation, and Racial Self-Hatred. The Assimilation subscale represents a version of an identity grounded on something other than race and black culture. Miseducation measures the extent to which a person accepts as accurate ideas about black people that are in fact negative stereotypes. Finally, the Racial Self-Hatred subscale is made up of items where the person is actually describing the self with clearly negative terms—that is, "I dislike being black," and so on. Surprisingly, the Miseducation pattern suggests that a black person can hold negative perceptions of the group yet psychologically compartmentalize these beliefs such that the person does not apply the generalization to a description of one's self, despite being a member of the group. To demonstrate this point, let us examine the influence of deindustrialization on black life.

When deindustrialization hit black communities hard, the closing of factories and loss of jobs practically forced black people to turn to the streets to generate income (Payne, 2017). In effect, black inner-city communities became the site of crime, gangsterism, and drug addiction, repeating history, as when working-class Irish, Jewish, and Italian immigrants turned to gangsterism for relief from the ravages of poverty. Rather than focus on root causes, the media and government officials began to attack the *psychological integrity of black men, in particular*, and passed draconian crime "prevention" legislation that over time resulted in the school-to-prison pipeline. At both the state and federal levels, black people supported such governmental and police actions, in part because black public opinion stood in agreement with the stereotypes anchoring such actions. Miseducation was in evidence for black people who otherwise viewed their own personal identity as positive, as the stereotypes were "compartmentalized" and *did not apply to them personally*. Although he pushed for passage of the crime package as well as legislation revamping welfare legislation that hurt poor black people, blacks voted overwhelming to re-elect President Bill Clinton in 1996. Miseducation can seem like an extension of the concept of self-hatred, but research using the CRIS continues to show the two concepts are distinct. Eventually, the black community came to understand the way the new laws "targeted" black people and black males in particular, but years had passed, and thousands of black males were already in prison.

Identity, Eudaimonia, and Meaning in Life

Some of you must be wondering why I am considered an expert on black identity, given that my analysis shows that black people may experience eudaimonia whether or not they embrace a black identity. In this section I try to demonstrate that identity is less a psychological construct than a *social-cultural-political* variable. Bear with me as I try to explain.

Social identity, or what I prefer to call the "existential self," is only one, albeit an important, layer of the self-concept. In psychology we tend to lump everything about the person into the vessel known as the "self-concept," and we go a step further and assume that each layer of the self is woven through and across each layer such that the dynamics of one layer are assumed to be intricately related (correlated/connected) to the other. This may be accurate in a clinical setting, where the personal history of a client shows us how her or his personality evolved and, subsequent to that, how her or his existential self emerged. But what may be true for one individual does not apply to another. This sense of interconnectivity dominates our understanding of people of color and, for that matter, any group holding a nominal identity subject to denigration and oppression by the majority group. While never the intent, such a perspective can lead to a *distortion* of our understanding of the general humanity of such groups, especially when we present theories suggesting that ethnic/racial identity is prescriptive. *As psychologists, our starting point should always be that we are discussing human beings and the amazing variability they bring to any psychological topic under consideration.*

When I am wearing my socio-cultural-political hat, I want as many black people as possible to make race and culture highly salient to their existential self. However, as a psychologist and humanist, I should expect that in a large sample of human beings who are black, and who exhibit "good enough" psychological personality traits, *their unique social histories* should ultimately explain how they inscribe the meaning of race, if it is in fact inscribed at all, because there are any number of experiences that can turn one black person toward race salience and other factors that "cause" them to look elsewhere for meaning in life. To think otherwise is to in effect deny black people of their humanity, because as human beings, African Americans are not hardwired to be black and thus can be expected to vary in the way each incorporates *or not* the salience of race within their overall existential frame—how they make meaning of life. Thus, in psychological studies of black people, holding a particular type of social identity is not correlated with eudaimonia, because as human beings, black people, despite their oppression, construct personal meaning through a broad range of pathways, and this variability speaks to their general humanity.

That said, research to date shows black identity is "normative" in the statistical sense that most black people evidence an existential self for which "race" and "black culture" are inscribed. While there is no guarantee that such inscription will provide a pathway to better mental health, holding a black identity means that whatever talents, skills, interests, and competencies are part of that person's self-concept will probably be shared with the community, *making it stronger in a socio-cultural-political sense.* Identity is about making meaning in life, and when a black person embraces blackness, she or he is likely to add socio-cultural-political strength to the community, even if, at the deep-structure level, the person is a flaming neurotic. If the person is more normal than not at the level of self-esteem and personality, all the better, because that means in transacting her or his skills, talents, and so on with other members of the community, she or he will be more effective and competent. On the other hand, many a black meeting has been a challenge to run, given that one person, who, while supportive of the group's agenda, is nonetheless interpersonally incompetent and drives everyone up the wall. Nigrescence may not lead to better mental health, but it can result in a meaning-making system that helps a person find *purpose in life.* The black social movement pressed black people to change the level of importance they ascribed to being black, and this change in mindset resulted in black people bringing all sorts of skills and talents to the table. Poets became black poets, psychologists became black psychologists, historians became black historians, artists became black artists, academics formed black studies programs.

Psychology needs to take ownership of its tendency for having made racial-ethnic identification *prescriptive*—that is, something almost "required" of the person—as if identity was hardwired. That sets up a *binary hypothesis* where in the study of an ethnic group, persons who identify as ethnic or racial are assumed to evidence higher levels of eudaimonia than members of the same group who do not. This binary hypothesis overlooks or is blind to human plasticity; human beings, whether members of a stigmatized group or not, will make meaning in life through social identity categories thought to be beyond the reach of the persons who are stigmatized. By way of example, at the very moment that some black people were drawn toward revitalization through Nigrescence, others were experiencing a religious peak experience, where they felt closer to God than ever before. At the level of the individual, finding God rather than Nigrescence will sustain a person's eudaimonia, and, likewise, another person awakened by Nigrescence, rather than God, will benefit psychologically as much as if she or he had experienced a religious conversion. In both exemplars, change will result in the person's *existential self*, with thoughts (social cognitions) reinforcing the person's newfound connection to God dominating the religious convert, while thoughts forging a new and stronger connection between the person and the black community is at the heart of Nigrescence.

In their preoccupation with eudaimonia, psychologists tend to overlook the power and value of identity, in large measure because it is so close as to be taken for granted. *Identity focus, content, and belonging* reveal what actions and commitments a person will evidence in *everyday life*. Nigrescence awakened people to the way in which a person can contribute to the health and wealth of the black community. At the time I became entranced by Nigrescence, I had advanced skills in psychology, from both an academic (teaching, research) and experiential (counseling, administration) framework. Thereafter, the focus of my writing, research, and teaching was very black focused. Even as I have evolved a more interlocking and humanist perspective, my works discover *humanism through the particular, because all that one needs to know about humanity can be unearthed in the study of black people.* There has been no change in my level of self-esteem, but my thinking has become more textured, dense, and complicated. Don L. Lee entered Nigrescence with literary and poetic talent, and thereafter his poems were decidedly grounded in blackness. The same narrative is true of Nikki Giovanni and Gwendolyn Brooks. Jeff Donaldson was an extremely gifted artist going into the movement, and he brought the AfriCOBRA aesthetics movement to

Howard University. Starting out with the goal of becoming a scholar, Reiland Rabaka, who is forty-five years young, has written eleven scholarly books, all on some aspect of the black experience, and is now considered a preeminent scholar of Africana studies.

When an individual anchors his or her existential self in connection to community through the mechanisms of personal talents and skills, the community is made stronger and more viable. Recall in the Yip and Cross (2004) study involving one hundred Chinese participants, forty-four were Chinese-focused, nineteen exhibited a bicultural orientation, and twenty-nine an American-focused orientation. That means sixty-three out of one hundred were in some way engaged by ethnicity. Given some were academics, others artists, and still others scientists, that means a majority were in some way engaging a Chinese sense of self in their everyday activities and accomplishments. The sum total of their activities probably resulted in a stronger Chinese community.

We do not need another study on the relationship of identity to well-being or self-esteem. Rather, we need qualitative diary studies, using the daily diary schedules developed by Janet Swim or Tiffany Yip. Their measures capture detailed information about daily activities along with attitudinal and emotional data allowing the researcher to explore the connection, if any, between the person's declared identity and the way identity is enacted and lived in everyday activities. We need more research on the *content of a person's existential framework* and its linkage to everyday activities. While the individual black person has many options for achieving personal eudaimonia, the strength of a community depends upon how many persons become attached to the community and, in so doing, *what gifts they bring to it.*

Can Black Identity Be Defined?

Success at defining what black identity is has been hard to come by. Ironically, more success has transpired in pinpointing racial self-hatred. In the beginning of my academic career, black self-hatred was taken for granted, and I have made it a point to strip it of myth and exaggeration, as I explore in the chapters ahead. That said, work with the construction and application of the CRIS has helped us to understand that there really is a fraction—a small fraction mind you—of black folk who do dislike themselves for racial reasons. I believe a negative or positive valence wraps around the sense of self, as it unfolds between infancy and childhood, and this will steer the person toward positive (or negative) meaning-making beliefs. I am very suspicious of the idea that blackness per se "causes" self-hatred or self-love. I think black people are harmed at an early age, and this makes them vulnerable to self-hatred as adults, when "race" becomes a blanket under which to hide the actual origins of one's pain. In any case, when a respondent scores high on the CRIS *Racial Self-Hatred scale*, they also tend to score low on whatever measure of well-being is included in the study.

That said, what specific beliefs and ideas define a positive black identity? Earlier we saw where the Afrocentrists tried to make this task easier by arguing the centrality of the Egyptian Mystery System and attracted few adherents outside the Association of Black Psychologists. Blackness is not so much a mystery as the object of constant variation. In our work with the CRIS, the one factor that pops out time after time is the word "salience." But here again, how far should one take this factor? The Afrocentrists tried to develop a comprehensive checklist on black values, dress, rules about who to date or marry, and so on, but one can imagine the immediate rejection by black folk at the thought of such limiting prescriptions.

Perhaps the most important obstacle constraining one's ability to settle on a definition is the fact that, while we are humans of African descent, our stay in the United States has been long enough that we are very much "American" in how we think, imagine, critique, create, dream, and contemplate. Although we tend to reject, at the surface level, the philosophy of individualism, we nevertheless are each the product of a socialization experience that at every turn reinforced *individuality* or the sense that each of us is a "unique" person. This sense of uniqueness is both a value and a potential deficit. *As something valued*, it results in what can be called "black style," as expressed in music, sports, literature, and poetry: the instrumental "sound" when playing the saxophone, trumpet, and so on; the vocalese of each black singer and/or composer; and the presentation of self, as in the way each black man enters the barbershop, or sisters present themselves in a crowded space. *As a deficit,* it causes one to "resist" agreement, compromise, and conformity, and, in the case of the current topic, it gets in the way of our coming to consensus on how to define blackness and black identity. Thus, while there is general agreement that the construction of one's existential self being black and one's connection to the black community should be accorded importance, priority, and salience, "how much" and to "what degree" are causes of a never-ending debate, and one is left with ambiguous "identity categories" such as nationalism, biracialism, humanism, and multiculturalism. By way of example, in the development of the CRIS, we found each and every category had "subsets" so that there seemed to be three or four types of nationalism, and the same was true for the categories Pre-encounter (Negro) and Multicultural. For example, while constructing the CRIS, most intriguing were the subsets we had to wade through for Multicultural, as some people liked the category Multicultural if it did not include white people [only people of color], while others wanted to make certain it did not include LGBTQIA persons. We decided to select the most inclusive set of items, thus our Multicultural scale has the awkward title Multicultural Inclusive.

Consequently, after forty-plus years in the field, the best I can do is to repeat: "*There is no one way to be black.*" In the hands of ideologues, a lack of consensus is problematic, but from the vantage point of humanism, it is less a problem and more the reflection of the inherent tendency of human beings to strive for difference and individuality, which in this instance happen to be persons of African descent. *Our inability to define in simple terms what blackness is represents less a failure than the affirmation, confirmation, and celebration of our greater humanity.*

Summary of Chapters 2 and 3

While originally conceived as a period piece tied to the events of the 1960s and 1970s, Chapter 2 explores evidence that shows Nigrescence—the abrupt change in black consciousness leading to a state of being woke—to be a recurring theme in black history. Thus, while the term "Nigrescence" is connected to a very contemporaneous discourse, the phenomenon of wakening, consciousness-raising, and striving to be woke has been ever-present throughout black history. Cultural awakening is imbedded in the racial narratives of people of color across the globe, and earlier episodes, as experienced by Africans, were documented by Frantz Fanon and Albert Memmi. In the aftermath of the assassination of Martin Luther King Jr., African Americans seemed to spontaneously react in a pattern shown to be amazingly similar, as documented by four black psychologists positioned at different locations across the United States. The similarity among the models was explained by the fact that although attending four different universities, the curriculum for each included a heavy dose of *transpersonal-existential psychology*. The Maslowian perspective—involving a hierarchy of needs and ever-expanding consciousness that accompanies awareness—clearly guided the identity-change narratives constructed by each author. To describe this process of psychological awakening, the term "Nigrescence" was borrowed from the French African literary movement known as Negritude. Thus, Nigrescence speaks to the *process* of developing black consciousness.

An encapsulated summary of the models starts with the mindset guiding a person's *meaning-making* system *before* experiencing a jolt to change. Following an Encounter, the person is caught between a rock and hard place, as a struggle ensues between the old identity, which is now the object of distain, and the desperate thrust to "figure out" the details of the consciousness level, yet to be achieved. This in-between state of perturbation and Dissonance can lead to extreme acting-out, where the person feels compelled to demonstrate her or his new self in dramatic and even dangerous actions. The stress of the middle stage cannot be sustained, and if the person moves forward, a sense of not being black enough is replaced by a period of resolution and Internalization of the new perspective. In a manner of speaking, the old way of making meaning of race and one's positionality in the world is replaced by a new meaning-making perspective.

While transpersonal psychology helped explain the underlying frame of reference employed by the four authors in the construction of their amazingly similar narratives, dissonance theory helped explicate the tumult that accompanies what amounts to a change in one's thinking. The chapter ended with a thick narration of the way Nigrescence changes thinking without necessarily changing personality. Friendship patterns may change, organizational affiliation may change, aesthetic preferences may change, types of literature read may change, political frame of reference may change, hairstyle may change, tendency to decorate one's body with African jewelry and clothing may change, types of social events attended may change, and so on, but the person's personality profile and transactional skills will remain intact. The person may feel "new," but that is because there has been such a radical revamping of his or her existential self and, for adults, personality is typically taken for granted. *In effect, Nigrescence tracks a radical change in one's thinking about race and one's relationship to that meaning.* As a counternarrative to the way the majority of black folk make blackness a component of their meaning-making system, a section emphasized that a critical number of black people make something other than race and black culture foundational to their beliefs systems. Lastly, a lifespan model was reviewed to demonstrate the range of social identity stances found among black people.

Chapter 3 focused on issues that emerged after the Nigrescence models became a common feature in discourses on blackness. As the four models were authored by males, the male-centric bias of the models was explored from a black feminist perspective. In particular, the way black male anger distorts Nigrescence was accorded considerable importance. In addition, the importance of intersectionality was examined. An Afrocentric critique of Nigrescence was explored in considerable detail. Nigrescence was often accompanied by social mobility in the lives of many; however, deindustrialization acted as a counterweight to personal uplift and pushed many into the quicksand of unemployment and a downward spiral. One section revisited the concept of Pre-encounter and Negro to show that what changes with

Nigrescence is the restructuring of one's belief systems or existential self, with personality left relatively unchanged. The relationship, if any, between choice of reference group and eudaimonia occupied a great deal of space in the current analysis. Uncovered was the fact that persons born with an ascription find meaning in life in which the ascription may or may not be accorded salience. While most black people make blackness a part of their meaning-making system, others, by way of divergent socialization experiences, end up seeing the world through a lens for which race places a minor role, if at all. Finally, the absence of consensus on how to define black identity was traced to the weight black people accord individuality, which while producing amazing innovation in sports, jazz, and hip-hop, impedes political consensus. Diversity in black socio-political-cultural thought was shown to be a general human tendency, rather than something specific to black people. Thus, ironically, the lack of consensus on what it means to be black was demonstrated to be a celebration of the underlying humanity of black people, rather than an ideological "flaw."

4

Double-Consciousness and the Performance of Identity

Irving Goffman's 1956 dramaturgical analysis (Goffman, 1956/1978)—centered on the importance of everyday social interactions—was anticipated over 150 years ago, with the appearance in 1903 of W.E.B. Du Bois's concept of "double-consciousness":

> It is a peculiar sensation, this double-consciousness, this sense of always looking at one's self through the eyes of others, of measuring one's soul by the tape of a world that looks on in amused contempt and pity. One ever feels his two-ness,—an American, a Negro; two souls, two thoughts, two unreconciled strivings; two warring ideals in one dark body, whose dogged strength alone keeps it from being torn asunder.
>
> The history of the American Negro is the history of this strife—this longing to attain self-conscious manhood, to merge his double self into a better and truer self. In this merging he wishes neither of the older selves to be lost. He does not wish to Africanize America, for America has too much to teach the world and Africa. He wouldn't bleach his Negro blood in a flood of white Americanism, for he knows that Negro blood

has a message for the world. He simply wishes to make it possible for a man to be both a Negro and an American without being cursed and spit upon by his fellows, without having the doors of opportunity closed roughly in his face. (Du Bois, 1903, pp. 2–3)

In this chapter I want to venture beyond the classification implications of twoness and examine it with a teleological lens, by exploring the meaning and performance implications of twoness. As much as anyone following the travail of emancipated Africans—men, women, children, and families—Du Bois observed firsthand how they fashioned a double-tiered sense of self to *survive tyrannical whiteness*. Exchanges with white people were filtered by a veil or mask, meant to disguise and protect the black performer's authentic self; however, in the presence of trusted black folk and exceptional whites, the veil was lifted, revealing the person's *real personality or quiet self*, as Kevin Quashie defines it (Quashie, 2012).

During the nadir of the black experience (circa 1877 to the turn of the twentieth century), it was dangerous for black people to present themselves as transparently human. However, total avoidance of white people was impossible, even for blacks living in all-black towns, thus twoness not only carried labels and definitions—"veil" and "the hidden self"—it also referenced variations on the *performance of self*: one premised on fear, vigilance, and caricature; the other on authenticity, creativity, and spontaneity. The crudity of the shift belies the fact that, over time, double-consciousness would give way to the sophisticated modern-day *code-switching*, as practiced by my father, when carrying out his work as a Pullman porter, or by my mother, when a maid for white households, or by myself at Princeton, as I sought to demonstrate my worthiness for a doctorate in psychology. The past fear of being labeled an Uncle Tom has changed in the present to anxiety over being too good at code-switching, raising the specter of an *imposter syndrome*. Paradoxically, in another sphere—namely sports—African American athletes continue to set and break long-established records, and are the role models for all athletes, including whites. This chapter concerns black identity enactments, because performing different styles of blackness continues to have relevance for purposes of survival as well as success.

To better comprehend what aspects of the psyche are manipulated during modern-day code-switching, I start with a brief summary of the components of the self-concept. A holistic picture of the self-concept requires information about personality as well as social identity. Personality, temperament, and interpersonal competence emerge at birth, and the attachment experience with the mother is generally foundational to future successful socialization of a child. As the infant child gains mobility and rudimentary interactional skills, key personality traits emerge between infancy and early childhood, taking on clearly recognizable dynamics by age twelve, and some would say even sooner. With age and continued experience, these traits—or ways of interacting with other humans—become more elaborate and sophisticated, while maintaining their essence. Thus "shyness" and holding back at age twelve may turn into a reserved style by age twenty-two, where one mostly observes or enters a conversation near the middle or end of an exchange, if at all. Likewise, a confident, energetic, exploratory style at age twelve may result in a bombastic, seemingly fearless and forward person at age twenty-two. Of course, a strong negative or outright traumatic experience can disrupt one's trajectory. One's unique personality style and private thoughts tend to define one's *interior self*, or *quiet self*, positioned behind the Du Boisian veil/mask for purposes of protection. For the sake of discussion, this interior view defines PI (private identity, or personal identity).

Traits, styles, and competences do not simply pop up or appear from thin air but emerge from everyday interactions or "experiences" with people that over time are transformed into pleasant or horrific developmental memories embedded in one's conscious, subconscious, or unconscious. Memories of the way we are constructed and become "human" may be triggered in reaction to a poem, lyrics to songs, or literary works by the likes of James Baldwin, Maya Angelou, or bell hooks, who, with imaginative, crafted, and transcendent prose, help people remember their upbringing. It is why we listen to music, attend plays, or read novels, because the narrative about someone else's life touches to the core the way we feel and think about our own.

Social identity, or "group" identity, refers to social labels, categories, and groups that can originate from outside groups who have the *power to name and classify*, or it can originate with persons (representatives) from inside the group, based on the group's history and legacy. Social identity is declarative and shallow during childhood through preadolescence—as in proclaiming oneself to be Jewish, or African American, or gay—because one's capacity for contemplative, philosophical, and existential ruminations are brain dependent, and advanced prefrontal cortex development begins during adolescence and levels off at around age twenty-five. It is fascinating that precocious youth may assimilate highly complex scientific theorems and formulas at an early age, while being unable to disentangle interpersonal relationships. One's capacity for deep thinking and reflection lies in wait until the prefrontal cortex progresses toward maturation. Thereafter, being Jewish, gay, trans, or black takes on a deeper philosophical and "examined" quality. Stated another way, a child can be taught that she or he is a person of African descent at an early age, but it is not until one's higher-level brain functions evolve that one can turn a label into the basis for finding meaning in life, as in a reference group orientation. Finally, group identity turns the human being into an abstraction that provides very little insight into the make-up of one's PI—private or personal identity. Amazingly, much of the discourse in black psychology revolves around research conducted solely at the group-identity level, leaving relatively untouched the analysis of the range of PI patterns to be found among black people, even though, ironically, PI is a better measure for any discussion of universal human traits.

The emergence of our capacity to experience the self at a deeper level—at either the group or PI level—was captured by Erik Erikson's psychosocial stages of identity development (Erikson, 1956). Erikson's narrative is most often referenced when seeking a developmental explication for the unfolding of personality, social identity, and reference group orientation. Erikson was a humanist, and his developmental stages ring true across cultures; however, humanism meets its match when the focus of attention is on the socially stigmatized. Faced with that predicament, stigmatized humans must evolve double-consciousness, where one's sense of self performs the *identity work* expected and demanded by those with the power to stigmatize—ultimately for purposes of exploitation that result in the lopsided distribution of wealth and power—as differentiated from the stigmatized person's private, interior self that is hidden behind the veil or mask. The ability of the stigmatized to obfuscate goes a long way in explaining the origins of resilience.

This is the conundrum of double-consciousness—to live a life knowing the *other* sees one's blackness, Jewishness, gayness, transgenderism, or disability (visual or hearing impairment, etc.) as reason for treating them as less than human, which in turn requires one to have to develop the psychological wherewithal to survive such attempts at dehumanization. If the stereotype is without legal and societal restraint, the other might rape, brutalize, or lynch, in which case one's very existence is in jeopardy. If there is enough sociopolitical progress that limits how far the *other* can express their disdain and hatred, the resulting contempt, conceit, and sense of superiority can be countered, and sometimes negated, by *stigma management* involving mindfulness and key interpersonal enactments that protect, disarm, and even make a black person's well-being possible.

Addendums to the Psycho-Social Stages

Given the inherent limitations of Erikson's model to account for positive psychological development of members of oppressed and stigmatized groups, a number of scholars have tried to address the dilemma with what can be considered *addendums* to Erikson's psychosocial model. James Jones's concept of TRIOS shows how certain attitudes, beliefs, and values help one cope with racism (Jones, 2003), as does Wade Boykin's Triple Quandary thesis (Boykin, 1986). Protection, within-group connectivity/pride, and mainstream success are themes emerging from the tripartite model of minority identity proffered by Daphna Oyserman and Kathy Harrison (1998). They suggest that, by early adolescence, black youth exhibit a multidimensional group identity structure in order to negotiate three worlds, or types of situations: (1) experiences with racism and discrimination, (2) black cultural experiences, and (3) experiences within mainstream society. Howard Stevenson (Stevenson & Arrington, 2009) and his students at the University of Pennsylvania focused on the socialization messages of black parents that stressed *protective* socialization, or awareness of the existence of racism, and *proactive* socialization, meaning conversations and activities stressing an appreciation for black culture at the emotional (pride), cognitive (historical awareness), and behavioral (attendance and participation of black events) levels. Written for a popular and general audience, Nancy Boyd-Franklin and Anderson Franklin's (2001) text titled *Boys into Men: Raising Our African American Teenage Sons* avoids academic jargon, but themes permeating each chapter include what I call in this chapter vigilance (protection, or *buffering*), strategies for success within school and general society (*code-switching*, or proactive behavior within mainstream settings), an openness to cross-cultural and cross-racial relationships (*bridging*), a sense of cultural identity (feeling of *attachment-bonding* with black culture and black people), and being true to oneself (individuality and individuation).

All of the addendums to Erikson's analysis operate at the group-identity level. The one exception can be traced to the work of Margaret B. Spencer, the Marshall Field IV Professor of Urban Education at the University of Chicago, as she takes the analysis another step to show that cutting across black parental concerns for identity protection and cultural engagement is the goal of *self-actualization* (Spencer, 1995). In effect, she emphasizes three themes: (1) identity protection, (2) a positive collectivist orientation, and (3) flowering of the child as a unique human being (individuation and individualism). To be clear, Spencer is not advocating the philosophy of individualism but the notion of optimal personal growth, where the youth's in-born proclivities and learned skills are allowed to blossom, take hold, and mature.

Complementing these motivational analyses and taking their cue from Goffman's dramaturgical analysis and the presentation of self in everyday life (Goffman, 1956/1978), scholars have attempted to match behaviors with each group-identity component to show how a particular identity thrust is enacted. That is, what does identity protection look like? What behaviors are triggered when operating within the mainstream? However, before moving to the presentation of such enactments, we need to remember that blacks have had to adjust and manipulate divergent *ecological settings* that range in degrees of freedom, from closed and highly oppressive to settings more open and thus subject to manipulation. These settings include:

- *Closed ecologies*, where the oppressor's power and control approach the absolute, making personal agency difficult to impossible, as during slavery and modern-day incarceration
- Entrapment ecologies, or *Faustian Dilemmas*, where black poor are drawn into behaviors that readily lead to incarceration
- *Open but constrained ecologies*, where the law and social circumstances made agency possible but difficult, as was true of black life from the end of Reconstruction in 1896 all the way to the beginning of modern-day black protest in the mid-1950s
- *Open, expansive ecologies*, as experienced by wealthy sectors of the black community from the 1970s to present

The Psychology of Buffering

Buffering as Endurance and Survival

Black people work to negotiate spaces over which they have some control and room to maneuver; however, *slavery and incarceration* are ecologies that by definition radically limit the degrees of freedom available to black manipulation. Thus, we need to differentiate between incarceration buffering and everyday buffering, which takes place in everyday black life outside of prisons. In highly confined and constricted spaces (prison and slavery) emphasis is less on manipulation or management than just achieving *survival*, plain and simple. In either setting, blacks became, and to this day remain, experts at "matching" unqualified evil with physical and psychological *resolve, endurance, grit, survival, and resilience.*

In the face of insurmountable odds, blacks turn to survival as the immediate objective. After being viciously flogged, raped, or severely punished and bought to the brink of insanity as a slave, or, in the present, forced to spend lengthy periods of time in solitary confinement, the individual slave/prisoner responded and responds in a variety of ways that made it possible to stay connected to one's humanity in the face of being treated like a subhuman. In recent history, one of the most improbable examples of a black prisoner making the best of an impossible situation is the story of Richard Phillips (Associated Press, 2019). After Phillips spent forty-seven years in prison, new evidence about the crime showed he was innocent, and he was exonerated. While incarcerated, he taught himself to paint using watercolors, and he exited prison with a spectacular cache of works. After his release from prison, the state found reason to delay payment of funds awarded to persons wrongfully imprisoned. Consequently, selling his paintings now provides his sole means of support. Given the excellence of his paintings, he has managed to sell works at a price that makes for a comfortable life. In an interview, Phillips stated: "I didn't actually think I'd ever be free again. This art is what I did to stay sane." Prison art and prison art therapy are well-documented ways prisoners salvage their humanity (Bernstein, 2010; Kornfeld, 1997; Merriam, 1998; Shailor, 2010; Sheets, 2019). In some instances, slavery, as well as imprisonment, produces nihilism and a sense of being *broken,* and, ironically, at the other end of the spectrum, the never-ending solitude can promote deep reflection and religious-like epiphanies, as happened to Malcolm X in his conversion to the Black Nation of Islam. Countless black inmates find solace in Jesus Christ.

At the fiftieth anniversary of the founding of the Africana Studies and Research Center at Cornell University, Professor John Bracey, the former chair of Africana Studies at the University of Massachusetts–Amherst, made the following statement (April 13, 2019) apropos to what I seek to summarize about endurance and survival; the following are not his exact words but capture the sentiment of his amazing tribute to black endurance: *They stacked us in slave ships and we survived the journey; they enslaved us yet we were there to take advantage of emancipation; during Jim Crow they lynched us by the thousands yet here we stand today; they segregated us and gave us inferior schools, yet today we survive and celebrate the fiftieth anniversary of black studies.*

Buffering and Everyday Living While Black

In most communities and for most individuals, the line between incarcerated life and everyday existence outside of prison is clear and unambiguous. However, walking while black, banking while black, doing Starbucks while black, doing work to spiff up one's property while black, barbecuing in a public park while black, or just passing through an open space while black can result in death when a person or persons observing you is your white neighbor with a gun, a white Starbucks manager, or, of course, the police, regardless of the officer's race or ethnicity. There is such an amazing consensus by white Americans from all walks of life—and too often among blacks themselves—that black boys and men in particular are a threat to the well-being of anyone and everyone. Given that white society expects law enforcement to be at the forefront of societal protection, there is little wonder actions by the police are behind the heavy toll of deaths experienced by black men and women in the course of carrying out their mundane daily activities. Note my stress on both genders, because somehow reports on police shootings are "gendered" by highlighting the shooting of black males, while making the not-infrequent deaths of black girls and women invisible (Brown et al., 2017). If black males are turned into caricatures of criminality, black girls are seen as adult before their time (Fordham, 1993; Gibson et al., 2014). Studies show that in school black girls are subject to more frequent and harsher disciplinary treatment, driven by stereotypes held by teachers and school administrators who perceive black girls to be older than their actual age, thus literally robbing black girls of their childhood and youth (Priest et al., 2018). Research shows that black girls are viewed as problematic starting as early as kindergarten (Zimmerman, 2018). Black women face another challenge that can be as lethal as a bullet fired from a gun: inadequate prenatal and postnatal health care (Grimes, 1994). Black women are at greater risk of dying in the aftermath of giving birth, as research shows they are at greater risk of pregnancy-induced hypertension and obesity (Lederman, Alfasi, & Deckelbaum, 2002; Lieberman et al., 1987), among other things (Blake et al., 2007). *The point being, psychological buffering is employed by both genders, in the present as in the past.*

Everyday buffering speaks to the psychological capacity and skill to protect oneself in the face of micro (subtle) or even macro (obvious) racial aggressions (Sue et al., 2007). Buffering can take on more concrete actions as one moves down the social class ladder, for poor people are typically treated more crudely. The ability to read a policeman's mood can mean the difference between a beating or threats to one's life. Fear for the well-being of black boys propelled the writing of two best-selling books, one by none other than Ta-Nehisi Coates (2015) and another by the Princeton University scholar and mother Imani Perry (2019), both of which are formulated as letters to their black male progeny. Not surprisingly, black concern for preparing black boys for everyday life is the focus of several recent studies, with Dawn Marie Dow (2019) examining concerns voiced by middle-class black mothers, and Abril Harris and Ndidiamaka Amutah-Onukagha (2019) analyzing those of working-class mothers. Harris and Amutah-Onukagha found black mothers could not control

> the stereotypes and beliefs associated with black masculinity; thus, the mothers in this study were forced to ensure that their sons self-policed their own identities and behaviors to limit contact with the police and ensure their sons safety during police interactions. While these mothers did not internalize society's characterization of their sons, many of the strategies were created based on an understanding of how young black men are racialized among police officers. (Harris & Amutah-Onukagha, 2019, p. 440)

While life or death tropes foreshadow the narrative about racism and black males, one should not lose sight of the way buffering plays a role in the everyday lives of black girls and women. Themes of vigilance, apprehension, protection, and buffering are present throughout Dani McClain's text (2019), which focuses on raising black girls.

In the aftermath of a tragedy, some black people find protection and survival in an extremely controversial identity mechanism—*forgiveness*. Jennifer Berry Hawes (2019, pp. 72–76) observed the way family and friends of the nine African Americans killed in the rampage inside Charleston's historically black Emmanuel Church on June 17, 2015, found a path to grace and forgiveness toward the white racist killer. At the bond hearing, observed by Dylann Roof through a televised hookup, the unrepentant, hate-filled, evil youth with the choirboy face sat motionless and silent, as, one by one, African Americans suffering from excruciating pain connected to the loss of a loved one spoke into the microphone and uttered words of forgiveness. As Hawes describes the scene:

> Her voice broke with sorrow, but she sounded warm and strong. Roof's destiny was in God's hands now. Her destiny remained in her own. What if she didn't forgive this killer? She wouldn't go to heaven, and that's where she would find her baby boy. She had to get there. Other family members spoke after her, echoing similar themes, those at the heart of Christianity: repentance, love, mercy, forgiveness. Sobs filled the background. Chief Mullen sat in awe. The bond hearing lasted just thirteen minutes, but it had only begun to reverberate across Charleston and the nation. (Hawes, 2019, pp. 77–76)

Their actions stunned the community, and news of their words of grace moved the then president of the United States—Barack Obama—to attend a special vigil honoring the memory of the murdered African Americans, when, in perhaps his most magnanimous moment as president, he led the audience in singing the hymn "Amazing Grace." In his sensitive review of Hawes's book, Chris Lebron ventured to say that forgiveness was part of the survivors' struggle to bring closure to the disaster, so that they might each find a sense of psychological peace and resolution (Lebron, 2019).

The Cost of Buffering

At its core, forgiveness represents the "internalization" of the emotions and feelings aroused by racism, which, for the purpose of discussion, we can call *race-related stress*. The same is true regarding our earlier discussion of *incarceration buffering*, when the person matches evil, physical punishment, and solitary confinement with a superhuman ability to take and absorb the punishment as a way to survive and thus live another day. Forgiveness and learning to "just take it" result in the partial dissipation of racist energy; however, the remaining negative stress is absorbed and eventually transformed into *high blood pressure*, a diagnosis commonplace among African Americans (Blascovich et al., 2001). In her book titled *Breathe*, and subtitled *Letters to My Sons*, Perry describes the physical costs of buffering and vigilance: "Hypervigilant panic is our misfortune, so much so, in my case, that the system for my body's protection has turned on me. To the lupus I have. To the sarcoidosis and congestive heart failure Byron had. And even when the body doesn't go awry, the hurt can make you trip over yourself, chasing a sweet spot to avoid feeling the pain up close. Moments of grace that can kill you. No, you just have to learn to live with the ache" (Perry, 2019, p. 37).

The Psychology of Black Functioning in Open Spaces

Racism is ubiquitous, so technically there are no free, open, and uncontaminated spaces, and it would be a mistake to suggest that educated and well-to-do blacks never have to endure, "take-it," or manifest resilience. The life stories of Maya Angelou or Jackie Robinson or Bill Russell tell us otherwise. However, being black, educated, and well-to-do can and does make a difference in one's life experiences and trajectory. In a theoretical article I coauthored (Cross, Smith, & Payne, 2002), we describe the psychological mechanisms critical to *double-consciousness identity work*. Stigma management, which is akin to the TRIOS concept of self-preservation, consists of buffering, code-switching, and bridging—three psychological mechanisms—while a second category, labeled *attachment-bonding*, depicts the identity work related to transacting one's personal-private self as well as one's relationship to black people and black culture. Taken together, the operations make black thriving—eudaimonia—possible. Ultimately, the capacity of individuals is not enough to ensure well-being, and members of stigmatized groups band together to root out oppression, allowing organizations such as the NAACP or Southern Christian Leadership Conference (SCLC) to initiate legislative forms of buffering and so on. Of course, black people also turn to social protest movements such as Black Lives Matter (Khan-Cullors, 2018).

Code-Switching: I used to know instantly that my wife was speaking to a white person when she answered the phone at our home. The casual speaking style, laced with Ebonical elocution markers, disappeared and was replaced by a speaking style—not unlike that of Nat King Cole—where every word seemed to end in the letters *d* or *t*. Code-switching speaks to the development of bicultural competence that allows one to function, at a high level, within two cultural realms: the mainstream community and the black community. In their study of strategies used by black mothers to prepare their sons for everyday racism, Harris and Amutah-Onukagha (2019) report themes of vigilance combined with code-switching. These same mothers openly encouraged their sons to seek out and engage opportunities within mainstream society. We are left with an image of a black person comfortable and competent in mainstream contexts as well as within the black community—of someone with the wherewithal to move back and forth between their community and the mainstream. When one thinks about buffering as compared to code-switching, it becomes clear that to live a successful black life can be complicated, to say the least. In situations calling for buffering, one's psychological state is geared toward vigilance, identity protection, and moving away from white people, while code-switching involves moving toward, entering, and *being successful within white spaces*. When the formerly oppressed gain status and find themselves in situations once considered white spaces—workplace, hospital, auto dealership, teacher's conference, exchange with the cable repair person, and so on—they often feel the need to defer to the white person's presumed way of communicating and interacting. The "switch" happens so quickly that the stigmatized person has almost no recollection of it, as captured by Shani Jamila:

> Over the years I learned to censor myself and adapt to different surroundings, automatically tailoring my tongue to fit the ear of whatever crew I was with. . . . White people automatically got a very precise speech, because I knew every word out of my mouth was being measured and quantified as an example of the capabilities of the entire race. Around Black people I slipped into the vocabulary I felt more comfortable with but remained aware that I was being judged. This time it was to see how capably I could fall back onto "our talk" without sounding like a foreigner. (Jamila, 2019, p. 349)

After the civil rights movement gave way to black power, some sectors of the white community responded by eliminating the most obvious forms of discrimination, making it possible for African Americans—and women in general—to enter formerly all-white, all-male spaces as employees, customers, professionals, undergraduate and graduate students, and so on. Racism retreated a few steps, but after the stigmatized gained a foothold, racism reappeared in the form of an obstacle to promotion, tenure, and favorable job performance reviews, and as last-minute roadblocks in the home mortgage or car loan process, and so on. Eventually, African Americans made inroads across every conceivable layer of white America and now find themselves living and functioning in those once-restricted spaces, working, and in some cases being part of the leadership supported or serviced by whites, as teachers, insurance agents, college professors, and top-flight medical physicians, to mention but a few cases in point. African Americans have mastered the decorum, interaction codes, rules of engagement, and cultural styles preferred by white people and white institutions. While black college students fully grasp the need for code-switching, any hint of condescension on the part of an instructor will draw a response from the students.

Although headway has been made in eliminating or minimizing racism in white spaces, black women often must double down, as they simultaneously negotiate the dynamics of race and gender, with discrimination and harassment emanating not only from white men but from black men as well. In such situations, competence, dedication, and standards are not enough, as black women's participation in the Me Too movement has made clear. In a manner of speaking, black women are often forced to be ready to adopt a *buffering stance*, even as they execute code-switching.

Code-switching has led to one of the most fascinating dilemmas faced by every category of humans who depend on stigma-management skills to achieve success within white spaces: the *imposter syndrome* (Breeze, 2018; Clance & Imes, 1978; Dancy & Brown, 2011; Ewing et al., 1996). One example is when a person so racializes the area into which he or she seeks admission and recognition that such strivings are mistaken as a form of cultural passing, causing the person to feel guilty and ashamed, rather than proud. Another example is when a person feels "fake," "unreal," not belonging, or like a fraud, with the associated fear that he or she is not up to the task, resulting in unrealistic strivings for perfection. The person seeks a way to make clear that she or he remains "black" in consciousness even though associated with the activity, field, or position otherwise linked to whiteness. In a series of studies, Kevin Cokley and his students at the University of Texas have demonstrated the link between imposter strivings, perceived discrimination, and mental health (Cokley et al., 2013; Cokley et al., 2017; Dancy & Brown, 2011; Stone et al., 2018).

In extreme cases, some light-complexioned African Americans have used their physiological ambiguity to code-switch in a way that can only be considered daring, the best example of this being Walter White. White ventured into the mouth of the lion, using his ambiguity to attend and record white behavior at lynchings, resulting in his famous text *Rope and Faggot: A Biography of Judge Lynch* (White, 1929/2001). Mentioning Walter White facilitates movement from the sublime to ridiculous in a modern-day phenomenon called "blackfishing," where "some" white people, especially some white women, have manipulated their appearance to be mistaken as black women—"reverse" code-switching. At the fifty-first meeting of the

Association of Black Psychologists held in Orlando, Florida, July 24–27, 2019, a small group of female black psychologists held a forum to discuss blackfishing. Participants took turns expressing bewilderment, astonishment, anger, and contempt at the practice. All in all, the discourse could pass as a script from an episode of the *Dave Chappelle Show*.

Bridging: Culture shifting and code-switching generally bring black individuals into close and repeated contact with a goodly number of white people and can lead to deeply felt and meaningful personal relationships with "some" whites. In white organizations and white spaces, a black person experiences all types of white interactions, some highly scripted, formal, and stiff; others casual; and a few that are profoundly deep and meaningful. When a black person opens herself or himself to such relationships, this is called *bridging*. Often what starts out as a mentoring relationship moves to another level. In any case, long-term success within white spaces is built on relationships, as noted in any introductory human resources textbook. In a recent *New York Times* article, David Gelles (2019) reports on the rise of Thasunda Brown-Duckett, a black woman, within JP Morgan Chase, and in a byline as well as in a quote from Brown-Duckett herself, mention is made of the centrality of relationships in her promotion through the system. Bridging has taken on a multicultural connotation, given the changing demographics in modern business circles.

The Self behind the Veil

Attachment-Bonding

Racial consciousness and the transactional triangle of buffering/code-switching/bridging reveal how black people manage stigma, thus explicating one of the two selves captured in Du Bois's concept of double-consciousness. We now turn to the way black people enact a connection to black people and black culture as well as nourish and sustain their personal/private view of self. Just as personality is not hardwired and must be shaped by countless interactions with nurturing parents, kin and non-kin, so it is that a sense of belonging to a particular group—to *any* group—evolves over time and experience. At birth, one's birth certificate may show nominal categorization, as required by most states, for gender, race, and ethnicity. To have meaning, "black" identity must be acquired, achieved, and internalized, again, through exchanges with one's loved ones and into adolescence, when the input of playmates, friends, neighbors, and schoolmates takes on extraordinary importance. As a person's prefrontal cortex equips him or her with the capacity to reconfigure and rearrange the inputs and suggestion of others, the person becomes an existential powerhouse and may end up with a frame of reference and worldview far removed from what appeared as a previously affirmed identity commitment. And, after all is said and done, the person may have an "aha!" moment and through Nigrescence reconfigure that sense of identity. If one keeps in mind the tremendous plasticity in the human condition, then it should not come as a surprise that there is no one (correct) way to be black, and many blacks simply do not anchor their social sense of self on race and black culture.

Another factor driving the range of social identities black people exhibit has to do with variance in one's ecological setting. A black person born and raised in rural or urban sectors of Mississippi cannot be expected to "see" and interpret the world as might a black person from Duluth, Minnesota. Construction of worldview will also be influenced by gender, sexual orientation, religious-spiritual beliefs, and so on and so forth. Experience and learning must result in a sense of attachment to "a" group that, as Erikson wrote, involves a combination of exploration and commitment. One of the great accomplishments of the civil rights and especially the black power movement was the spread of literature and information, making it easier and more accessible to explore black culture and black history. The Internet and mass media in general have further made information about blackness readily at hand.

Public education still has somewhat of a mixed track record in educating black youth; however, the continued reality of residential segregation of the races increases the probability that black youth will wade in the waters of blackness at the point that their prefrontal cortex is moving toward maturation, thus allowing them to dig deeper and find more convincing evidence and information pointing toward the embrace of a black identity. Once the choice is made, exploration can be experienced on multiple fronts. Youthful blackness can be explored and expressed through hairstyles, clothing and dress, tattoos, ear piercings, a broad swath of musical genres, popular dance, alternative pronunciation of words and alternate (black) meanings for words and phrases, rich and varied presentations and representations of black life in Hollywood movies and TV shows and sitcoms, the black imprimatur in all college-level and professional sports, and so on. In effect, positive messages and information about the black experience are easy to come by. Participation and immersion in any number of these cultural options can result in a sense of *attachment and bonding* to black culture, black people, and the black experience. At adolescence, most black youth explore and seek a match between their personal, in-born gifts and proclivities and an avenue of expression in blackness. From this mixture evolves tomorrow's Biannca Prince, Ted Short, Binta Cross, Maya Angelou, James Turner, Saidiya Hartman, Henry Louis Gates Jr., or Reiland Rabaka.

Attachment-Bonding, Code-Switching, and Creativity

I have become friends with the amazing scholar of black culture Reiland Rabaka (2011), and, during one of our exchanges, he provided insight into the relationship between *attachment-bonding*, *code-switching*, and *innovation*. As he is a jazz drummer, the discussion centered on black music. While my original notion of code-switching involved entering white spaces for the purposes of employment or receiving services such as schooling, health care, sports, and so on, Rabaka pointed out that much of black art involves first learning and engaging with the foundations of a Western way of doing art and, second, seeing things differently, thus producing something artistically "new." Jazz resulted when African Americans entered white musical spaces to play European instruments (saxophone, flute, bass violin, drums) but ended up performing with a sense of space, rhythm, and syncopation traceable to Africa and the Caribbean. The Modern Jazz Quartet dressed in formal attire befitting players in a symphonic orchestra and began each selection by performing a highly scripted opening, with solo freelancing intertwined thereafter, ending with a return to the opening script. Gil Evans and Miles Davis collaborated to produce two long works, one based on the opera *Porgy and Bess* and another derived from classical Spanish composition (*Sketches of Spain*). Nina Simone, who began as a classical pianist, played jazz solos that clearly showed the influences of Bach, in particular, as was also true of Dave Brubeck. Bill Evans's work integrated the sensibilities of Debussy, Ravel, and other European romantics. Jimi Hendrix invented cultural loops, starting with a black-blues sensibility fused with a white rock-and-roll aesthetic, then he looped back to outrageous electronic blasts and flourishes that could be classified as neither black nor white. It became the Hendrix sound! The Broadway hit musical *Hamilton* is another example of innovation resulting from the fusion of a black aesthetic—this time hip-hop—with European history and culture.

One of the most startling examples of code-switching leading to innovation involves the life and times of Leroy Graves, the renowned conservationist associated with Colonial Williamsburg (Watson, 2018). Born poor and attending school only through the fifth grade, Graves was hired in 1967 to work on the maintenance crew for Colonial Williamsburg. During his lunch period, he often made himself invisible while watching experts refurbish colonial furniture in the Department of Collections. He taught himself every facet of furniture restoration. Eventually, his sophisticated expertise made it possible for him to be called upon to authenticate whether a piece was original or a fraud. In addition, he solved one of the most pressing problems confronting restoration. Over time, the original wooden frames are nearly destroyed with tacking and retacking, given each new restoration. He developed a method that did not require nails or tacks; it is used the world over and known as "the Graves Method." Having first mastered to the "T" every aspect of conservation practice, Graves then added his new insights, making for a stunning exemplar of code-switching mastery followed by innovation. He is the author of *Early Seating Upholstery: Reading the Evidence* (Graves, 2015).

Innovation can work both ways, as Picasso's otherwise European aesthetic was radically transformed upon his exposure to African art and African sensibilities about movement, form, and shape. The composer Steve Reich freely admits that the music of Thelonious Monk, John Coltrane, Miles Davis, and other jazz giants was a source of inspiration in the evolution of his approach to modern composition. Exemplars of code-switching and black creativity can be made across the arts and humanities.

The point is that code-switching is more than finding ways to fit in, conform, and be accepted. It can serve as a point from which to see things differently and think with renewed imagination and creativity. From baseball legend Willie Mays's waist-high basket catches to gymnast Simone Biles's triple-double back flip on the floor and double-twisting, double dismount from the balance beam; Michael Jordan's acrobatic gyrations; Biggie Smalls's infectious grunts or Tupac Shakur's mesmerizing poetry; the bending and curling of notes by Sarah Vaughan; the overlooked skills of NASA's "hidden figures" (Mary Jackson, Katherine Johnson, and Dorothy Vaughan [Shetterly, 2016]); and the lyrical sounds of Duke Ellington, African Americans have provided America with an amazing array of gifts, made possible by explosive cultural creativity generated by code-switching, cultural-sharing, and synthesis of worldviews.

The reader will be forgiven if I have made it appear that being black, feeling black, and espousing a black identity is typical. However, in her exploration of black families, Beverly D. Tatum (1997/2003) reported that black parents differ in the importance—salience—they accord race and black culture in the socialization of their children. Thus, from the very beginning of a black child's exposure and discussion about life, he or she may be guided in a direction such that as an adult she or he may embrace "something other than race and black culture" in making sense of the world. This too explains why one is practically forced to discuss not what black identity is, rather what is the *range of black identities* (plural) found in a large sample of black people.

Intragroup Buffering

While multiple and wide pathways to a positive attachment to blackness overshadow negative pathways, the fact of the matter is that racism is alive and well in the United States and is constantly churning out negative racialized messages about blackness and black people. Consequently, most mature black youth and adults need an intragroup-buffering component as part of their social identity to help filter out negative propaganda broadcasted by racists from outside the community. However, in many instances, this negativity may be produced by some blacks themselves, thus the need to filter internalized racism emanating from nearby. Many black people do not recognize the role of deindustrialization in the creation of the street-level drug trade that has ensnarled so many black youth, and many a black scholar, politician, and prognosticator has looked for flaws in black youth themselves as a possible "explanation" for the school-to-prison pipeline (Rempson, 2016). Here, internalized racism is not so much a dynamic of the individual as a form of collective cultural miseducation.

Individuation and Individuality

A while back, I went through a heavy travel schedule and after getting stuck in the check-in screening line for what seemed like an interminable length of time, I decided to cough up some cash and join a service called Clear, which uses biometrics to quickly identify who you are and thus speed the check-in process. In my case, I use the system's ability to identify me through the analysis of my retina, or retinal vasculature intercept, which is as unique and reliable as my fingerprints. By late adolescence, a human being is the result of millions of interpersonal interactions with parents, siblings, relatives, fictive kin, associates, and friends, resulting in individual traits, habits, attitudes, and behaviors unique to every person. When combined with certain inborn tendencies like temperament or one's right-handed versus left-handed proclivity, and so on, a person's personal psychology profile is nearly as unique and differentiated as fingerprints or retinal patterns. The process of this uniqueness is called "individuation" and the end product is "individuality." It is perhaps the most important and powerful concept associated with the philosophy of humanism, in which it is presumed that we are all from the same species.

In some sectors of black studies and black psychology, the trilogy of individuation, individuality, and humanism is mistaken as advocacy of a *philosophy of self-centeredness* that acts as a counternarrative to collectivism. Nevertheless, it is important in the study of the psychology of the black experience to include in our analysis a clear understanding that we are first and foremost "human beings" and, if anything, we are primed at birth to experience *human plasticity* in all its glory. When a person's socialization has reached its peak, between the ages of early adolescence and the point of maturation of the prefrontal cortex (i.e., age twenty-five or thereabout), our human mechanisms for receiving and apprehending information; our integration of inputs into our existing worldview; the attitudes we hold about topics x, y, and z; and the behavior we exhibit in the aftermath of receiving-processing-internalizing and acting on a situation are unique to each person. What better example than to think of the score and lyrics for the song "Tenderly" and then recall its unique performance by the likes of Louis Armstrong, Johnny Mathis, Ella Fitzgerald, Nat King Cole, Bill Henderson, Bill Withers, Betty Carter, Sarah Vaughan, Pearl Bailey, or Billy Eckstine. This sense of individuality is a statement of fact and, as noted by Spencer (1995), must be accounted for in the discourse on black identity. Linda Clark Strauss and I (2005) conducted a fourteen-day daily diary study that explored how often black college youth attending a predominantly white university actually made use of racial identity enactments in everyday life, and the category "just being myself" appeared alongside the racial enactment categories. Buffering, code-switching, and bridging were all categories selected for activities calling for protection, mainstream activities, and friendship activities across racial lines. However, the most frequently checked category was "just being myself," which we took to mean an expression of individuality.

Summary and Conclusions

In this chapter I began with a discussion of the experience of slavery and its counterpart in the present—incarceration—because both are closed systems where human agency is minimized, strictly surveilled, and controlled through violence. Slavery and incarceration underscore themes of survival and the herculean task of salvaging one's sanity. As slaves and then prisoners, blacks learned to endure, take it, live for the next day, amplify personal willpower, and survive to a point that gives new meaning to the term "resilience." In the forced solitude of contemporary confinement, most do nothing but count the days, while others reshape their identities, conquer hatred and anger, find God, and internalize blackness. One of the greatest black leaders of the twentieth century—Malcolm X—reshaped his identity during meditation while incarcerated. In slavery, and continuing through the mid-1960s, blacks lived within the fascist underbelly of the United States, and protection and self-preservation were of primary concern, especially for blacks living in the rural South. It did not take much to trigger jealous, insecure, and uneducated white sociopaths into fits of uncontrollable rage, whose ruthless behavior was often publicly encouraged by members of law enforcement, government officials, and cultural elites. To this day, "living while black" in earshot of the police presents a continued concern, especially for young black males.

Although not a psychologist, W.E.B. Du Bois has influenced and, in some ways, guided the psychology of the African American experience, past and present. His unflinching perception of black people as human steered him away from biogenetic tropes, and he was exposed to cutting-edge humanistic and socioeconomic theorizing while studying for a Ph.D. in pre–World War I Germany. In *Black Reconstruction* he documented black agency and self-determination, but eleven years before its publication he had already documented black uplift (Du Bois, 1924/2007). Du Bois approached the end of slavery and the ex-slave's entrance into a democratic society as an unplanned "natural" social experiment. He showed how the vast majority of slaves—destitute, landless, illiterate—progressed at an uneven pace, given the uneven support forthcoming from federal and state agencies plus philanthropic organizations. *The Philadelphia Negro* (Du Bois & Eaton, 1899) constituted the "results" section of this natural experiment. Given the ex-slaves' rapacious appetite for education and uplift, as documented in *Black Reconstruction*, Du Bois wanted to track how *literacy plus enlightenment coupled with opportunity* transformed and produced change.

In *The Philadelphia Negro* he essentially documented the type of black society the South "could have generated and benefited from" had it been able to look past vengeance and retribution to see, instead, the gifts the ex-slaves wanted to create and share with the South. Instead of feeding off black motivation, hunger for education, enlightenment, and uplift, the South—elites and common folks alike—regressed into a mindless stupor of hate, bloodlust, and cultural sociopathy, forecasting attitudes and violent behavior we tend to associate with Hitler's Germany or South Africa's apartheid regime. Du Bois theorized that, in being treated as a caste, the majority of black people, and especially those locked into poverty, had little wiggle room to accumulate wealth and education, and their salvation required life behind a mask of racial consciousness. However, in also studying black people who managed to achieve and experience uplift between the end of slavery and the turn of the twentieth century, Du Bois uncovered the way blacks thought, felt, and acted *behind the mask*, thus leading to his analysis of *double-consciousness*. Behind the mask or veil—as Du Bois sometimes referenced it—black people experienced and reflected upon their humanity, hidden from and denied by the larger white society.

First postulated in 1903, the concept of double-consciousness explained—with remarkable accuracy—findings from a research project conducted nearly seventy years later. After recording no difference in the level of self-esteem between white and black adolescents—a finding that startled the field—Morris Rosenberg and Roberta G. Simmons (1971) also found black youth were cognizant of society's devaluation of blackness and preference for whiteness. However, the youth evidenced a sense of black beauty and worth, shielded by their racial consciousness "mask." When asked to explain themselves, they noted that their personal sense of attractiveness was derived from the supportive and complimentary beliefs/perceptions communicated to them by *other black students*, even if the larger society did not reinforce these affirmations. In this example, code-switching takes on the broader and encompassing meaning of a complete cultural shift. White oppression was successful in causing black progress to stagnate, and E. Franklin Frazier would have one believe that rural poor black people entered a cultural void of their own making. Writers like Zora Neale Hurston and Langton Hughes thought otherwise. They uncovered human beings who, although "poor," nonetheless carried on a profound relationship with God; evidenced moral standards for self, progeny, and community; created a minimalist cuisine that satisfied; played games rich in social interactions; composed music from the rhythms of their heartbeats; and evidenced a capacity to bring up children like those who participated in the Rosenberg and Simmons study. Furthermore, these writers demonstrated that black poverty was not, as proposed by Frazier, self-inflicted, but the result of systematic oppression requiring the collusion of state and federal agencies, pronounced "legal" in surreal decisions by the U.S. Supreme Court.

Erik Erikson explicated stages of human self-actualization that fall woefully short in capturing the dynamics of double-consciousness, thus setting the stage for a handful of mostly black psychologists who proposed addendums to Erikson's work, stressing (1) experiences with racism and discrimination, (2) black cultural experiences, (3) experiences within mainstream society, and (4) experiences tied to the expression of one's individuality. These *addendums* showed how racism required of black people a partitioning of consciousness into two domains: one designed to negotiate constraints on their humanity by the larger racist society and another that allowed expression of their awareness of being a full-fledged human being. In the days of racial segregation, this meant a highly sensitive sense of *vigilance* and, when possible, outright avoidance of white people altogether. Today, this on-guard vigilance is mediated, to a certain extent, by one's social class standing, where working-class and poor blacks are particularly vulnerable to the sometimes-lethal actions of law enforcement. However, the modern social movement Black Lives Matter has not failed to attract members of the black middle class and elites.

Black protest in the 1960s and 1970s created pathways into every nook and cranny of American society, and for blacks with a college degree and more, avoidance of white people was no longer an option. Rather, the new circumstances required a psychological mindset and various identity enactments making it possible to be highly successful within once-sacrosanct white spaces. This meant being motivated to *enter, perform, and be highly successful within white spaces*, even if for some there was the risk of experiencing an *imposter syndrome*. Besides enacting *code-switching*, one had to be prepared for and open to possible deep and meaningful friendships with "some" white people (bridging), because success within most organizations is partly driven by relationships. In addition, a rise in one's status meant getting used to being *serviced and attended to* by white people, rather than the other way around, as it was now white doctors, nurses, school teachers, and bank tellers who serviced them. Because residential housing segregation remains the reality across the United States, and because black people tend to marry persons from the black community, most black people find themselves re-entering black spaces after 5 P.M., true even for former president Obama, as the White House—servants and support staff aside—became a middle-class black space occupied by his black wife and their black children.

While code-switching presents an element of one-way accommodation and fitting in on terms dictated by the larger society, it also provides the basis for understanding black creativity, innovation, and, yes, even black genius. Jazz, black poetry, black literature, and black contributions to the fine arts show black artists first mastering elements of European artistic expression. Thereafter black artists find ways to twist, turn, and "play" with mainstream perspectives to discover and produce new notes and sounds, new combinations of colors, new choreography, new shapes, changes in the literary canon, and more.

Behind the mask of stigma management, blacks experience themselves as human beings, and this tends to be a shared experience, as most blacks identify as black; thus, one's "human side" is enacted before black audiences. Strauss and I (2005) found that when blacks recorded being in a state of "just being myself," white people were seldom present, while it was not uncommon for other blacks to be present. That said, many blacks experience their humanity while according limited salience to race and black culture, including those exhibiting an identification with white mainstream culture, as in an assimilationist stance. Large-scale surveys (Bobo, 1988; Powers & Ellison, 1995) show black people embrace a wide range of beliefs about the human condition and meaning making. This diversity of opinion further affirms black humanity because human beings in general evidence plasticity across a wide range of opinions, feelings, and affiliations. *Black "diversity" is not a problem or cultural flaw, it is an expression of black humanity.* Finally, we touched upon the multiple influences in socialization practices, biogenetics, and culture that make each (black) human being unique. One is reminded that *individuation and individuality* are as much a part of black psychology as any topic.

As this is an educational narrative, I have described the various identity protective and proactive mechanisms separately, when in fact the two mechanisms are dance partners. We end with the *dance of twoness* as lived by Jackie Robinson. In breaking the Major League Baseball color barrier, Jackie Robinson fused buffering, code-switching, and innovation. He dared to enter a white space (Major League Baseball), found ways to psychologically protect himself (buffering), exhibited a masterful level of understanding and competence about the way the game should be played (code-switching), introduced innovations (stealing home base as a base runner), and eventually had white associates (bridging) who enjoyed his company (Pee Wee Reese) or provided him some degree of in-house protection at the level of management (Branch Rickey). His success was the sum of all these parts. Besides courage, daring, resilience, and persistence, he showed the ability to be flexible in his blackness, displaying not a Johnny-one-note expression but a repertoire of identity skills and enactments. The first year on the field, he followed Branch Rickey's advice and held everything "in," paying a price rather early in life, dying from a combination of diabetes and heart disease at the relatively young age of fifty-three!

5

Interrogating the Deficit Perspective

In chasing down the origins of the deficit perspective on black identity, culture, and family structure, one discovers the influence of two solo voices plus a male ensemble. We first encounter W.E.B. Du Bois, who conducted the earliest sociological studies on black culture and family life, and his *double-consciousness* trope remains foundational to the modern discourse on blackness. Then there is E. Franklin Frazier, whose work on the black family pinpoints the actual origin of the *negative* legacy of the slavery trope that continues to find relevance to this day, as in Joy DeGruy's important book *Post Traumatic Slave Syndrome* (DeGruy Leary, 2005) as well as in Joe L. Rempson's self-published work on the woes of the so-called black underclass (Rempson, 2016). Last, there is the all-male choir, consisting of the faculty for the Department of Sociology at the University of Chicago (circa 1890–1940) under the direction of Robert Ezra Park, who, rather than Du Bois, is incorrectly credited with founding the first American department of sociology. In point of fact, Du Bois accomplished this years earlier at Atlanta University. In the production of his now infamous 1932 dissertation on the black family subsequently published as a book in 1939, Frazier would in fact "reference" parts of Du Bois's research while avoiding those aspects of his narrative that challenged Frazier's core propositions. Frazier claimed slavery left black people embracing an extremely primitive and deeply flawed culture inclusive of weak family dynamics, which, along with the pressure of urban living, combined to produce disastrous social results such as youth delinquency and criminality, unhinged sexual behavior, broken marriages, and out-of-wedlock births. Du Bois thought otherwise.

Both Du Bois and Frazier agreed that the end of slavery marked the start of an historic "natural" social experiment through which observers such as themselves could track the ex-slave's transition and progress from slavery to freedom. Before Frazier's doctorate was awarded in 1932 (Frazier, 1932), Du Bois provided four "reports" on the progress made by ex-slaves, the first involving a subsample drawn from the 40,000 black folk living in Philadelphia (Du Bois & Eaton, 1899). His narrative in this first report is fairly upbeat, as he is able to show *social change* as reflected in differential patterns of adjustment, using a form of cluster analysis summarized by Saidiya Hartman:

> The 40,000 Negroes of Philadelphia, including 9,675 living in the seventh ward, could be divided into ranks of grades, ascending from the bottom rung to the aristocracy. Grade One: families of undoubted respectability earning sufficient income to live well; Grade Two: the respectable class living in decent homes and steadily employed; Grade Three: the poor, not always energetic or thrifty, but with no touch of gross immorality; Grade Four: the lowest class of criminals, prostitutes, and loafers, the submerged tenth. By his admission, these were moral categories rather than class designations. Poverty and crime were not the natural condition of the Negro, contrary to popular belief. . . . His visual graphics offered a true portrait of the Negro as changing and variable, not an outcast of evolution. (Hartman, 2019, pp. 112–113)

The influence of theories of social adjustment developed by the Chicago School of sociology must have emerged between the publication of *The Philadelphia Negro* in 1899 and Du Bois's study of the Negro American family in 1908, because missing in the first work is any reference to the civilization-assimilation trope, while in the latter, Du Bois makes mention of the Chicago School's "theory" integrating genetics, culture, and assimilation. While these terms and the theory are given their due in his 1908 work, Du Bois also finds his way back to his major themes of change and possibility. After reviewing a table on black family structure, in the 1908 publication he says: "Twenty-five years ago, they would have been far worse than today, and while there is no perceptible change of moment in statistics of 1890 and 1900, most of the tendencies are in the right direction, and a healthier home life is in prospect" (Du Bois, 1908, p. 31).

The Chicago School of sociologists cut their teeth tracking the adjustment of ethnic groups, such as the Irish, Italians, and Eastern European Jews. Viewed from the perspective of eugenics, these were inferior groups, with Negroes positioned at the base of either the cultural or racial hierarchies. Each group entered the United States with an inferior cultural foundation, and their challenge was to become assimilated. Park and his associates suggested that otherwise inferior groups can learn to mimic or imitate aspects of the new culture, but complete assimilation—assumed to be a long and arduous process—was fundamentally impossible for members of groups that were genetically inferior from the beginning (Fine, 1995). Creators and advocates of this frame of reference made up the membership of Frazier's dissertation committee. With this in mind, one might question the authenticity of his dissertation and book; however, down the line, Frazier had every opportunity to revisit, and, if necessary, change or modify his narrative, but this never happened. Thus, while one can assume Frazier must have been under the influence of, if not subject to outright duress from, his committee of dedicated white racists, the fact of the matter is, later in his career, when he clearly put distance between himself and the University of Chicago, he continued to take "ownership" of his family study. In the absence of any recorded modification, then assistant secretary of labor and future senator Daniel Patrick "Pat" Moynihan drew a straight line between his observation of broken family statistics recorded in the

1960s (Moynihan, 1965/1997) and Frazier's depiction of broken family dynamics recorded in 1939.

Du Bois stressed ex-slaves' agency, vision, and motivation in *Black Reconstruction* (Du Bois, 1935). *The Souls of Black Folk* (1903) finds Du Bois coming to terms with the reality that the white South's war on black people had successfully turned most black people into paupers trapped in a caste-like status, yet he remained adamant in trying to document *what could have been*, and his 1924 book documents the emergence of black educators, inventors, and industrialists, many of whom were once slaves (Du Bois & Gates, 1924). Supporting this perspective is an observation made by the University of North Carolina sociologist Guy Benton Johnson, who in 1933 wrote:

> The white South has long proceeded on the assumption that the way to maintain her safety and integrity and to promote progress is to follow a policy of excluding the Negro from direct participation in the social, economic, and political order. The obvious effect of that policy has been the maintenance of differentials between whites and Negroes which have not only retarded the progress of the Negro toward social and economic adequacy, but have retarded the social and economic well-being of the whole south. (Johnson, 1933, Memorandum of a Proposed Study)

The phrase "legacy of slavery" does, in fact, appear in Du Bois's 1908 publication, but usually as an afterthought and not a central tenet. In *The Philadelphia Negro*, Du Bois reported that black men and women aspired to marriage and a two-parent household, but delayed marriage *when financial circumstances* made this wish problematic. In this finding he comes close to presenting evidence that social class and not some legacy of slavery impediment was blocking progress. The themes of oppression and uplift, captured in Du Bois's use of the phrase "the problem of the color-line," drove Du Bois's infographic presentations at the 1900 Exposition des Negres d'Amerique, held in Paris, France (Battle-Baptiste & Rusert, 2018).

That ex-slaves could, in *one generation*, experience uplift is an impossibility in the theory of Negro adjustment Frazier would eventually advocate. In both his dissertation and book, Frazier's discourse references Du Bois's work, with the exception of *Black Reconstruction*; however, given Du Bois's transparent, repeated, and obvious emphasis on the ability of ex-slaves to achieve uplift—for some even in one generation—Frazier totally discounts this possibility and links "civilized" Negroes to once-free black communities and/or privileged mulattoes. Writing in 1939, Frazier cites no evidence of uplift achieved by Negroes who were common field hands during slavery. Ironically, while Frazier sees himself extricating the analysis of the Negro condition from the tentacles of eugenics theory, he loses sight of the fact that terms like "civilized" and "assimilated" are foundational to the eugenics narrative and would trigger in the imagination of the informed as well as lay reader the eugenics vision, even though that was not Frazier's intent. The racism embraced by members of his committee found resonance in Frazier's voice. The eugenics-oriented white members of his committee were probably pleased.

Frazier's Dissertation

In discussing Frazier, one needs to differentiate between his dissertation, published by the University of Chicago in 1932, and his famous text published in 1939, also by the University of Chicago Press. While sections of the dissertation anticipate the fatalism openly expressed throughout the 1939 book, this characteristic is balanced in the dissertation by an ecological frame—typical of scholarship emanating from the Chicago School perspective—that conjures in the mind of the reader notions about *process and change*, such as new migrants moving from the status of dregs of society to that of contributing homeowners and literate citizens. In repeated reference to the lifestyles, occupations, family structure, and sexual behavior of folks in one zone as compared to other zones, Frazier seems to be forecasting a difficult but mildly optimistic future for the Negro in urban life. In the dissertation, his phrasing makes clear to the reader that one cannot talk about "the" Negro as if belonging to a homogeneous group, a point he first made in 1929 in an essay, ironically titled "La Bourgeoisie noire," included in the famous anthology of Negro literature edited by V. F. Calverton (1929). However, it should be added in passing that this essay bears little resemblance to the book of the same title published in 1957. In the 1929 work, Frazier wrote: "As a matter of fact, the Negro group is highly differentiated, with about the same range of interest as whites.... Class differentiation among Negroes is reflected in their church organizations, educational institutions, private clubs, and the whole range of social life" (Frazier, 1929, pp. 379–380).

The dissertation opens with a comprehensive, full-throttle critique of the then favored literature on "race" and eugenics that saw Africans at the base of the civilized hierarchy and slavery as an ill-fated matching of two groups said to be at opposite ends of the civilization spectrum. Frazier's critique establishes a beachhead for humanism, but he holds back ideas about the "pathology of racism" that got him fired from Atlanta University (Frazier, 1929). In the dissertation, he says without qualification that the release of the Negro from slavery saw a people embarking on the journey toward greater civilization and eventual assimilation. In line with Robert Ezra Park's assumptions, Frazier states slavery stripped slaves of their African roots, while making it difficult to impossible to learn and internalize the new culture. In the dissertation he uses the terms "culture," "civilization," and "assimilation" as theorized by Park and other intellectual colleagues from the University of Chicago. However, he goes on to introduce the image and dynamics of the Chicago black community as forming a series of ecologically distinct "zones," where Zone 1 embraces new migrants evidenced by family instability, poverty, and juvenile delinquency. The progression across other zones is accompanied by a decrease in such social markers until one reaches the zone where the black residents have intact families headed by men, the poverty rate is reduced, the range of occupations varies, and home ownership is more common (Frazier's misogyny is discussed shortly). His forewarning about the need to avoid lumping all blacks in one category plus the heavy emphasis on zones combine to communicate a sense of "progress" by Negroes in urban centers. Thus, if the front end of the dissertation embraces the Chicago School metatheory on civilization and assimilation, the heart of the work voices constrained *progress and hope*. At this point in the dissertation, Frazier appears to be in alignment with Du Bois, who used, as previously discussed, a version of the "bad-to-good" zones trope in *The Philadelphia Negro*.

Frazier's 1939 Book

In his 1939 book, Frazier's clear explication of his intellectual frame, as tied to theorizing by the Chicago School, disappears, only to reappear in the final pages: "It appears that the travail of civilization is not yet ended.... The gains in civilization will in the future as in the past be transmitted for generations through the family" (Frazier, 1939, pp. 487–488).

Rather than make explicit that the intellectual scaffold on which the book is based is derived from Park and the Chicago School, Frazier switches gears and constructs an amazingly engaging narrative that, if one had first read his dissertation, causes confusion, as the dissertation is not as onerous, critical, and fatalistic as the book. The dissertation outlines "problems," not fatal flaws, and the zones trope suggests possible change in the distant future. Rather than recapitulate the theoretical tropes of the Chicago School, Frazier researched hundreds of narratives written or spoken by blacks and presents them in ways that make it appear that blacks themselves are articulating the theoretical prepositions that in the dissertation are associated with the Chicago School. Thus, in his dissertation, we are presented with the voices of his white mentors. In the book, those same theoretical points are constructed from the words and minds of black people. *This manipulation is what makes the book so compelling.* It is only with a second or third reading and going back and forth between the dissertation and the book that one comes to the realization that in his book, Frazier *weaponized black stories* to make it appear that blacks themselves believe they are the ones establishing his frame and that he is merely conveying their points of emphasis. Du Bois's 1908 study of the black family also makes heavy use of quotes and passages; however, in Du Bois's hands the effect was to *humanize black people*, while Frazier's analysis paints a picture of black people suffering from a "unique" form of poverty—impervious to intervention—that is, the negative legacy of slavery, or what thereafter is referenced as the *deficit perspective on black culture*. It is black people themselves who confess to falling apart at the end of slavery, who describe aimless wandering following Emancipation, freewheeling sexual behavior, the central role of mothers, and the distancing of black men. The one exception is Frazier's heavy reliance on the historical writings of Ulrich Bonnell Phillips (1929), who took it as a given that Africans were culturally backward as well as biologically inferior, and he viewed slavery as an institution that *partially but incompletely* civilized Africans. In effect, he applied the "need for civilization trope" as much as anyone, whether he was describing blacks as slaves or freedpersons.

Phillips was in many ways Du Bois's nemesis, as Du Bois wrote about slavery and Reconstruction from the bottom looking up, while Phillips coveted the perspective gained from the vantage point of the slave owners and, later, Southern Redeemers (Smith, 1980). Given Frazier's flair for constructing point-counterpoint in the first chapter of his dissertation covering the eugenics literature, for some reason he forgoes such an approach in his book. Instead, he constructs a narrative on the effects of slavery that presents Phillips's as the last word on the subject, and, given the complete neglect of those aspects of Du Bois's analysis that countered Phillips, Frazier's fatalism "feels" like the truth, and hope of repair or intervention seems out of the question. In future writings, others would translate his fatalism into the concept of the black underclass (Sides, 2006). In 1965, Moynihan captured that same fatalism in his now famous regurgitation of Frazier's prediction of the inevitable crumbling of the black family through internal faults, not societal forces such as social class. Whether intended or not, Frazier shrouds poverty in a blanket of racial-cultural-civilizing tropes and helps people to conclude there is something uniquely *racial-cultural* about black poverty. In digesting Frazier's analysis, a reader could be forgiven for thinking that Frazier actually believed in black cultural inferiority, and, as the term "civilizing" is foundational to the intellectual infrastructure of the genetic narrative, many readers probably assumed Frazier came perilously close to affirming his people's biogenetic inferiority. That he struggled with a propensity or "need" to unearth black fault lines and human foibles seems confirmed by his over-the-top critique of the black middle class (Frazier, 1957).

But what of the zones so prominently featured in Frazier's dissertation? While central to the dissertation, the table explicating the zones does not appear in the book until page 305, long after he has established the *futility and intransigence* of lower-class black existence. Furthermore, he builds a racial wall around those black families that in the dissertation seemed to forecast progress Frazier argues that the most "civilized" segments of the black community are descendants from free Negro communities and mulattoes. According to Frazier, free Negroes lived under conditions that made it possible for them to assimilate the social mores of whites, and, in his discussion of mulattoes, he comes ever so close to suggesting mixed people are prone to be more civilized, as a consequence of being part white. As the offspring of illicit relationships (e.g., dalliances and/or rape), mulatto children were often treated differently and given access to education, freedom, and the ability to go to Europe for education and worldly experiences, and so on. Frazier makes note of these unearned privileges, but his emphasis is on "race" rather than entitlements. He actually constructs a table (Table 25, page 427) noting the "color of grandparents of 311 persons listed in the *Who's Who in Colored America* for 1928–29." By linking previous free Negro status and racial status (mulatto) to his "zone of the most civilized Negroes," Frazier practically eliminates any discussion of uplift processes and suggests, instead, that lower-class Negroes are stuck in poverty in perpetuity: a permanent underclass. In the otherwise compelling and erudite narrative of pathology and cultural backwardness found in his 1939 text, Frazier makes highly circumscribed reference to Du Bois's work and certainly does not engage Du Bois's fundamental conclusion that ex-slaves are capable of uplift. Frazier came to his conclusion not by producing a study of the scope of *The Philadelphia Negro* but by articulating an unproven theory of assimilation and, after studying the most destitute segments of the black community, generalizing his findings as *truths descriptive of black people in general.*

Once Du Bois declared that he was a radical socialist, this made it possible for his enemies to classify him as a *propagandist and not a scholar.* The negative legacy of slavery and the culture-of-poverty tropes dominated the discourse on race and made all-the-more invisible the dynamics of social class in the lives of black and white working-class people. Du Bois gave voice and factual evidence to the perspective that *literacy leads to enlightenment, which, when rewarded with opportunity, results in uplift.* He thought his study *The Philadelphia Negro* documented this, and the primary purpose of his text *The Gift of Black Folk* was to provide further evidence of how rapidly black people could "rise," all of which was underplayed, if not dismissed outright, in Frazier's zest to define black people and black culture as incomplete in their development. Frazier followed through with a devastating stereotype of black human backwardness and social incompetence that made Du Bois's collection of uplift stories appear fanciful and not even vaguely relevant. However, it turns out that Du Bois, not Frazier, had a more prophetic vision. During the period that Frazier was busy constructing his pejorative vision, University of North Carolina sociologist Guy Benton Johnson wrote a research proposal, the rationale for which contained this comment: "During the early years of freedom, the Negroes in this country have made remarkable progress. It would probably not be exaggerating to say that in educational and economic attainments the average Negro today is better qualified to discharge the duties of citizenship than were the masses of white men when they were granted the right of full and free manhood suffrage" (Johnson, 1933, Study Outline).

As happened with impressions about black self-hatred emanating from the Clark doll studies, Frazier's trope about black family instability and inferiority became invulnerable to critique. Du Bois's perspective—carefully crafted from real data—was shunted aside for a narrative that fails to incorporate facts about one-generation uplift easily available to those who could read. Social attitudes dramatized in *The Birth of a Nation*, alongside Frazier's depiction of blacks as undercivilized, dominated the public image of black people from the 1920s through the publication of the Moynihan Report in 1965. As it is, the culture of poverty trope is alive and well in Rempson's reaffirmation (2016).

A Theory without Predictive Power

It is nothing short of amazing that Frazier's culture of poverty thesis has had such a long shelf life. First of all, his prediction of deterioration of black families went unfulfilled, as the census reports for 1940 and 1950 failed to reveal a constant uptick in the percentage of broken black families (Gutman, 1976). In addition, Frazier's theory that black families from rural backgrounds could not socialize black youth to become productive citizens was called into question, not from the results of another scholar's research but in the social history of black sharecroppers migrating to the West Coast.

The first edition of Frazier's book on the Negro family was published in 1939, and unbeknownst to Frazier, every facet of his theory was *tested and found wanting* in the experiences of black sharecroppers migrating from the Deep South's Black Belt to California. Not that racism was missing in the perceptions and attitudes of white Californians, but, as Josh Sides puts it, for Negroes of the time, Los Angeles was a paradox:

> It was a city where white supremacy was as central to white self-perception as it was in Southern Mississippi, but anti-Black violence was quite limited. It had one of the highest proportions of black home ownership of any major city as well as an extensive network of racially restrictive housing covenants designed to minimize black residential mobility. It was a city where the presence of an extraordinarily diverse multicultural and multiethnic neighborhood population mitigated the harshest effects of racial segregation in neighborhoods and schools but exacerbated those effects in the workplace. Finally, it was a city in which the black community delicately balanced competing desires for both activism and accommo-

dation. These paradoxes, of course, were the products of the city's early history. (Sides, 2006, pp. 12–13)

Urban areas in California presented opportunity spaces akin to the first twelve years of Reconstruction, when the ex-slaves exploded from the grips of slavery and carved out a level of progress and uplift that stunned white elites. In pre–World War II California, black migrants easily found work and were able to accumulate enough savings to buy homes, send progeny to the same high-quality schools as whites (K–12 and college), and were able to participate and excel in sports at the collegiate athletics level. An early example of what was possible shows Ralph Bunche graduating from UCLA with honors in 1927 (summa cum laude, and Phi Beta Kappa). In 1939, the year in which Frazier's book on the black family was published, UCLA made room for the offspring of black sharecroppers, one the progeny of a poor black family from Cairo, Georgia, the other from the cotton fields of Texas (Johnson, 2017). The Robinsons of Georgia saw their son—Jack Roosevelt Robinson, better known as Jackie Robinson—grow into an accomplished baseball player who integrated major league baseball. His classmate from Texas—Thomas Bradley—became the first black mayor of the city of Los Angeles. At UCLA they were joined by two additional African Americans, Kenny Washington and Woody Strode, to form the four black Bruins of UCLA of the late 1930s and early 1940s (Johnson, 2017). It would be decades before any predominantly white college-level institution would allow four black athletes to be members of any major collegiate team. Their life trajectory made mincemeat of Frazier's civilization trope and demonstrated without a doubt that human beings—black human beings—could achieve *uplift in one generation*, just as Du Bois had demonstrated in *The Philadelphia Negro* and *The Gift of Black Folk*, which explored one-generation social mobility for black educators, inventors, and business owners (Du Bois & Gates, 1924). Given how Frazier's theory was totally incapable of explaining the black uplift that occurred in the first twelve years of Reconstruction, as well as the evidence of social mobility for black sharecroppers who migrated to California, it becomes clear, in hindsight, that the damage wrought by Frazier's work was avoidable.

Delinquency Rates

Frazier's perspective turned on evidence showing high levels of black delinquency. He theorized that incompetent black families were not capable of effectively socializing progeny and saw high delinquency rates as a critical "proof" for his theory. In many ways, his prediction of black criminality was as influential as statistics on family illegitimacy. Lee Rainwater put it this way: "It is the central thesis of this paper that the caste-facilitated infliction of suffering by Negroes on other Negroes and on themselves appears most poignantly within the confines of the family and that the victimization process operates in families and prepares and toughens its members to function in the ghetto world, at the same time it seriously interferes with their ability to operate in any other world" (Rainwater, 1966, p. 176).

Working within the same time period as Frazier (1920–1940) and the same urban center from which Frazier drew his family data (Chicago), Michael W. Homel studied the history of the establishment of segregated schooling in Chicago (Homel, 1984). In a section of his text covering family life, community, and schools, Homel's analysis of school segregation, while not focused on black family dynamics per se, nevertheless presents historical evidence that, when placed side by side with Frazier's work, provides a more plausible explanation for the rise of black youth delinquency than suggested by Frazier. For the same time period (1920–1940), Homel found that the white ethnic population had stabilized and had actually begun to decline precipitously and, by 1940, overcrowding was not much of a challenge for schooling white ethnic children. The opposite was true for blacks, as the constant influx of blacks migrating from the Deep South—especially from Mississippi, Arkansas, and Louisiana—overwhelmed the school board policy favoring racial segregation.

Citing a report on black enrollment dated 1941, Homel found that, although the system was designed for a maximum capacity of 18,800 black students, the actual enrollment was 28,673, or an overcapacity of 35 percent. A few of the elementary schools operated at 30–40 percent over capacity; however, the most dramatic overcrowding was at the *high school level*. DuSable High had an official capacity of 2,400 but was servicing 4,000. Phillips High was designed for 1,500 but was asked to service 3,600, or an overcapacity of 240 percent. These school enrollment figures are correlated with neighborhood density. Black areas of Chicago had 90,000 residents per square mile, while in nearby white neighborhoods the figure was 20,000 per square mile. Neighborhood overcrowding replicated school overcrowding (Homel, 1984).

Part of the problem was the school board's reluctance to build new schools in black neighborhoods. Even with the white school population in decline, new schools were more likely to be built in white rather than black districts. Given the limited investment in black school construction, the school board turned to other solutions to relieve the overcrowding issue, namely the use of temporary structures called portals and an attendance policy known as double shifts (Homel, 1984, pp. 79–80). In order to sustain school segregation, officials provided damp, dangerous, and unhealthy temporary portals. In another option that speaks directly to the rise in delinquency, the board instituted double shifts. School schedules were changed so that each day a school might function with two or more shifts. Rare in white neighborhoods, the number of multiple shifts in the ghetto rose from four in 1931 to seven in 1936 and thirteen in 1940. *Black students were spending 20 percent to as high as 40 percent fewer hours in school than white students.* Phillips High School was servicing 3,600 students and DuSable 4,000. The double-shift policy meant that both for the morning and afternoon shifts, nearly half the students enrolled at both high schools—3,800 black adolescents—were out of school, *without supervision*. Homel quotes school professionals, community leaders, and an alderman offering the same observation that the double-shift policy was turning black youth into truants (Homel, 1984, pp. 82–83). *In effect, coming to terms with the rise in black juvenile delinquency did not require postulation of a legacy-of-slavery trope.*

Frazier never makes mention of the double-shift school policy in his analysis, and this is surprising for several reasons. Historical evidence strongly suggests he should have known about double shifting. Double shifting was first documented in a report released in 1922 by the Chicago Commission on Race Relations titled: *The*

Negro in Chicago: A Study of Race Relations and a Race Riot, for which Frazier's friend, Charles S. Johnson, did most of the writing (Farber, 1995). "Indications of overcrowding are the average number of seats in a classroom, the average number of pupils per teacher, and the double-school or shift system.... Although there are no double schools in the group attended mainly by white Americans, one of the six attended mainly by Negroes and five of the schools attended mainly by children of immigrants are double schools" (Chicago Commission, 1922, p. 244).

That the double-shift policy was a key finding is underscored years later, when in an edited volume published in 1971, Anthony Platt highlighted the double-shift policy as a major precipitating factor in the cause of the 1919 Chicago race riot (A.M. Platt, 1971, pp. 109–110). Frazier was well connected to the Chicago Urban League (CUL), as was the chair of his dissertation committee—Robert Ezra Park—and as reported by Homel (1984), the league was one of the strongest voices to publicly denounce the double-shift policy: "The League was also an important part of the anti-overcrowding movement, assisting protests in individual school districts and participating in ghetto-wide effort. As early as 1935, Frazier T. Lane, director of the CUL's Civic Improvement Department, cooperated with the PTA representatives in a committee to investigate and complain about double-shift schools in black neighborhoods" (Homel, 1984, p. 136).

It is nearly impossible to imagine that E. Franklin Frazier did not possess knowledge about the school board's double-shift policy and its influence on the delinquency rate for black youth in the Chicagoland area. In both his dissertation and his book, Frazier references the Chicago Urban League as a major supporter of his work on black families. To repeat, his relationship with the CUL suggests he was an important consultant to the league's activities. It is possible members of his dissertation committee recommended that he not mention the double-shift policy. Then there is the possibility of Frazier being seduced by human hubris, where he became so enamored with his own theorizing as to preclude searching for alternate narratives. In a similar vein, that he references Du Bois when such referencing supported his civilizing trope, while studiously *avoiding*

Du Bois's research demonstrating black uplift, is perhaps even more disturbing than the failure to mention the double-shift information. His presentation appears airtight and leaves absolutely no room for dispute, as he never entertains *any* counternarratives, even though, in the case of Du Bois, Frazier was presented with a formidable voice constantly and repeatedly pointing out historical evidence that defies Frazier's emphasis on the Negroes' need for enhanced civilizing.

Frazier was obsessed with Negro sexual behavior. Just as the double-shift policy may have worked to distort the delinquency tendencies of black youth, Hartman has uncovered the way Frazier's analysis of black women was surface-level at best:

> With no proof of employment, [a black women could be] indicted for vagrancy under the Tenement House Law. Vagrancy was an expansive and virtually all-encompassing category; . . . it was an ubiquitous charge that made it easy for the police to arrest and prosecute young women with no evidence of crime or act of lawbreaking. In the 1910s and 1920s, vagrancy statutes were used primarily to target young women for prostitution. To be charged was to be sentenced because 80 percent of those who appeared before the magistrate judge were sentenced to serve time; some years the rate of conviction was 89 percent. It did not matter if it was your first encounter with the law. Vagrancy statutes and the Tenement House Law made young black women vulnerable to arrest. What mattered was not what you had done, but the prophetic power of the police to predict the future. (Hartman, 2019, pp. 241–242)

In effect, conjecture about the loose morals of black men and women said to be residual of the legacy thesis was premised in part on arrest records that were, in point of fact, a contrivance—a social illusion.

The above material deconstructs Frazier's perspective using resources readily available to Frazier himself. The point being, his theory was flawed from the very beginning, and its capacity to shape public opinion has less to do with the veracity of his research findings and interpretations and more to do with stereotypes already "in the air." While surely not his intent, Frazier's work supported stereotypes found in the narrative for the infamous film *The Birth of a Nation*. The movie stoked fears about the overall lack of civilization exhibited by blacks, and Frazier anchors his analysis with such tropes. The film painted black men, in particular, as hypersexual, and Frazier presented a comparative image of black men driven by sexual urges unconstrained by a culture riddled with sexual contradictions. The film's depiction of black people as pariahs sits comfortably next to Frazier's narrative showing black parents as incapable of socializing children to fit into society. Just as the film stimulated fear in the white viewer, so does reading Frazier's analysis provoke fear in any reader, let alone whites. Almost as important, acceptance of his thesis about a legacy of slavery would steer future scholars away from an analysis of social class, and direct them instead to a search for that "something else" that allegedly made black poverty more peculiar from white poverty.

Taking Turns Demonizing Each Gender

This chapter has taken on the deficit perspective as it applies to *black people in general*—black children, black women, and black men—however, a case can be made that the perspective targets black boys and black men disproportionately, given that the deficit literature depicts *black boys and black men as superpredators, out-of-control rapists, and otherwise criminally inclined*. In recent times, the predator trope was made popular during the 1988 presidential campaign, when George Bush and his campaign manager, Lee Atwater, used the horrific criminal behavior of one black person, Willie Horton, to racialize the campaign and make it appear that Bush's opponent—Michael Dukakis—was soft on crime. The Willie Horton trope infected social attitudes toward crime, and inner-city crime in particular, leading to hysterical and overly punitive social policies toward crime and culminating in the mass incarceration of African American adult and adolescent males (Anderson & Enberg, 1995; Hurwitz & Peffley, 2005). However, in modern times, nothing reveals both the existence and power of negative stereotypes heaped on male youth more than the story of the Central Park Five. In the absence of corroborating witnesses and DNA evidence linking any of five black youths to the crime, interrogating detectives and the chief prosecutor convinced *themselves* that the youth "must be guilty," because in their eyes black youth are savages capable of heinous acts (Byfield, 2014). In perhaps the most comprehensive presentation of the deficit analysis since the publication of Kenneth Clark's *Dark Ghetto* (K. B. Clark, 1965/1989), Rempson (2016) accepts as good science past as well as contemporary research showing that black boys and men are, in a few words, psychologically messed-up. Rempson is not oblivious to the power of social forces and oppression, but he presents arguments that the distorted and negative mindset of black males "prevents" them from recognizing and thus seizing opportunities right in front of them, such as understanding the value of education as a tool for protecting oneself from the ravages of oppression.

In a stunning and highly provocative analysis, Tommy J. Curry (2017) demonstrates that, when taken seriously, the deficit perspective seems compelling and leads a reader to the conclusion that black boys and men are animalistic superpredators. As a case in point, in a recent newspaper opinion piece by Harvard law professor Randall Kennedy (2019), he describes how one of the jurors who voted for Keith Tharpe's death decision later stated he believed the defendant was a "nigger," and he wondered whether black people have souls. Curry takes up the mantle of the late Frazier's devastating critique of the black middle class—*Black Bourgeoisie* (Frazier, 1957)—and repeats ad nauseam that middle-class blacks are afraid of the underclass, and that middle-class black scholars, in particular, have failed to study and capture the "interior spaces" experienced by black boys and men. At this point in his analysis, Curry seems unaware, ironically, that it was Frazier who originated the superpredator trope to begin with!

Curry, with insight and sensitivity, takes the reader beneath the predator stereotype to reveal black boys and men as *vulnerable human beings* who, like black girls and women, are frequently the object of sexual violence and, yes, even rape. Curry traces the origin of the superpredator stereotype to white slave owners' fears that black men lusted for white women and that white women in turn lusted for intercourse with black bucks. He explores lynchings that incorporated castration rituals and black boys being arrested for crimes simply because they were in the vicinity, and ends his historical tracking of the stereotype by noting its inclusion in *Black Macho and the Myth of the Superwoman*, by Michele Wallace (1978). Curry meticulously documents how, as was true for black girls and women, black boys and men were the object of sexual fantasies and violations during slavery, genital mutilations during lynchings in the South (circa 1900–1930), and, in the present, the insertion of instruments like screwdrivers and revolvers by white police into the anuses of arrested black boys and men under the guise of searching for drugs.

Curry fails to include the works of Yasser Payne (Payne, 2006), Michele Fine (Fine et al., 2004), and Ann Ferguson (2010), all of whom anticipated Curry's vulnerability thesis by ten years or more. Also missing is reference to Anastasia Curwood's (2008) amazing deconstruction and critique of Frazier's work that exposes Frazier's fundamental sexism. Frazier attacked women's power, suggested female-headed families were by definition inferior and incapable of socializing children to be productive human beings, and claimed that, if the mother was absent a male partner, black families exhibited diminished progress over time (Curwood, 2008). Frazier theorized that slavery left the black family too dependent on women, and he supported a hierarchy of men over women. Frazier tied African American problems to the feminization of the race, as did his mentor, Park, who referred to black folk as the feminine race: "Frazier's gender and sexual politics, with his emphasis on hierarchical gender roles and the practice of normative heterosexuality, while not unusual for his time, are notable for the fact his work has heavily influenced scholarship and policy debates on African American families" (Curwood, 2008, p. 334).

When combined with Curry's, Curwood's analysis reveals that within the deficit discourse the *genders take turns being the source of all evil* in the diagnosis of social and psychological problems in the black community, with women being the bone of contention in the past, men more so in the present.

Finally: Bringing the Power of SES and Poverty to the Surface

Ten to fifteen years after the publication of the Moynihan Report on black families, white people, *who were never slaves*, began to exhibit addiction patterns, family breakup statistics, and overdose death rates previously thought impossible, given the presumed strengths of white families. In Robert D. Putnam's masterful book titled *Our Kids: The American Dream in Crisis* (2015), the changing family dynamics for white people living in Port Clinton, Ohio, are shown to be typical of changes occurring among white families throughout the United States, especially for those living in areas tagged with the label "Rust Belt," such as central New York, Pennsylvania, West Virginia, Ohio, Indiana, Iowa, Michigan, Illinois, and Wisconsin.

Putnam pointed out these statistics about white families: skyrocketing rates of white juvenile delinquency, quintupling of white single-parent households, increase in white unwed births from 20 percent to 40 percent, and an increase in white child poverty from 10 percent in 1999 to 40 percent in 2013 (Putnam, 2015, p. 21). Likewise, in her case study titled *Falling from Grace*, Katherine Newman (1998) found father abandonment, divorce, and lower academic aspirations in children happened to white families—*all within one generation*. In addition, white people began to exhibit a phenomenal addiction to drugs, starting with methamphetamine (Reding, 2010), then opioids, and eventually heroin (Macy, 2018). By 2017, 70,000 drug overdoses were recorded in the United States, the majority occurring among whites. In 2016, the drug-related overdose rate (per 100,000) was 25.3 for whites, 17.1 for blacks, and 9.5 for Hispanics. In other words, the rate was 50 percent and 167 percent higher for whites than for blacks or Hispanics, respectively (Berezow, 2018; Seth et al., 2018). The iconic image of the average drug-addicted person shifted from Willie Horton to Emily Groth, a blonde youth from Sioux Falls, South Dakota (Kennecke, 2018).

There is close to universal acceptance that the primary forces explicating the fall from grace of white families and entire white communities can be traced to *deindustrialization and globalization*.

According to Barry Bluestone and Bennett Harrison, "deindustrialization" means the "systematic disinvestment in the nation's basic productive capacity. Controversial as it may be, the essential problem with the U.S. economy can be traced to the way capital—in the forms of financial resources and of real plant and equipment—has been diverted from productive investment in our basic national industries into unproductive speculation, mergers and acquisitions, and foreign investment. Left behind are shuttered factories, displaced workers, and newly emerging ghost towns" (Bluestone & Harrison, 1982, p. 6).

Continuing, Bluestone and Harrison then show how deindustrialization evolves into globalization:

> This does not mean that corporate managers are refusing to invest but only that they are refusing to invest in basic industries of the country. U.S. Steel has billions to spend, but instead of rebuilding steel capacity, it paid 6 billion to acquire Marathon Oil of Ohio. General Electric is expanding its capital stock, but not in the United States. During the 1970s, GE expanded its worldwide payroll by 50,000, but it did so by adding 30,000 foreign jobs and reducing its U.S. employment by 25,000. RCA Corporation followed the same strategy, cutting its U.S. employment by 14,000 and increasing its foreign work force by 19,000. It is the same in the depressed automobile industry. (Bluestone & Harrison, 1982, p. 6)

The backstory for deindustrialization begins in the 1940s. During World War II, access to white male participation in the workforce dropped, as most were recruited into the armed forces to fight the war. This loss of manpower was replaced by workforce participants once shunned by industry—women and people of color. Within urban centers, factories producing war armaments were accessible to ghetto residents primarily through public transportation. These urban-centered industries remained active through World War II, the Korean War, and, to some extent, the war in Vietnam. Robert Morley (2005) points out that during World War II, U.S. manufacturing capacity literally supported the winning of the war, and thereafter remained exemplary, with Ford, GM, Maytag, and other offerings as household names. Then, within a short period of time, the manufacturing base of the American economy began to evaporate. According to Morley, manufacturing represented 53 percent of the American economy in 1965, falling to 39 percent in 1988 and only 9 percent by 2004. This represents a loss of over 7 million good-paying jobs once held by workers with education levels of a high school degree or less. Bluestone and Harrison (1982) would have found this to be a serious undercount, because when the ripple effects of plant closings are figured in, the total jumps to tens of millions more jobs lost. When the failing plants became part of a corporate buyout, retirement and pension funds were often raided, stripping another source of worker support and making the community even poorer and more vulnerable to decay.

Blacks, more so than whites, were disproportionately affected by the *first round* of deindustrialization (see Goozner, 1990).

> Blacks are especially hard-hit because they are increasingly concentrated within central cities and in those regions of the country where plant closings and economic dislocation have been most pronounced.... To add to the inequality of burden, nonwhite minorities also tend to be concentrated in industries that have borne the brunt of recent closings.... The nearly immutable code of last hired first fired, combined with entrenched patterns of housing segregation, have left minorities at a real disadvantage when plants close down, retail shops move out, and economic activity spreads to suburbs and beyond. (Bluestone & Harrison, 1982, pp. 54–56)

Stephanie Coontz noted the biggest losers were undereducated black males who could, by the dint of hard work and strenuous effort, make an adequate income to support marriage and a family (Coontz, 1991, p. 245). In the 1950s, over 50,000 people were once employed at the Gary U.S. Steel Plant, the Inland Steel Plant, and the Standard Oil Refinery (Brady & Wallace, 2001). The subsequent rise in the percentage of the Chicagoland population receiving Aid to Families with Dependent Children was shown to be directly correlated with the rise in unemployment connected to the closure of these plants (Brady & Wallace, 2001). This scenario played out in black communities across America. As the residents of black ghettos in Chicago, Cleveland, Detroit, and Philadelphia responded to unemployment with a drop in marriage rates, an increase in out-of-wedlock births, and increases in drug addiction, street crime, and gang behavior, Moynihan and others saw this as the fulfillment of the *Frazier prophecy about black culture.*

It is with an understanding of the dynamics of deindustrialization that one must approach the Moynihan Report (Moynihan, 1965/1997). Recall Frazier set the stage by claiming black poverty was somehow "different" from ordinary poverty because, in addition to socioeconomic forces, black poverty stems from the added element of the legacy of slavery. That is, black poverty results in part from external socioeconomic forces, but is in addition an "internal" problem related to a lack of civilization. Moynihan did not fabricate the statistics supportive of his narrative, but in his inability to find evidence that white families were suffering too, he fell back on the similarities of his findings with that reported by Frazier in 1939. Deindustrialization would not spread to white communities for another ten years, and the spatial isolation of the two communities—that is, the factor of residential segregation, with ghettoes over here and white communities over there—helped sustain the *illusion* that something other than socioeconomic forces were at play.

Interestingly, the term "deindustrialization" was seldom if ever used during the first phase, when it was enveloping black communities, but found almost immediate application in explicating economic downturns in white communities. Black people, and black youth in particular, found their racially segregated communities the logical site for underground economic ventures based on illicit activities. Given that history shows that black street life replicates the behavior of past periods of Jewish, Italian, and Irish gangsterism, the emergence of black gangsterism should not have been a surprise, nor should it have been "explained" through highly racialized tropes. Murder and mayhem are part of white ethnic group gangsterism, and to strip discussions of black crime of its presumed peculiarity, it helps to be reminded of this ethnic gangsterism. Otherwise astute observers and scholars, even in the face of readily available socioeconomic evidence and unemployment rates staring them in the face, have gravitated toward racial explanations for black crime rather than socioeconomic trends. The drama of gangsterism, hip-hop culture, and Frazier's shadow has drawn observers toward racial and cultural tropes, the primary and worst example being the Moynihan Report.

One of the most disconcerting examples of the power of the deficit perspective to turn fact into fiction was played out in the late 1990s. In February 1992, *USA Today* published a graphic depiction of the ripple effects felt throughout Perry, Florida, in the aftermath of the closing of a factory that was the primary source of employment for undereducated, low-income, (mostly) white Perry residents (Stone, 1992). At the top of the poster-like infographic were the faces of a cluster of white adults (one African American)—now unemployed—and beneath their faces was a series of squares each representing a business or service doomed to be shuttered as a result of the factory closing. Arrows crisscrossed to connect various enterprises so that the entire matrix presented a clear and gripping picture of what happens to a community when it is the victim of sudden, massive unemployment. The only thing missing was a depiction of the cycles of drug addiction—first meth, then opioids—and the accompanying narrative was focused entirely on "social forces," with not a word mentioned about the personal psychology of the now unemployed.

In July of the same year, the *New York Times* (Toner, 1992) ran a string of articles in front-page coverage supportive of a change in the welfare laws being advocated by then president Bill Clinton. The series focused on black people, and these concepts were baked into the analysis: personal responsibility, cultural deficits, immature decision making, and irresponsible black males, who, out of "choice," were unemployed. In the *USA Today* article, unemployment resulted from systemic forces producing a category of people captured by the label the "worthy poor," while the *Times* series depicted behavior disconnected from societal forces and dripping in *personal choices* allegedly incentivized by an outmoded welfare system. The "worthy poor" merit our sympathy, while the urban poor require passage of a draconian welfare law that incentivizes through punishment, shaming, and tough love. The latter comes remarkably close to the type of policy statements found in the rhetoric of white leaders of the KKK during the Klan's Second Wave between 1920 and 1930 (Pegram, 2011).

Part of the problem involved the spatial separation between black and white communities, making for an *intellectual vacuum* that seduced and teased scholars into imagining race-linked theoretical constructs, while blinding them to the power and dynamics of inequality. Today, the destructive force of deindustrialization is easier to grasp because it is so evident in both communities. However, when confined to black and Latino communities, the *"must be something wrong with black folk"* trope found easy access into the worldview of Moynihan, as it did to Frazier, when he first allowed the inferior culture and legacy of slavery tropes to trump his understanding of the power of social class. It is often overlooked that Frazier's initial observations were made on one of the poorest wards in the city of Chicago, marked by punishing poverty. Furthermore, at the time of his data collection, circa the late 1920s and early 1930s, black people were treated as a caste and their employment opportunities were phenomenally low.

Deindustrialization reared its head in all-white communities beginning in the 1980s, and, to repeat, though white folks were never slaves, the subsequent deterioration in their communities followed to the letter the negative consequences first observed in segregated black communities. *Race should have lost its explanatory power* because deindustrialization showed that when once-employed Americans—black or white—experience drastic changes in their socioeconomic circumstances, as happens when out of work with little hope for re-employment, the human beings caught in this Faustian Dilemma evidence downturns in their humanity, such as alcohol or drug addiction, rise in drug overdose death rate, family abandonment, divorce, child abuse, single-parent households, diminished academic aspirations in children, rise in poverty rate, and so on. However, in an amazing turn of events, political machinations converted a common and shared problem (loss of employment related to deindustrialization) into a race problem, where whites were made to believe the source of their downturn was racial rather than traceable to systemic economic forces, as captured by Robert Wuthnow (2019) in his book, appropriately titled, *The Left Behind: Decline and Rage in Small-Town America*.

The Real Legacy of Slavery: A Race War and Southern White Fascism

After the Civil War, greed, dominance, and a thirst for privilege found everyday white Southerners participating in outrageous acts of inhumanity on the bodies of helpless black people (Allen et al., 2000). It is more than ironic that in a well-documented history of one group killing over 4,400 people of color, we somehow focus on the legacy of slavery as it theoretically influenced the contemporary lives of blacks, yet little mention is made of the legacy of slavery as experienced by Southern whites. After a lynching, mothers in attendance would return home and feed their babies, children would go out to play, and men would return to their chores. This kind of human disconnect is referenced in psychology as *sociopathy*. The death of Emmett Till in 1954 and the Charlottesville March in 2017 show that aspects of this legacy can be documented up to the present. In an important empirical study by Avidit Acharya, Matthew Blackwell, and Maya Sen (2000), they found that whites living in areas of the South today that in 1860 had high concentrations of slaves are more likely to identify as Republican, express colder feelings and resentment toward blacks, and oppose affirmative action. The article is titled "The Political Legacy of American Slavery" and makes for a far stronger case of a legacy of slavery than any work alleging a legacy of slavery facing modern blacks.

When, during the first twelve years of Reconstruction, it became obvious that blacks were advancing at a pace that would position them to be more educated than the average white person (Du Bois, 1935; Gates, 2019), black schools were shut down, and it would be forty years before they would reappear (Anderson, 1988, pp. 188–

193). We typically think of the American Civil War as a horrific singular event; however, there were *two wars*. The second was a *race war* that saw the white South defeat, using violence and political shenanigans, black communities throughout the South. Lynchings and pogroms were the most demonstrative forms of social control, but legislative machinations were equally effective, as will become clear shortly. The African American experience in the Deep South from the end of Reconstruction into the early 1960s was akin to living not within a democracy, but in a cluster of Southern states that presented a facade of democracy. In actuality, the Southern states were a collection of fiefdoms, overseen by governors whose fascistic mindsets anticipated what the world would witness in Hitler in the 1930s. The South was governed by a one-party system that energized politics through the constant infusion of sociopathic hatred. Sociopaths in the uniforms of law-enforcement officials led the way to lynch-mob rule and ritualized the display of inhumanity, making possible the frequent burning alive of human beings, the use of butcher knives to cut off the arms of black prisoners, and the use of blowtorches to disfigure as well (Dray, 2007). Lynch-mob participants often brought their children to the lynch scene for a form of bizarre socialization in race relations, as captured on the front jacket of the text *Without Sanctuary: Lynching Photography in America* (Allen et al., 2000), a photographic macabre memorial to Southern white cultural sociopathy. The 2017 Unite the Right march in Charlottesville, Virginia, was a reminder that the South's attraction to fascism and violence simmers just below the surface of white human beings who, from a distance, seem ordinary.

As whites controlled resources and the instruments of power and through the use of political violence, two developmental patterns emerged. First, educational, commercial, and strategic resources were heaped on white citizens and white families, allowing them to experience *accelerated advancement*—that is, to achieve social mobility at a rate not possible had resources been distributed equally. Second, black Southern communities experienced *accelerated marginalization and underdevelopment*. This pattern can be traced well into the twentieth century, as made evident in the earlier discussion of Homel's exposé of the Chicago School Board's use of outrageously inferior and unhealthy temporary portals and the policy of school shifts that pushed black juveniles into truancy (Homel, 1984). However, the most alarming example concerned the administration of the World War II GI Bill benefits. Southern senators made certain benefits were administered disproportionally to white GIs, and created nearly insurmountable obstacles for black GIs, especially regarding benefits meant to create wealth, as in Veterans Administration home loans. For example, in a 1947 survey of thirteen Mississippi cities, only 2 of the 3,229 VA-guaranteed loans were made to black GIs. *In effect, the GI Bill was a massive socialistic support system representing affirmative action for white GIs and their families* (Katznelson, 2005), notwithstanding Suzanne Mettler's surreal counternarrative arguing that blacks benefited as much as did white GIs (Katznelson & Mettler, 2008). Thus, while World War II GI benefits practically made the growth of the white middle class possible in Mississippi (and throughout the United States), its racialized administration not so much "blunted" but suppressed and exaggerated the lack of growth of the black middle class (Katznelson, 2005; Turner & Bound, 2003). This set the stage for the explosive growth of the black underclass in the 1960s and 1970s (Pager, 2008). "In the south, the GI Bill functioned in a manner deeply consistent with white supremacy and racial segregation across the board; as a result, for the majority of black veterans it was reprehensively retrograde in ways that, more than any other cause, widened the gap between white and black Americans in the decades after 1945" (Katznelson & Mettler, 2008, p. 523).

In allowing states to administer the GI benefits, the federal government in effect joined and supported the South's war on blacks. Of course, not to be forgotten are the scores of black GIs who, upon returning from the war, were abducted while in uniform and lynched, in many instances because they looked "too proud" (Dray, 2007). Even though evidence of racism in the administration of GI benefits was made known to federal authorities as early as 1947, nothing was done because, the way the bill was written, states' rights in the administration of the benefits were sacrosanct. Between 1934 and 1962, the Federal Housing and Veterans Administrations distributed 120 billion dollars in home loans, only 2 percent of which was awarded to black people and people of color (Lipsitz, 1998). Going further, the government, in cooperation with banks and the real estate industry, made certain that 2 percent was for housing in less desirable areas, meaning these homes did not increase in value as did white homes.

If collusion between federal agencies, banks, and the real estate industry helped to limit black access to wealth through home ownership, other forms of government-private conspiracies found ways to strip black families of farmland. In an investigative report published in *The Atlantic*, Vann R. Newkirk (2019) outlined how over one million black farmers had their farms taken from right under them through machinations orchestrated by local and federal farm agencies and Wall Street. We see the same type of legislative mumbo jumbo in bills passed under the guise of the drug-related law-and-order thrust, resulting in the school-to-prison pipeline (Wald & Losen, 2003), even though the propensity to use drugs is the same for blacks and whites. While states like Colorado have gone out of the way to pass laws and enact policies to make casting an election ballot *easier*, Southern Republican governors and state attorneys are working hard to *suppress* black voting rights, a right for which in the 1960s scores of black and white supporters were beaten and in some cases murdered (Berman, 2017; Musgrove, 2018). The phrase "white privilege" is more illuminating than most can comprehend.

Over time, the blockage of black social mobility has positioned blacks to be disproportionately represented among the poor and working classes. In 2020, with the onset of the COVID-19 pandemic, that positionality was lethal. Worldwide, the virus proved more deadly for those who, at the point of infection, suffered medical preconditions such as hypertension, diabetes, and asthma, ailments more apt to be experienced by poor people. Before the development of a vaccine, the only way to suppress the spread of the virus was to practice social distancing—a practice nearly impossible for poor people to execute due to overcrowded residences, and, as they were disproportionately employed at jobs requiring use of public transportation and workplaces involving multiple contacts (e.g., bus drivers, positions in grocery stores and warehouses, etc.), their rate of exposure to the virus far exceeded that of middle-class and wealthy people who had the protection afforded by having living spaces occupied by one person, couples, or small- to medium-sized families. With the exception of those connected to medical professions, middle- and upper-income families were not employed in jobs requiring constant and numerous social interactions. For poor people, social distancing was, for all intents and purposes, impossible to observe—the result being that poor blacks and people of color, had, on average, numerous opportunities to come in contact with carriers of the virus. The virus collided with the medical preconditions previously noted, resulting in a death rate for poor people, and black people in particular, that reached astronomical proportions. The virus proved as successful in exposing the structural flaws in society as racial pogroms and lynchings.

Summary of Chapter 5

This chapter critiques Frazier based on material readily available to Frazier to show how odd it is that his work became so important despite the ease with which its veracity can be called into question. Here I find inspiration from the writings of George Makari (2015, pp. 473–474), who, in his book *Soul Machine*, describes the vacuous claims of phrenology in language and phrasing that perfectly suits my perceptions of Frazier's work. Long before putting pen to paper, Frazier found himself deluged by opinions proclaiming blacks less than human. Frazier embraced propositions based on correlational thinking that, when he converted his dissertation into a book, he *hardened correlational data into truths* confirmed not by new data but a reaffirmation of the original correlation, even though his thinking was riddled with subjectivity, folklore, and everyday prejudices. That he followed up his treatise on the black poor with an intellectual diatribe against the black middle class leads one to entertain the perception that Frazier was uncomfortable with some aspects of his blackness. Frazier provided "research" that complemented preexisting beliefs and myths perpetuated by the South. He probably had no idea that, rather than subjecting his theory to research that would interrogate it, future scholars and spokespersons alike would *repeatedly* take his framework as a point of departure, thus resulting in the sequential reaffirmation rather than contestation of myth. Remember, it was more than forty years before Herbert Gutman's work (1976) would appear, and, even in the face of Gutman's retort, people continued to cling to Frazier, as if Gutman's findings were of limited relevance.

Poverty drove Irish, Polish, Russian, and Italian women to the streets and prostitution, yet when Frazier saw black women faced with the same social class pressures, he saw culture in place of social class. Punishing poverty enticed black men and women to street life, and in this they replicated gangsterism first developed by white immigrants, but this was unacknowledged by Frazier, even though during the time he was writing his dissertation, Chicago was the site of the 1929 Saint Valentine's Day Massacre. White crime could morph into celebrity, but, in Frazier's mind, black crime provided "proof" of cultural damage. Whites who were never slaves succumbed to poverty brought on by deindustrialization with a loss of hope and a despair once linked to the legacy of slavery. In a capitalist society, once coherent and proud communities saw the rise of vulgar human behavior in the face of losing livelihoods. When towns or regions suffered collapse—within a compressed time period—hope-filled white communities turned into an underclass, with a rapper like Eminem singing their woes.

One cannot "blame" Frazier for four generations of scholars—black and white—who allowed his theory to reign supreme because of their timidity. And in the process, we seemed to hang Du Bois out to dry. Frazier is dead, and it is not an insensitive activity to challenge his work. He was human, humans are flawed, and his work suffered mightily. It is always the following generation's duty to reread, reconstruct, and, where necessary, tear down and replace bad research and erroneous theory. Black progress made during the first twelve years of Reconstruction was no fluke, and thereafter a small percentage of black folk broke through rigid racial barriers constructed by white Southern Redeemers. Had these daring people been studied more closely, we would have discovered the linkage between literacy that leads to enlightenment and, when they are afforded the opportunity, the ability of black men and women to reach higher heights, just as the Enlightenment philosophers predicted. Former slaves were positioned to spread K–12 education throughout the South. Frederick Douglass proved we were equal; Eugene Bullard, the black World War I pilot, proved we were equal; Lucile Buchanan, the first black to graduate from the University of Colorado, proved we were equal; Jack Johnson, the boxer, proved we could be superior.

Ironically, we are faced with the same narrative today. How many potential black poets have we imprisoned for publicly smoking a joint? How many potential black female astronauts died prematurely, while giving birth, because of inadequate health care? As Curry might say: How many sensitive, vulnerable black boys have we turned into sociopaths even though they are missing the genetic marker? After being imprisoned time and again, black men and women are left dumbfounded by insight into the twisted piece of human junk they have become in their frantic struggle to bring home the bacon. Theirs is a replay of an earlier saga told by poor Eastern European Jews, by illiterate Irish and Italians, who, within a depleted environment, found nourishment suckling from society's underbelly.

When deindustrialization hit white America in full force, whites, who were never slaves, started to exhibit social pathologies once thought unique to black folk. In the aftermath, race should have lost its explanatory power, but, in a bizarre twist of fate, it became a wedge issue splitting white and black voters in the 2016 presidential election. Of primary concern to this observer is the power of the deficit perspective to shut down imagination regarding what did or did not happen to black folk during and after slavery. It painted a very limited picture of the agency slaves exhibited in the immediate aftermath of slavery, so thoroughly documented by Du Bois (1935) in *Black Reconstruction*. Once the flaws in Frazier's theorizing are recognized, one is practically forced to reimagine what *cultural and psychological assets* ex-slaves exhibited when exiting slavery. Such re-imagining is the focus of Chapter 6.

6

Slavery, Trauma, and Resilience

Decoupling Intent from Effects

While E. Franklin Frazier's analysis of the effect of slavery on modern black life outlived its usefulness and relevance, its lasting influence has been in the realm of mythmaking. Frazier saw ex-slaves as in need of civilizing, and his use of that word reveals the larger notion of *slavery resulting in damage,* which Frazier and others expanded on, with considerable imagination, to concepts like "the matriarchy" or "the mark of oppression." As noted in Chapter 1, this is the "must be" hypothesis, where the starting point in any analysis of the legacy of slavery is the "damage" *it must have caused* the captive Africans. Let's reference this stance as the "100 percent evil" perspective in that both the system of slavery and its influence on the captive Africans are assumed to narrate evil, both regarding intent (the action of those in power) and outcome (the damage experienced by the enslaved). This perspective forces one to predict that at the point of Emancipation the now free Africans would exhibit dysfunctionality, pain, and confusion as well as a limited capacity for planning and cooperation. It is this type of thinking that made Du Bois's text *Black Reconstruction* (1935) seem so "radical," because, rather than confirm Frazier's prediction of self-immolation, he presented page after page of historical evidence showing the ex-slaves exhibiting agency, an attribute not predicted by a deficit perspective.

In effect, Du Bois decoupled "intent from consequence," making the observer aware that as evil as the system may have been in both *intent and execution*, the human beings caught in the middle did not always respond as predicted. When an observer perceives black people stereotypically, theory becomes formulaic, where x is thought to produce z; but when black people are understood to be human, as did Du Bois, x may produce z plus a range of additional attributes linked to the unpredictable solutions and reactions human beings invent-construct-imagine in the moment and that are generally not accounted for in the mind's eye of those who oppress.

Currently, the biographies of Frederick Douglass and Booker T. Washington are generally categorized as exceptions to the rule, meaning they were born and raised as slaves, but happenstance intervened and, as can occur in some sort of "random" pattern, they managed to exit slavery with personality traits and levels of interpersonal competence that defy explanation, thus the two appellations thought to apply to their circumstances—happenstance and randomness. But suppose, as we do in psychology, that the humanization (or dehumanization) of a human being is never explained by happenstance, because outside of temperament, very little about being human is 100 percent hardwired at birth. "Traits" and "personality characteristics" result from exposure to ways of knowing and ways of doing taught to the evolving infant-child in the course of innumerable daily interactions. Personality traits do not just appear, pop up, and take full form by happenstance. A child absorbs ways of perceiving, knowing, feeling, and acting by "watching-copying-imitating" through "interactions" with other human beings. It is in this sense that every human being is a "social construction" and every "biography" tells us who the important figures were in shaping that person's life, including the likes of Frederick Douglass or Booker T. Washington.

Of the two, Washington may be the most intriguing. His story shows him possessing the qualities of fortitude, daring, developed intelligence, and extraordinary leadership skills. But rather than use his own story as a model for what other ex-slaves could do, he was convinced by some—especially Robert Ezra Park—that ex-slaves must see themselves as uncivilized and in need of intense training, practice, and experience, even though slaves built, ran, and maintained plantations in the first place. As previously mentioned, Park went on to head the Department of Sociology at the University of Chicago and was the chair of the dissertation committee for E. Franklin Frazier. Booker T. Washington literally invented a path for others that was contradicted by his own life story. Once the "100 percent evil" stance takes hold, the scholar-observer-activist has very little wiggle room in which to operate, because intent and consequence become inextricably linked, as believed by Washington, *despite the fact that such a narrative did not explain his own development.*

Modern scholarship on the slavery experience—penned by the likes of Herbert Gutman and John Blasingame—has dramatically decoupled *intent and consequence* to produce a voluminous historical literature that explicates slave culture, slave community, and slave aesthetics, meaning a narrative told looking from the bottom up, rather than the top down. As an example, of the subfields of study that result from this approach, Wilma King (2011) was able to devote an entire text to the experiences of slave youth: *Stolen Childhood: Slave Youth in Nineteenth-Century America.* The new research reveals the way ex-slaves, *viewed from the perspective of their being human,* were more resistant, resilient, and agentic than previously thought possible.

In this chapter, the objective is to provide a *psychological addendum* to the contemporaneous historical discourse on slavery by explicating how a segment of the slave population, the size of which is still unknown, exited slavery with interpersonal competence and confidence that, in large measure, made it possible for them to record—after slavery—success across a broad range of achievement categories: business, farming, skilled crafts, and education, as documented by Du Bois, no less, and not Frazier. *While the legacy of slavery points to trauma, a complete depiction must also account for protective factors, ingenious ways of surviving, and resilience.* The second part of this chapter links black socialization practices emanating from slavery to instances of black social mobility observed in the present. Emancipation triggered a social movement for uplift among the slave community, and modern studies of such movements show participants displayed a messianic, supercharged mindset, making achievable *fantastical* individual and group aspirations.

Newborn Slave Infant: Breeding versus Birthing

The passage of the 1807 law abolishing the slave trade meant that slave owners could best expand their wealth through birthing, or what they saw as "breeding." Thus, between 1807 and the end of slavery, birthing within the slave community itself, and not the importation of new slaves from Africa, became the way to increase wealth, with the qualifier "potential," because an infant had to be transformed into a grown person before investment and wealth were actualized. The infant had to be developmentally socialized. Such a situation placed constraints on the owner's capacity to be evil, for example, to maim, mutilate, rape, or kill, because it was only when the infant grew into an adolescent or adult that the slave, as property, could increase the owner's wealth. Furthermore, the ultimate paradox of slavery is that one human being (the owner) needed slaves who exhibited positive attributes, for example, positive albeit accommodating attitudes, interpersonal competence, and intelligence, because these human qualities helped the slave *anticipate, carry out, and fulfill* the orders and desires of the owner. Only the delicate and nimble hands of the *socialized* slave could pick the cotton; only a *socialized* slave could act as a surrogate to the owner's children; only a *socialized* slave could satisfy lust that leads to rape and forced intimacy. In short, the slave community's ability to raise fully *socialized* progeny did not prevent them from experiencing evil whims of the owners, and, after achieving positive socialization in the slave quarters, some slaves would be killed for no rhyme or reason. Nevertheless, from 1807 onward, birthing presented the slave community with *greater latitude in the expression of their own humanity* and in shaping the personality of newborn infant slaves.

The drive to increase one's wealth (the owner's agenda), accompanied by directives to the slave overseers and the slave community to protect and nurture the infant (again, the owner's agenda but an objective easily agreed to by the community), made it possible for the community to fashion an ecology of positive child development (slave community's agenda), resulting in a new member of the community who identified, supported, helped sustain, and, where possible, protected the community (slave community's agenda), in addition to contributing, inevitably, to the owner's enterprise (the owner's agenda). Thus, the intent of the owner was to "breed," but the response of the community was to birth, care for, nurture, and inculcate prosocial attitudes that, paradoxically, also helped the slave perform tasks and actions benefiting the owners. We need to stop confusing slavery with complete and total dehumanization. It was a horrid experience in human containment, but within its boundaries and walls the inhabitants did not cease being human.

Most important is the understanding that the prosocial attitudes and interpersonal competence resulting from the way slaves were socialized by the slave community in preparing the slave to function within the slave system did not "disappear" at the point of freedom. Rather, the ex-slaves could now use their psychological strengths in pursuit of personal happiness and well-being *after slavery*. Psychological assets were "portable" in the sense that, once developed, they could be put to use in the service of the owner or, in freedom, become tools in support of one's agenda as a freedperson. To say that slaves resisted is an understatement, and an important sign of slave resistance was the ability to make possible a *positive ecology of human development*, within which they could help mothers and their infants transact what today we know as the attachment-bonding experience, and, thereafter, help the slave child develop interpersonal competence and prosocial attitudes. The science and psychology of child development reveal that positive attachment and early childhood development is overwhelmingly driven by human contact and human interactions, independent of the *physical surroundings*, which can vary from rural poor environs to highly privileged contexts.

Research by Wilma King

The foremost expert on the experiences of slave childhood and slave youth is the award-winning historian Wilma King (2011). King points out that passage of the 1807 Act Prohibiting the Importation of Slaves placed a premium on the birthing of new slave children—especially male infants. In the logic of slavery, black bodies were a "commodity," and slave infants represented increased wealth. Quoting the instructions of a Mississippi slave owner to his overseer, King wrote: "The children must be particularly attended to, for rearing them is not only a duty, but also the most profitable part of the plantation business" (King, 2011, p. 57).

As a corollary of reproduction, Southern, more so than Northern, owners tolerated and even encouraged conjugal relationships, and marriage (jumping the broom) was not uncommon. Thus, many infants had identifiable parents with whom to openly and frequently interact: "Bondservants formed binding relationships, established conjugal unions, and developed memorable lives within the confines of bondage. Many slave-owners acknowledged marital relationships, recorded births by family units, and insisted upon monogamy. They reasoned that marriage and children fostered 'happiness' and worked against restiveness" (King, 2011, p. 39). King notes that while owners sought to encourage birthing, the state of medical knowledge and the general conditions for birthing were notoriously dangerous for all Southerners: "Enslaved mothers . . . could not control physical conditions that fostered high incidences of mortality and morbidity among their children. . . . Infant mortality rates were high, and communicable diseases were color-blind in Antebellum America. Slave-owners and slaves alike lived with sickness and death" (King, 2011, p. 57).

King's analysis supports the proposition that attachment and positive child development was possible during slavery. Mothers cherished their infants and invented ingenious garments with which to carry their infants to the fields so that breastfeeding could continue during the day, even as the mother toiled in the field or wherever her work assignment took her. Most importantly, King found records showing that on large plantations *nurseries* were run by elderly, infirmed slaves—generally women. The nurseries reflected the importance of fictive kin in a child's development and probably became the repository for the exchange of caregiving techniques and ideas: "Children became attached to caregivers and entered into fictive kin relationships that could serve them well if major changes, such as marriage, relocation, or death occurred within the owners' household and resulted in separation of slave families" (King, 2011, p. 63).

King made it a point to repeatedly stress the importance of fictive kin and the community at large: "If enslaved girls and boys enjoyed a childhood, it was because their parents and fictive kin made that possible. They stood between children and slaveholders or others who sought to control boys and girls psychologically and break their will to resist. Loving adults tried to protect them from emotional and physical harm regardless of its source" (King, 2011, p. 30).

As an aside, Imani Perry reminds us of the continued importance of fictive kin in modern African American social relations. When a person contested her sons' reference to Byron as Uncle Byron, she explained by what standard he was, in fact, an uncle: "You insisted. Of course, he was. . . . This is our culture. It is a beautiful thing, you know. Back in slavery times, when the nation and its laws said we had no right to family, to the kinship structures of blood and law, we made another set of relations, bindings, family. Family is more than that, we testified. And we kept it up, and we hold it, even when it might look like we have assimilated. Even after death" (Perry, 2019, p. 36).

Returning to King, her historical analysis reveals that an as-yet-unknown proportion of slaves experienced *positive attachment and positive child development*. King's analysis also shows that during slavery, the community exhibited positive, strong, and effective child-rearing practices, contradicting proclamations to the contrary by Robert Ezra Park and his doctoral student, E. Franklin Frazier. That black youth with strong positive personalities were, after childhood, subjected to rape, beatings, extreme forced labor, and forced relocation (sold to another owner) means that the horrors of slavery existed side by side with the capacity of the slave community to fashion a positive ecology of human development. Naturally, the question arises: How are trauma and conditions for positive personality development intertwined?

Slavery and Trauma

Contemporary research on the effects of trauma indicates that if a person has a positive and reasonably strong personality *before* experiencing the trauma, the greater the probability those strengths will help moderate post-trauma reactions, making the expression of resilience possible (Griffin et al., 2009; Peterson et al., 2008). There can be no doubt that, in a general sense, being a slave and functioning in the slavery system involved multiple traumas, for some even unimaginable horrors. However, as George Bonanno (2004) has noted, a rigid conceptualization automatically linking trauma to *dysfunctionality* must be rejected, otherwise how to explain the many ex-slaves who rapidly achieved success within a short time after exiting slavery? Furthermore, slave culture included strong spiritual and religious beliefs, qualities helpful in mitigating stress and trauma (Peres et al., 2007). The personality strengths ex-slaves evidenced years after slavery can only be explained, from a human development perspective, by the fact that somehow during slavery the community was able to construct a reasonably successful ecology of human development in the midst of an otherwise inhumane system. These extant strengths made success after slavery more likely and helped make resilience a more probable outcome, where dysfunctionality lurked.

It is important to emphasize that evidence of positive personality development in slaves does not contradict trauma theory. To the contrary, given it is understood that pre-existing personality strengths cannot so much minimize but *mitigate* the full impact of a trauma, knowledge of the two brings to light the human qualities constantly making an appearance in slave narratives: resilience, endurance, flexibility, pliability, pain tolerance, plasticity, and capacity to bounce back (Bontemps, 1969; Judy, 1993). Given the recent epoch of the mass incarceration of black people, and given that we understand incarceration replicates in many ways what it was like to be a slave, there is no coincidence that the same qualities help us understand how incarcerated black people salvage their humanity while in prison.

Black People Seen as Normal

W.E.B. Du Bois was perhaps the first scholar to record "normal" black agency from records showing freedpersons craving education: "The eagerness to learn among Negroes was exceptional in the case of a poor and recently emancipated folk. Usually, with a protective psychology, such degraded masses regard ignorance as natural and necessary, or even exalt their own traditional wisdom and discipline over 'book learning'; or they assume that knowledge is for higher beings, and not like us. The American Negro never acted this way" (Du Bois, 1935, pp. 637–638).

The science of social movements shows that when a human is socialized to hold one set of beliefs and then comes upon information—beliefs—that radically call into question the veracity of the old beliefs, this discovery of the "new" way of understanding life is experienced at the level of the individual person as an "epiphany." Should the change in belief become a group phenomenon, we have a "social movement." Emancipation triggered epiphanies and a social movement among the previously captive Africans, as the juxtaposition of being a "slave" in one instance, and a free person in another, released a torrent of dissonance that quickly transformed into motivational energy, targeting change *in each individual as well as the community as a whole*. Although most were illiterate, all coveted practical knowledge gained by observations made of the behavior, actions, and thinking, not of poor and common white people, but of white elites. Thus, while their material conditions defined them as members of the *lumpenproletariat*, agents of Northern benevolent societies, the Freedmen's Bureau, and members of free black communities helped the ex-slaves shape an ideology for change involving education, voting rights, land ownership, and societal protection of mind, body, and soul.

When demands of ex-slaves were combined with resources and help from those friendly to their cause, what became achievable within a short span of time was, in a word, *incredible*. Du Bois recorded how, under Union Army general Nathaniel P. Banks, New Orleans and the State of Louisiana established black schools throughout the state, including in rural districts. When this system came under threat, the ex-slaves resisted—for example producing a thirty-foot-long petition showing the "marks" of 10,000 ex-slaves (Du Bois, 1935, p. 644). At minimum such behavior suggests an amazing degree of human agency, drive, motivation, vision, and planning—a far cry from Frazier's lack-of-civilization trope. The Africana scholar-historian Sundiata Keita Cha-Jua, after researching ex-slaves' creation of the all-black town Brooklyn, Illinois, depicted the coming together of ex-slaves in this way:

> Most African Americans who lived in Brooklyn in 1870 to 1886 were recent migrants from former slave states of Tennessee, Missouri, Mississippi, Kentucky, and Virginia. In the sixteen years between their acquisition of citizenship rights and their assumption of political power, African Americans strengthened their institutions, consolidated themselves around freedom-conscious culture, shaped new militant leadership, and molded themselves into a community. African American success at running their own institutions and organizations and a profound belief in their own efficacy, as the majority population, created enormous potential for them to take political control. (Cha-Jua, 2000, p. 115)

The success of many former slaves was not a random statistical event but a predictable outcome when it is understood that many former slaves walked out of the horror chamber with a level of interpersonal competence, once solely enacted in support their owner's enterprise, but now, in freedom, used to help turn one's personal agenda into reality.

Another window for uncovering and peering into the minds and competence of ex-slaves are stories pointing to the success of children born to parents who were once slaves, as was true for William Pickens (1916/1991) and Lucile Buchanan (McLean, 2018). Both were highly successful progeny born to parents who were once slaves, even though Frazier argued that slavery left the ex-slaves in a cultural void wherein they had not the cultural capacity to raise progeny capable of uplift in a short period of time. Their *second-generation success stories* show that black parents did in fact process the humanity and cultural grounding to produce highly intelligent, motivated, and successful offspring. Pickens would progress from rural schools in the South to the halls of Ivy at Yale, where he graduated Phi Beta Kappa and mastered multiple European languages. He also held a key managerial post with the nascent NAACP. His biography, published in 1916, received considerable coverage in the black community and among black intellectuals in particular.

Buchanan's success was monitored by the NAACP's publication *Crisis*. The journal reported how, after fulfilling all the requirements for an undergraduate degree from the University of Colorado, Buchanan was not allowed to publicly accept her diploma, nor was she pictured in the yearbook. She was pictured in the 1918 edition of *Crisis* (McLean, 2018). As previously noted, Frazier, for whatever reason, seemed to deliberately overlook facts and observations about ex-slaves who found educational and material success right out of slavery, as did he fail to mention cases of second-generation patterns of success recorded by the likes of Pickens and Buchanan. Du Bois, having been exposed to the writings of Immanuel Kant and adherents of the philosophy of Enlightenment, relished singling out ex-slaves who seemed to perform the impossible in defiance of prognostications to the contrary by supporters of eugenics.

Solving the Riddle of One-Generation Uplift

The foremost expert on the history of black education in the South has traced this legacy of positive black achievement motivation into the twentieth century (Anderson, 1988), and a good example is revealed in the life and times of Charles Nelms, whose story follows him from picking cotton to the chancellorship of a university (Nelms, 2019). In opening his narrative, Nelms states that all blacks of his generation who grew up in the Arkansas Delta had grandparents who were either slaves or direct descendants of slaves. As a child, Nelms was taught how to pick cotton: "My earliest memory of being in the cotton field was September 1951, just a week following my fifth birthday. There I stood on that hot and humid day in my cotton flannel shirt and my patched and faded overalls" (Nelms, 2019, p. 2).

Then, in a narrative eerily like the one repeated across the South following Emancipation, Nelms describes how his uneducated sharecropper parents provided vision and motivation for their ten children. As uneducated parents they still understood the importance of literacy in relationship to power, wealth, comfort, and identity:

> Amid an environment that was, for all intents and purposes, devoid of books and reading materials, my parents still had this phenomenal belief in education.... My parents were phenomenal for several reasons. One is their unwavering faith in the power of education, although they possessed little themselves. Their belief in education's power to transform lives inspired me since childhood. My parents were also deeply committed to land ownership and voting. Among those who have been dispossessed and disfranchised, their profound belief in the trinity of education, voting, and land ownership motivated my siblings and me to commit ourselves to all three without questions. (Nelms, 2019, pp. 6–7)

Subsequently, Nelms went on to a distinguished career in higher education, including being appointed chancellor of North Carolina Central University in Durham, and he held important administrative positions at Indiana University Northwest in Gary. Nelms's story offers a window into understanding what is meant by uplift, so important to Du Bois's observations about Reconstruction, as well as James Anderson's extension of Du Bois's narrative in his seminal work, *Education of Blacks in the South, 1860–1935* (1988). From Nelms's description of his parents' worldview, it is clear they were not using poor whites as a reference group, rather they defied their proletariat status and used *educated whites* as a reference in communicating a philosophy of life to Nelms and his siblings. It is this energy and vision that led to the social movement for education formed by ex-slaves following emancipation (Spencer et al., 2003). Thus motivated, schools or cultural instructors outside the home taught progeny Standard English and other social as well as technical skills. In this scenario, progeny are not prisoners of the absence of certain kinds of knowledge by illiterate parents. Once students were motivated, they were *taught critical skills by others*, but the parents, who were ex-slaves, provided the life force, energy, human motivation, and a you-can-do-this attitude, communicated through Ebonics. Black parents did not have to be middle class themselves to produce progeny who would attain middle-class status through education, experience, and opportunity.

Du Bois more so than Frazier understood this, and while Frazier downplayed and practically suggested uplift of the common black person was close to impossible, Du Bois spent time actually recording one- and two-generation uplift stories (Du Bois, 1924/2007). Documentation of uplift experienced by ex-slaves can also be found in Rayvon Fouché's text, titled *Black Inventors in the Age of Segregation* (2003), as well as the seldom-referenced work published in 1893 by M. A. Majors, M.D., titled *Noted Negro Women: Their Triumphs and Activities* (Majors, 1893), which, as the title suggests, focused on black women. While the majority of the cases cited were women from free black communities and/or mulattoes, at least thirteen of the cases were ex-slaves who achieved uplift, one generation after slavery.

Nelms reflects solely on the ideas his parents conveyed in helping him construct his philosophy of life and meaning-making system, and he seemingly takes for granted how they socialized him to be a *well-rounded human being*. Consequently, I take the liberty to restate Nelms's recollections about his upbringing so that two points are emphasized: First, his parents socialized him to be a person of *character and interpersonal substance*, and, second, they communicated *vision and motivation*. The first factor—having a strong, positive, enabling personality—explains how he was able to transact their vision and philosophy in the classroom, when he was young and in college as a doctoral student. Nelms's parents spoke Ebonics and not Standard English, yet their capacity to effectuate attachment and personality socialization were not language dependent. And what of the "origins" of their capacity to effectuate positive human development? In all likelihood it is a carryover from experiences in slavery, passed down after slavery up to the present.

Such describes the state of mind, child-raising skills, and role-model capacities the slaves exhibited as they exited slavery. It explains how the parents of William Pickens and Lucile Buchanan, though former slaves and illiterate, provided the kind of positive psychological foundation and visionary worldview with which Pickens and Buchanan could become college educated. The sharecropper-to-uplift story was also told by Jackie Robinson and Los Angeles mayor Tom Bradley. And, to recall a point made previously, many of the scholars establishing black studies, myself included, were the offspring of working-class families, who, as was true in Nelms's case, raised us to be "good enough" human beings and motivated us to achieve beyond the station into which we were born. Our relatives and fictive kin were experts at grooming fairly polished personalities, and, after becoming "woke" through Nigrescence and involved in the black social movements of the 1970s, each of us took advantage of once-in-a-lifetime opportunities to become what at an earlier stage we never thought possible: members of the academy.

Hamilton Hatter, 1856–1942

My interest in ex-slaves who experienced attachment and positive socialization during their slave childhoods and subsequently recorded success *after slavery* was piqued by the discovery that one of my distant relatives was Hamilton Hatter (Caldwell, 1923; Miller, 1904). My father was born in Berryville, Virginia, and many of his kin are buried in the Milton Valley Cemetery of Berryville. In walking the grounds, I discovered there were four or five distant relatives named William Cross, but each had a different middle name, so instead of William the Fifth, I am Junior, after my Dad. I also discovered that one of the largest headstones belonged to Sarah Hatter Cross. The mere mention of her name would discombobulate my Dad, because he was physically abused by his own family, and Sarah, his grandmother, loved him without reservation. After visiting the cemetery, I decided to join two ancestor search websites, which eventually brought me into contact with genealogist Joyceann Gray, a distant relative on Sarah Hatter's side of the family. She informed me I was not the first Cross or Hatter to receive an advanced degree, because that was Hamilton Hatter, who walked out of slavery and within twenty years headed an institution of higher education.

According to Caldwell (1923) and Miller (1904), Hatter's life story is complicated, as he was neither an exemplar of a free Negro nor was he a mulatto. His status fell in between ordinary slave and being somewhat privileged. Hamilton's maternal and paternal grandparents were slaves; however, his father, Frank, was a free Negro at the time of Hamilton's birth, while his mother—Rebecca—was a slave. His father found work nearby, thus Hamilton knew and interacted with both his mother and dad (and possibly his paternal and maternal grandparents) while growing up, a fact bound to account for the psychological strengths he exhibited as an adult. The point being, his father aside, Hamilton's upbringing was heavily influenced by persons who were themselves slaves. Rebecca was owned by the Asquith family of Virginia, whose pharmacy and real estate business was based in Charles Town; thus, Hatter's childhood was spent in an urban rather than rural context. His first nine years—his formative years—were spent as a slave. Hatter had ten siblings, and it is likely he was exposed to early childhood education, given his urban environment. As a young adult he worked as a builder, mechanic, and sawmill manager, paying for his enrollment and graduation from Storer College located atop Harpers Ferry (the John Brown Memorial is located on the grounds of what was once Storer College). Moving to Maine, he attended two religious schools affiliated with Storer College and eventually graduated from Bates College in Lewiston, Maine, in 1878. He returned to Storer, teaching courses in Latin, Greek, and mathematics, and was a Storer trustee until 1906. His activities in support of the Republican Party brought him to the attention of Governor Virgil A. Lewis, who selected Hatter to be the first principal for the newly developed Bluefield Colored Institute, made possible by the Morrill Act of 1890, and which was renamed Bluefield State College in 1943. In a spiteful response to the gains of the civil rights movement of the 1960s, the Virginia Department of Education appointed a new white president, and, with the support of the department, terminated the employment of all the black faculty and staff of Bluefield and changed the student body to predominantly white. Ironically, one of the buildings on campus carries Hamilton Hatter's name, and a permanent historical marker just off campus shows Bluefield originated as a colored institution and only later became Bluefield State, a white college.

We know from contemporary studies of child development that much of Hatter's personality, drive, positive temperament, and effective prosocial skills can only be understood as a *window into his socialization* as a child by the black slave community. That is, he did not "just happen"—rather his humanity, character, and interpersonal competence are "constructions" resulting from everyday interactions and exchanges with persons who, at the time, were themselves slaves. Because he was born in a context that encouraged conjugal relations, his status as slave was softened by the fact that he could identify and interact with both his father and mother. Certainly, his urban surroundings were not as brutal as that of being a slave on a plantation. Nevertheless, he is part of that overlooked critical mass of slaves who exited slavery reflecting a level of humanity that previous discussions of slavery thought impossible, given that damage and a negative legacy was the order of the day. He was like the ex-slaves who founded Brooklyn, Illinois, and, pushing forward to the present, he was a mirror image of the black men who came into view as I sat atop the barber's chair on the South Side of Chicago in the 1940s.

Yes, starting with the positive human development that began in slave nurseries on plantations in Alabama and Mississippi, and likely all the large plantations throughout the South, a straight line—marking black competence at raising human beings to be positive, strong, and resilient—connects the slaves Booker T. Washington, Frederick Douglass, Harriet Tubman, and so on, and subsequently runs through Reconstruction, where it joins the likes of Hamilton Hatter, Lucile Buchanan, and William Pickens, and so on, and, at the turn of the twentieth century entwines Jack Johnson, Madame C. J. Walker, Major Taylor, Du Bois as well as Frazier, and so on, and then dances about Harlem to impale Zora Neale Hurston, Langston Hughes, Jean Toomer, Jessie Fauset, Duke Ellington, Bessie Smith, and so on, and, during the 1940s and 1950s, moves onward to pierce Miles Davis, James Baldwin, Toni Morrison, Charles Nelms, attorney Robert L. Tucker, Jackie Robinson, and Tom Bradley, and so on, and advances into the 1970s, enveloping Henry Louis Gates Jr., William E. Cross Jr., Reiland Rabaka, James Turner, Brendesha Tynes, Ruby Mendenhall, Beverly Vandiver, Yasser Payne, Robert Harris, and Helen Neville, all of whom joined the academy after first being birthed and socialized among the black working class. This line connects all of us to slavery, not through the machinations of those who operated under the illusion of "owning" us, but through the spirit of those who survived and left a mark in the soil.

I never felt comfortable with the deficit thesis, because growing up on the South Side of Chicago, and later within the small ghetto that was the Evanston black community, many of the black men and women—descendants of slaves—who cut my hair, took my pennies in exchange for Juicy Fruit gum, delivered our mail, took my transfer on the bus, clustered around my father on his job as a Pullman porter, or knocked on our front door as a prelude to a date with one of my older sisters could certainly be called characters, but few, very few, were broken or pathological. I did not make the connection at the time, but the black men I viewed while sitting atop the barber's chair were cut from the same cloth.

The great tragedy of our times is that normal black people are mired in the socioeconomic malaise called deindustrialization. Like ghetto dwellers of the past—the Irish, Italians, Eastern European Jews, and others—black men and women, as Yasser Payne has pointed out, turned to the streets to make a living only to discover it is a trap, a Faustian Dilemma, constructed by elites motivated by the belief that black people are undercivilized. This negative image was derived from the deeply flawed dissertation and subsequent book written by E. Franklin Frazier. W.E.B. Du Bois presented a brilliant counternarrative; however, Frazier's mythmaking won out, and the stereotype of the undercivilized black person in the image of Willie Horton helped white and black politicians alike feel self-assured when passing legislation that ultimately branded otherwise positive black men as criminally inclined, and black women as avatars of licentiousness. *If found to be gay, lesbian, or transgender, the imagery becomes all the more distorted.*

More so than social scientists, black playwrights, poets, and literary figures better told and continue to tell the story of our humanity. Rather than being confused and misled by lives of pain, sorrow, and astonishing achievements, black artists frequently find a way to juxtapose *opposite streams of meaning making*. For me, personally, writing this work has drawn me closer to Maya Angelou's captivating phrase: "I know why the caged bird sings."

Closing Comments

So much of the analysis of the contemporary black condition is dependent on an observer's depiction of the psychology of black people as they—once captive Africans—exited slavery. This preoccupation with the proposed damage wrought by slavery has its academic origins in the writings of E. Franklin Frazier, along with the academy's suppression of research presented by W.E.B. Du Bois. It is ironic that Frazier meant to produce an analysis in contradistinction to the view of his time, which declared black people genetically inferior, period. In his eyes, showing black people to be culturally inferior somehow removed the stench of biological inferiority. This distinction is very much with us in contemporary discussions of black criminality, as Americans simply have no memory of the relationship between crime and poverty in the social history of immigrants from Europe. The first time I taught a course on the topic, some students thought me anti-Semitic in mentioning the Jewish Purple Gang of Detroit, or Jewish prostitution in late eighteenth-century New York City. Likewise, Yasser Payne's work shows that contemporary black street life is full of otherwise "normal" black people, who, through the forces of racism, poverty, and systemic inequality, are literally made to accept the underbelly of society as their place of employment.

I was born on the South Side of Chicago, when my family lived on St. Lawrence Boulevard, and today our Englewood neighborhood is depicted on the TV show *Chicago P.D.* as the center of Chicago's black gangs. Surely the trajectory of my life would have been different had I been born in 1970 rather than 1940. My salvation was to become an Africana scholar, with an obsession to deconstruct the deficit perspective. My original frame of reference was black nationalistic; however, two humanists, namely the late Urie Bronfenbrenner and the still active and marvelous Margaret B. Spencer, asked me—no, demanded of me—that my explications of black psychology be consistent with the writings of humanists, not nationalist ideologues.

I cannot express to you, the reader, how stunned I was to discover that Hamilton Hatter, a distant relative raised as a child in slavery by slaves, rose from the ashes of slavery to become an erudite, highly educated, and amazingly accomplished educator. In my familiarity with Frazier's cultural inferiority trope about the legacy of slavery, Hatter's story simply did not make sense. Thus, for those that have read my narrative up to this point, I trust I have shown how slavery, as an otherwise closed system, found slaves digging tunnels beneath what the slave owners thought were impenetrable *psychological* barriers. I request that, in place of the word "slave," you, the reader, substitute the word "human," because that makes it easier to keep in mind these human tendencies: ingenuity, imagination, resistance, creativity, empathy, and a drive to be human, as in raising and caring for infants and children of the community, such that when all these human attributes were combined and inculcated in progeny, the evil of one's oppressors was diluted and made slightly less onerous. However, it was in freedom that the true human capacities of so-called slaves were revealed, previously hidden behind what Du Bois called the "veil." It meant that people walking out of slavery were more prepared for freedom than many thought possible.

Thus, I leave you with this summary: In order to fully comprehend the agency, motivation, interpersonal competence, thirst for knowledge, and material success exhibited by former slaves within the first twelve years following Emancipation, we need to construct a new psychological paradigm. Most importantly, we need to keep in mind that their personalities, prosocial attitudes, and general psychological competence all resulted from the way they were raised as children in slavery, at the hands of human beings who were themselves slaves. This means the dehumanizing schemes of the elites were not as effective as originally designed, despite overwhelming historical evidence confirming the intent of slave owners was to fashion hell on earth. Thus, we need to decouple intent from consequence. For humans who spent infancy through childhood in slavery to subsequently display remarkable success as freedmen and freedwomen, when they reached twenty, thirty, or forty years of age, is historical evidence that something *profoundly human* happened to them as children, when the slave community shaped their self-concepts and informed their worldviews. Discovering the humanity of the enslaved is not romanticism, it is the comprehension of how humanity expresses itself, even under the most restrictive, punishing, and heinous conditions. It links to the way Jews in Nazi concentration camps coveted musical instruments and, before death, held concerts for the doomed. It is to understand how black men and women in the present survive years of solitary confinement. It is how the World War II Korean comfort women lived to tell their stories. It is to comprehend the origins of Martin Luther King Jr.'s remarkable letter from the Birmingham Jail; it is how Nelson Mandela walked out of prison with his humanity intact. We are birds that sing while caged.

References

Acharya, A., Blackwell, M., & Sen, M. (2016). The Political Legacy of American Slavery. *Journal of Politics, 78*(3), 621–641.

Adams, M. (2020). Introduction/Biography. Maurianne Adams Papers, Education Collection, Special Collections and University Archives, UMass Amherst Libraries. Retrieved from http://scua.library.umass.edu/umarmot/tag/education

Adams, M., Bell, L. A., & Griffin, P. (Eds.). (1997). *Teaching for Diversity and Social Justice*. New York, NY: Routledge/Taylor and Francis.

Alkalimat, A., Crawford, R., & Zorach, R. (2017). *The Wall of Respect: Public Art and Black Liberation in 1960s Chicago*. Evanston, IL: Northwestern University Press.

Allen, J., Als, H., Lewis, J., & Litwack, L. F. (2000). *Without Sanctuary: Lynching Photography in America*. Santa Fe, NM: Twin Palms.

Anderson, D. C., & Enberg, C. (1995). Crime and the Politics of Hysteria: How the Willie Horton Story Changed American Justice. *Journal of Contemporary Criminal Justice, 11*(4), 298–300.

Anderson, J. D. (1988). *The Education of Blacks in the South, 1860–1935*. Chapel Hill: University of North Carolina Press.

Associated Press (2019, January 18). Man Exonerated after 45 Years Sells His Prison Art to Support Himself. NBC News. Retrieved from https://www.nbcnews.com/news/us-news/man-exonerated-after-45-years-sells-his-prison-art-support-n960361

Azibo, D. A. Y. (Ed.). (1996). *African Psychology in Historical Perspective and Related Commentary.* Trenton, NJ: Africa World Press.

Banks, W. C. (1976). White Preference in Blacks: A Paradigm in Search of a Phenomenon. *Psychological Bulletin, 83*(6), 1179–1186.

Battle-Baptiste, W., & Rusert, B. (Eds.). (2018). *W.E.B. Du Bois's Data Portraits: Visualizing Black America.* Hudson, NY: Princeton Architectural Press.

Berezow, A. (2018). White Overdose Deaths 50% Higher than Blacks, 167% Higher than Hispanics. Retrieved from https://www.acsh.org/news/2018/04/05/white-overdose-deaths-50-higher-blacks-167-higher-hispanics-12804

Berman, A. (2017, November–December). Rigged: How Voter Suppression Threw Wisconsin to Trump. *Mother Jones,* pp. 24–31.

Bernstein, L. (2010). *America Is the Prison: Arts and Politics in Prison in the 1970s.* Chapel Hill: University of North Carolina Press.

Berry, J. W. (1976). *Human Ecology and Cognitive Style: Comparative Studies in Cultural and Psychological Adaptation.* New York, NY: John Wiley and Sons.

Best, S., & Kellner, D. (1999). Rap, Black Rage, and Racial Difference. *Enculturation, 2*(2), 1–23.

Blake, S. M., Kiely, M., Gard, C. C., El-Mohandes, A. A., El-Khorazaty, M. N., & NIH-DC Initiative. (2007). Pregnancy Intentions and Happiness among Pregnant Black Women at High Risk for Adverse Infant Health Outcomes. *Perspectives on Sexual and Reproductive Health, 39*(4), 194–205.

Blascovich, J., Spencer, S. J., Quinn, D., & Steele, C. (2001). African Americans and High Blood Pressure: The Role of Stereotype Threat. *Psychological Science, 12*(3), 225–229.

Bluestone, B., & Harrison, B. (1982). *The Deindustrialization of America.* New York, NY: Basic Books.

Bobo, L. (1988). Attitudes toward the Black Political Movement: Trends, Meaning, and Effects on Racial Policy Preferences. *Social Psychology Quarterly, 51*(4), 287–302.

Bonanno, G. A. (2004). Loss, Trauma, and Human Resilience: Have We Underestimated the Human Capacity to Thrive after Extremely Aversive Events? *American Psychologist, 59*(1), 20.

Bontemps, A. W. (1969). *Great Slave Narratives.* Boston, MA: Beacon Press.

Boyd-Franklin, N., and Franklin, A. J. (2001). *Boys into Men: Raising Our African American Teenage Sons.* New York, NY: Penguin Putnam.

Boykin, A. W. (1986). The Triple Quandary and the Schooling of Afro-American Children. In U. Neisser (Ed.), *The School Achievement of Minority Children* (pp. 57–92). Hillsdale, NJ: Lawrence Erlbaum.

Boykin, A. W., Franklin, A., & Yates, F. J. (1980). *Research Directions of Black Psychologists.* New York, NY: Russell Sage Foundation.

Brady, D., & Wallace, M. (2001). Deindustrialization and Poverty: Manufacturing Decline and AFDC Recipiency in Lake County, Indiana 1964–93. *Sociological Forum, 16*(2), 321–358.

Breeze, M. (2018). Imposter Syndrome as a Public Feeling. In Y. Taylor & K. Lahad (Eds.), *Feeling Academic in the Neoliberal University* (pp. 191–219). New York, NY: Springer.

Brehm, J. W. (2007). A Brief History of Dissonance Theory. *Social and Personality Psychology Compass, 1*(1), 381–391.

Bronfenbrenner, U. (1979). *The Ecology of Human Development: Experiments by Design and Nature*. Cambridge, MA: Harvard University Press.

Brown, M., Ray, R., Summers, E., & Fraistat, N. (2017). #SayHerName: A Case Study of Intersectional Social Media Activism. *Ethnic and Racial Studies, 40*(11), 1831–1846.

Buchanan, L., Bui, Q., & Patel, J. (2020, July 8). Black Lives Matter Puts Stamp on History. *New York Times*, p. A-15.

Burch, A., Cai, W., Gabriel, G., McCarthy, M., & Patel, J. (2020, June 16). How Black Lives Matter Reached Every Corner of America. *New York Times*, pp. 1, F5.

Byfield, N. (2014). *Savage Portrayals: Race, Media, and the Central Park Jogger Story*. Philadelphia, PA: Temple University Press.

Caldwell, A. B. (Ed.). (1923). *History of the Negro, West Virginia Edition: Hamilton Hatter*. Retrieved from http://www.wvculture.org/history/histamne/hatter.html

Caldwell-Gunes, R. M., & Parham, T. A. (2019). *The Bakari Project: A Lifeline for African American Adolescent Development and Success*. Unpublished manuscript.

Calverton, V. F. (1929). *Anthology of American Negro Literature*. New York, NY: Modern Library.

Casas, J. M., Suzuki, L. A., Alexander, C. M., & Jackson, M. A. (Eds.). (2016). *The Handbook of Multicultural Counseling* (4th ed.). Thousand Oaks, CA: SAGE Publications.

Cha-Jua, S. K. (2000). *America's First Black Town: Brooklyn, Illinois, 1830–1915*. Urbana: University of Illinois Press.

Chicago Commission on Race Relations. (1922). *The Negro in Chicago: A Study of Race Relations and a Race Riot*. Chicago, IL: University of Chicago Press.

Clance, P. R., & Imes, S. A. (1978). The Imposter Phenomenon in High Achieving Women: Dynamics and Therapeutic Intervention. *Psychotherapy: Theory, Research & Practice, 15*(3), 241–247.

Clark, K. B. (1989). *Dark Ghetto*. Middletown, CT: Wesleyan University Press. (Original work published 1965)

Clark, K. B., & Clark, M. K. (1939). The Development of Consciousness of Self and the Emergence of Racial Identification in Negro Preschool Children. *The Journal of Social Psychology, 10*(4), 591–599.

Coates, T. N. (2015). *Between the World and Me*. New York, NY: Spiegel and Grau.

Cokley, K. O. (2005). Racial(ized) Identity, Ethnic Identity, and Afrocentric Values: Conceptual and Methodological Challenges in Understanding African American Identity. *Journal of Counseling Psychology, 52*(4), 517–526.

Cokley, K. O. (2015). Afrocentricity and African Psychology. In J. L. Conyers (Ed.), *Afrocentricity and the Academy* (pp. 141–162). Jefferson, NC: McFarland.

Cokley, K. O., & Awad, G. (2013). In Defense of Quantitative Methods: Using the "Master's Tools" to Promote Social Justice. *Journal for Social Action in Counseling and Psychology, 5*(2), 26–41.

Cokley, K. O., McClain, S., Enciso, A., & Martinez, M. (2013). An Examination of the Impact of Minority Status Stress and Impostor Feelings on the Mental Health of Diverse Ethnic Minority College Students. *Journal of Multicultural Counseling & Development, 41*(2), 82–95.

Cokley, K. O., Smith, L., Bernard, D., Hurst, A., Jackson, S., Stone, S., . . . & Roberts, D. (2017). Impostor Feelings as a Moderator and Mediator of the Relationship between Perceived Discrimination and Mental Health among Racial/Ethnic Minority College Students. *Journal of Counseling Psychology, 64*(2), 141–154.

Collins, P. H. (2002). *Black Feminist Thought: Knowledge, Consciousness, and the Politics of Empowerment*. London, UK: Routledge.

Combahee River Collective (1977). Combahee River Collective Statement. Retrieved from https://combaheerivercollective.weebly.com/the-combahee-river-collective-statement.html.

Conyers, J. L., Jr. (Ed.). (2015). *Afrocentricity and the Academy: Essays on Theory and Practice*. Jefferson, NC: McFarland.

Coontz, S. (1991). *The Way We Never Were: American Families and the Nostalgia Trap*. London, UK: Hachette.

Cross, W. E., Jr. (1971). The Negro-to-Black Conversion Experience. *Black World, 20*(9), 13–27.

Cross, W. E., Jr. (1978). The Thomas and Cross Models of Psychological Nigrescence: A Review. *Journal of Black Psychology, 5*(1), 13–31.

Cross, W. E., Jr. (1983, Fall). The Ecology of Human Development for Black and White Children: Implications for Predicting Racial Preference Patterns. *Journal of Critical Perspectives of Third World America, 1*(1), 177–189.

Cross, W. E., Jr. (1991). *Shades of Black: Diversity in African American Identity*. Philadelphia, PA: Temple University Press.

Cross, W. E., Jr., Drinane, J. M., Owen, J., Schmidt, C. K., Raque-Bogdan, T. L., Hook, J. N., . . . & Ajibade, A. (2020). Uncovering Alternate Ethnic Identity Trajectories: A Cluster Analysis of the MEIM and Psychological Well-Being. *Race and Social Problems, 12*(2), 103–111.

Cross, W. E., Jr., & Fhagen-Smith, P. (1996). Nigrescence and Ego Identity Development: Accounting for Differential Black Identity Patterns. In P. Pedersen, J. Draguns, W. Lonner, & J. Trimble (Eds.), *Counseling across Cultures* (4th ed.) (pp. 243–270). Newbury, CA: SAGE Publications.

Cross, W. E., Jr., Smith, L., & Payne, Y. (2002). Black Identity: A Repertoire of Daily Enactments. *Counseling across Cultures, 5*, 93–107.

Curry, T. J. (2017). *The Man-Not: Race, Class, Genre, and the Dilemmas of Black Manhood.* Philadelphia, PA: Temple University Press.

Curwood, A. (2008). A Fresh Look at E. Franklin Frazier's Sexual Politics in *The Negro Family in the United States. Du Bois Review: Social Science Research on Race, 5*(2), 325–337.

Dancy, T. E., & Brown, M. C. (2011). The Mentoring and Induction of Educators of Color: Addressing the Impostor Syndrome in Academe. *Journal of School Leadership, 21*(4), 607–634.

DeGruy Leary, J. D. (2005). *Post Traumatic Slave Syndrome: America's Legacy of Enduring Injury and Healing.* Milwaukie, OR: Uptone Press.

De Salzmann, J. (2011). *The Reality of Being: The Fourth Way of Gurdjieff.* Boulder, CO: Shambhala Publications.

Dow, D. M. (2019). *Mothering while Black: Boundaries and Burdens of Middle-Class Parenthood.* Oakland: University of California Press.

Dray, P. (2007). *At the Hands of Persons Unknown: The Lynching of Black America.* New York, NY: Modern Library.

Du Bois, W.E.B. (1903). *The Souls of Black Folk.* Chicago, IL: A. C. McClurg.

Du Bois, W.E.B. (1908). *The Negro American Family.* Atlanta, GA: Atlanta University Press.

Du Bois, W.E.B. (1924). *The Gift of Black Folk: The Negroes in the Making of America.* Boston, MA: Stratford.

Du Bois, W.E.B. (1935). *Black Reconstruction: An Essay Toward a History of the Part Which Black Folk Played in the Attempt to Reconstruct Democracy in America, 1860–1880.* New York, NY: Russell and Russell.

Du Bois, W.E.B. (2007). *The Gift of Black Folk: The Negroes in the Making of America.* In Henry Louis Gates Jr. (Series ed.), *The Oxford W.E.B. Du Bois* series. New York, NY: Oxford University Press. (Original work published 1924)

Du Bois, W.E.B., & Eaton, I. (1899). *The Philadelphia Negro: A Social Study.* Philadelphia: University of Pennsylvania Press.

Erikson, E. H. (1956). The Problem of Ego Identity. *Journal of the American Psychoanalytic Association, 4*(1), 56–121.

Erikson, E. H. (1968). *Identity: Youth and Crisis.* New York, NY: W. W. Norton.

Ewing, K. M., Richardson, T. Q., James-Myers, L., & Russell, R. K. (1996). The Relationship between Racial Identity Attitudes, Worldview, and African American Graduate Students' Experience of the Imposter Phenomenon. *Journal of Black Psychology, 22*(1), 53–66.

Fanon, F. (1952). *Black Skin, White Masks* (Trans. Charles Lam Markmann). Paris, France: Gallimard.

Fanon, F. (1961). *Wretched of the Earth* (Trans. Constance Farrington). New York, NY: Grove Press.

Farber, N. (1995). Charles S. Johnson's *The Negro in Chicago*. *The American Sociologist, 26*(3), 78–88.

Ferguson, A. A. (2010). *Bad Boys: Public Schools in the Making of Black Masculinity*. Ann Arbor: University of Michigan Press.

Fine, G. A. (1995). Introduction: A Second Chicago School? The Development of a Postwar American Sociology. In G. A. Fine (Ed.), *A Second Chicago School? The Development of a Postwar American Sociology* (pp. 1–16). Chicago: University of Chicago Press.

Fine, M., Torre, M. E., Boudin, K., Bowen, I., Clark, J., Hylton, D., & Upegui, D. (2004). Participatory Action Research: From within and beyond Prison Bars. In L. Weis and M. Fine (Eds.), *Working Method: Research and Social Justice* (pp. 95–119). New York, NY: Routledge.

Fordham, S. (1993). "Those Loud Black Girls": (Black) Women, Silence, and Gender "Passing" in the Academy. *Anthropology and Education Quarterly, 24*(1), 3–32.

Foster, H. J. (1976). Partners or Captives in Commerce? The Role of Africans in the Slave Trade. *Journal of Black Studies, 6*(4), 421–434.

Fouché, R. (2003). *Black Inventors in the Age of Segregation: Granville T. Woods, Lewis H. Latimer, and Shelby J. Davidson*. Baltimore, MD: Johns Hopkins University Press.

Frazier, E. F. (1927). The Pathology of Race Prejudice. *The Forum, 70*, 856–862.

Frazier, E. F. (1929). La Bourgeoisie Noire. In F. C. Calverton (Ed.), *Anthology of American Negro Literature* (pp. 379–388). New York, NY: The Modern Library.

Frazier, E. F. (1932). *The Negro Family in Chicago*. Chicago, IL: University of Chicago Press.

Frazier, E. F. (1939). *The Negro Family in the United States*. Chicago, IL: University of Chicago Press.

Frazier, E. F. (1957). *Black Bourgeoisie*. New York, NY: Free Press.

Gardner, J., & Thomas, C. (1970). Different Strokes for Different Folks. *Psychology Today, 4*(4), 48.

Garza, A. (2016). A Herstory of the #BlackLivesMatter Movement. In J. Hobson (Ed.), *Are All the Women Still White? Rethinking Race, Expanding Feminisms* (pp. 23–28). Albany: State University of New York Press.

Gates, H. L., Jr. (2019). *Stony the Road: Reconstruction, White Supremacy, and the Rise of Jim Crow*. London, UK: Penguin Press.

Gelles, David. (2019, April 7). Black White Wealth. *New York Times,* Business Section, p. 4.

Gergel, R. (2019). *Unexamined Courage*. New York, NY: Sarah Crichton Books.

Gibson, P. A., Wilson, R., Haight, W., Kayama, M., & Marshall, J. M. (2014). The Role of Race in the Out-of-School Suspensions of Black Students: The Perspectives of Students with Suspensions, Their Parents and Educators. *Children and Youth Services Review, 47,* 274–282.

Gladwell, M. (2008). In the Air. *The New Yorker, 84,* 50–60.

Goffman, E. (1978). *The Presentation of Self in Everyday Life.* London, UK: Harmondsworth. (Original work published 1956, Edinburgh, UK: University of Edinburgh)

Goozner, M. (1990, September 3). Pay Inequity Grew in 80s, Study Finds. *Chicago Tribune*, p. 1.

Graves, L. (2015). *Early Seating Upholstery: Reading the Evidence*. Williamsburg, VA: Colonial Williamsburg Foundation.

Grier, W. H., & Cobbs, P. M. (1968). *Black Rage*. Eugene, OR: Wipf and Stock.

Griffin, G., Martinovich, Z., Gawron, T., & Lyons, J. S. (2009). Strengths Moderate the Impact of Trauma on Risk Behaviors in Child Welfare. *Residential Treatment for Children & Youth, 26*(2), 105–118.

Grimes, D. A. (1994). The Morbidity and Mortality of Pregnancy: Still Risky Business. *American Journal of Obstetrics and Gynecology, 170*(5), 1489–1494.

Gutman, H. G. (1976). *The Black Family in Slavery and Freedom, 1750–1925*. New York, NY: Pantheon Books.

Hardiman, R., Jackson, B., & Griffin, P. (2007). Conceptual Foundations for Social Justice Education. In M. Adams, L. A. Bell, & P. Griffin (Eds.), *Teaching for Diversity and Social Justice* (pp. 35–66). New York, NY: Routledge/Taylor and Francis Group.

Harris, A., & Amutah-Onukagha, N. (2019). Under the Radar: Strategies Used by Black Mothers to Prepare Their Sons for Potential Police Interactions. *Journal of Black Psychology, 45*(67), 439–453.

Harris, D. (2009). A History of Black American Feminism. In D. Harris (Ed.), *Black Feminist Politics from Kennedy to Clinton* (pp. 1–54). New York, NY: Springer.

Hartman, S. (2019). *Wayward Lives, Beautiful Experiments: Intimate Histories of Social Upheaval*. New York, NY: W. W. Norton.

Harvey, G. (Ed.). (2003). *Shamanism: A Reader*. London, UK: Routledge.

Hawes, J. B. (2019). *Grace Will Lead Us Home*. New York, NY: St. Martin's Press.

Helms, J. E., & Carter, R. T. (1991). Relationships of White and Black Racial Identity Attitudes and Demographic Similarity to Counselor Preferences. *Journal of Counseling Psychology, 38*(4), 446.

Henson, J. (1852). *The Life of Josiah Henson, Formerly a Slave*. London, UK: Charles Gilpin.

Homel, M. W. (1984). *Down From Equality: Black Chicagoans and the Public Schools, 1920–41*. Urbana: University of Illinois Press.

Hoppál, M. (1996). Shamanism in a Postmodern Age. *Folklore: Electronic Journal of Folklore, 2*, 29–40.

Hurwitz, J., & Peffley, M. (2005). Playing the Race Card in the Post–Willie Horton Era: The Impact of Racialized Code Words on Support for Punitive Crime Policy. *Public Opinion Quarterly, 69*(1), 99–112.

Jackson, B. W. (1976). *The Function of a Black Identity Development Theory in Achieving Relevance in Education for Black Students*. (Doctoral dissertation). University of Massachusetts–Amherst.

Jamila, S. (2019). Can I Get a Witness? Testimony from a Hip-Hop Feminist. In D. Hernandez & B. Rehman (Eds.), *Colonize This! Young Women of Color on Today's Feminism* (Rev. ed., pp. 346–356). New York, NY: Seal Press, Division of Basic Books.

Johnson, G. B. (1933). Proposed Study of Negro Participation in Government and Civic Affairs in the South, Folder 1252, dated December 2, 1933. G. B. Johnson Papers, University of North Carolina, Chapel Hill, NC.

Johnson, J. W. (2017). *The Black Bruins: The Remarkable Lives of UCLA's Jackie Robinson, Woody Strode, Tom Bradley, Kenny Washington, and Ray Bartlett*. Lincoln: University of Nebraska Press.

Jones, J. M. (2003). TRIOS: A Psychological Theory of the African Legacy in American Culture. *Journal of Social Issues, 59*(1), 217–242.

Judy, R. A. (1993). *(Dis)forming the American Canon: African-Arabic Slave Narratives and the Vernacular*. Minneapolis: University of Minnesota Press.

Kardiner, A., & Ovesey, L. (1951). *The Mark of Oppression: Explorations in the Personality of the American Negro*. New York, NY: W. W. Norton.

Katznelson, I. (2005). *When Affirmative Action Was White: An Untold History of Racial Inequality in Twentieth-Century America*. New York, NY: W. W. Norton.

Katznelson, I., & Mettler, S. (2008). On Race and Policy History: A Dialogue about the GI Bill. *Perspectives on Politics, 6*(3), 519–537.

Kennecke, A. (2018). Emily's Hope: A Personal Story of Loss in the Opioid Epidemic. Retrieved from https://www.keloland.com/news/eye-on-keloland/emily-s-hope-a-personal-story-of-loss-in-the-opioid-epidemic/1420662895

Kennedy, R. (2019, February 21). The Stench of Prejudice in Keith Tharpe's Death Sentence. *New York Times*, Section SR, p. 3.

Khan-Cullors, P. (2018). *When They Call You a Terrorist: A Black Lives Matter Memoir*. Edinburgh, UK: Canongate Books.

King, J. E. (2015). Dysconscious Racism, Afrocentric Praxis, and Education for Human Freedom. In *Through the Years I Keep on Toiling: The Selected Works of Joyce E. King*. Philadelphia, PA: Routledge.

King, W. (2011). *Stolen Childhood: Slave Youth in Nineteenth-Century America* (2nd ed.). Bloomington: Indiana University Press.

Kornfeld, P. (1997). *Cellblock Visions: Prison Art in America*. Princeton, NJ: Princeton University Press.

Kranish, M. (2019). *The World's Fastest Man: The Extraordinary Life of Cyclist Major Taylor, America's First Black Sports Hero*. New York, NY: Scribner.

Lebron, C. (2019, June 6). The Charleston Church Massacre and the Inspiring Journey to Forgiveness. *New York Times Book Review*, p. 13.

Lederman, S. A., Alfasi, G., & Deckelbaum, R. J. (2002). Pregnancy-Associated Obesity in Black Women in New York City. *Maternal and Child Health Journal, 6*(1), 37–42.

Lieberman, E., Ryan, K. J., Monson, R. R., & Schoenbaum, S. C. (1987). Risk Factors Accounting for Racial Differences in the Rate of Premature Birth. *New England Journal of Medicine, 317*(12), 743–748.

Lipsitz, G. (1998). *The Possessive Investment in Whiteness*. Philadelphia, PA: Temple University Press.

Macy, B. (2018). *Dopesick: Dealers, Doctors and the Drug Company That Addicted America*. New York, NY: Little, Brown.

Majors, M. A. (1893). *Noted Negro Women: Their Triumphs and Activities* (No. 161). Chicago, IL: Donohue and Henneberry.

Majors, R., & Billson, J. M. (1993). *Cool Pose: The Dilemma of Black Manhood in America*. New York, NY: Simon and Schuster.

Makari, G. (2015). *Soul Machine: The Invention of the Modern Mind*. New York, NY: W. W. Norton.

Marcia, J. E. (1993). The Ego Identity Status Approach to Ego Identity. In J. E. Marcia, A. S. Waterman, D. R. Matteson, S. L. Archer, & J. L. Orlofsky (Eds.), *Ego Identity* (pp. 3–21). Berlin, Germany: Springer.

Maslow, A. H. (1970). New Introduction: Religions, Values, and Peak-Experiences. *Journal of Transpersonal Psychology 2*(2), 83–90.

McClain, D. (2019). *We Live for the We: The Political Power of Black Motherhood*. London, UK: Hachette.

McInnis, E.E.M., & Moukam, R. R. (2013). Black Psychology for Britain Today? *Journal of Black Psychology 39*(3), 311–315.

McLean, P. E. B. (2018). *Remembering Lucile: A Virginia Family's Rise from Slavery and a Legacy Forged a Mile High*. Boulder: University Press of Colorado.

Memmi, A. (1991). *The Colonizer and the Colonized* (Trans. Howard Greenfeld). Boston, MA: Beacon. (Original work published 1957)

Merriam, B. (1998). To Find a Voice: Art Therapy in a Women's Prison. *Women & Therapy, 21*(1), 157–171.

Miller, T. C. (1904). *History of Education in West Virginia*. Chicago, IL: The Tribune Printing Company.

Milliones, J. (1980). Construction of a Black Consciousness Measure: Psychotherapeutic Implications. *Psychotherapy: Theory, Research & Practice, 17*(2), 175–182.

Monroe, L. (1990, October 10). Fatally Stabbed Professor's Care Assailed. *Los Angeles Times.* Retrieved from https://www.latimes.com/archives/la-xpm-1990-10-10-me-1835-story.html

Morley, R. (2005, December 15). The Death of American Manufacturing. *Philadelphia Trumpet.* Retrieved from https://www.thetrumpet.com/2011-the-death-of-american-manufacturing

Moynihan, D. P. (1997). *The Negro Family: The Case for National Action.* Washington, DC: Office of Policy Planning and Research, U.S. Department of Labor. (Original work published 1965)

Msimang, S. (2017). *Always Another Country: A Memoir of Exile and Home.* Melbourne, Australia: World Edition Publisher.

Musgrove, G. D. (2018). The Ingredients for "Voter Fraud" Conspiracies. *Modern American History, 1*(2), 227–232.

Myers, L. J. (1993). *Understanding an Afrocentric World View: Introduction to an Optimal Psychology.* Dubuque, IA: Kendall/Hunt.

Nelms, C. (2019). *From Cotton Fields to University Leadership: All Eyes on Charles, a Memoir.* Bloomington: Indiana University Press.

Neville, H. A., & Cross, W. E., Jr. (2017). Racial Awakening: Epiphanies and Encounters in Black Racial Identity. *Cultural Diversity and Ethnic Minority Psychology, 23*(1), 102–108.

Newkirk, V. R. (2019, September). This Land Was Our Land: How Nearly 1 million Black Farmers Were Robbed of Their Livelihood. *The Atlantic,* pp. 74–85.

Newman, K. S. (1988). *Falling from Grace: The Experience of Downward Mobility in the American Middle Class.* Detroit, MI: Free Press.

Oyserman, D., & Harrison, K. (1998). Implications of Cultural Context: African American Identity and Possible Selves. In J. Swim & C. Stangor (Eds.), *Prejudice: The Target's Perspective* (pp. 281–300). Amsterdam, Netherlands: Elsevier.

Pager, D. (2008). *Marked: Race, Crime, and Finding Work in an Era of Mass Incarceration.* Chicago, IL: University of Chicago Press.

Parham, T. A. (1989). Cycles of Psychological Nigrescence. *The Counseling Psychologist, 17*(2), 187–226.

Parham, T. A., & Helms, J. E. (1981). The Influence of Black Students' Racial Identity Attitudes on Preferences for Counselor's Race. *Journal of Counseling Psychology, 28*(3), 250–257.

Payne, Y. A. (2006). "A Gangster and a Gentleman": How Street Life–Oriented, U.S.-Born African Men Negotiate Issues of Survival in Relation to Their Masculinity. *Men and Masculinities, 8*(3), 288–297.

Payne, Y. A. (2017). Participatory Action Research and Social Justice: Keys to Freedom for Street Life–Oriented Black Men. In J. Battle, M. Bennett, & A. Lemelle (Eds.), *Free at Last? Black America in the Twenty-first Century* (pp. 265–280). New York, NY: Routledge. (Original work published 2006)

Pegram, T. R. (2011). *One Hundred Percent American: The Rebirth and Decline of the Ku Klux Klan in the 1920s.* Louisville, CO: Rowman and Littlefield.

Peres, J. F., Moreira-Almeida, A., Nasello, A. G., & Koenig, H. G. (2007). Spirituality and Resilience in Trauma Victims. *Journal of Religion and Health, 46*(3), 343–350.

Perry, I. (2019). *Breathe: A Letter to My Sons.* Boston, MA: Beacon Press.

Peterson, C., Park, N., Pole, N., D'Andrea, W., & Seligman, M. E. (2008). Strengths of Character and Posttraumatic Growth. *Journal of Traumatic Stress: Official Publication of the International Society for Traumatic Stress Studies, 21*(2), 214–217.

Phillips, U. B. (1929). *Life and Labor in the Old South.* New York, NY: Grosset and Dunlap.

Phinney, J. S. (1989). Stages of Ethnic Identity Development in Minority Group Adolescents. *The Journal of Early Adolescence, 9*(1–2), 34–49.

Phinney, J. S., & Ong, A. D. (2007). Conceptualization and Measurement of Ethnic Identity: Current Status and Future Directions. *Journal of Counseling Psychology, 54*(3), 271.

Pickens, W. (1991). *Bursting Bonds: The Heir of Slaves: The Autobiography of a "New Negro"* (Enlarged ed.). Bloomington: Indiana University Press. (Original work published 1916)

Platt, A. M. (1971). *The Politics of Riot Commissions, 1917–1970: A Collection of Official Reports and Critical Essays.* New York, NY: Collier Books.

Platt, T. (1991). *E. Franklin Frazier Reconsidered.* New Brunswick, NJ: Rutgers University Press.

Powers, D. A., & Ellison, C. G. (1995). Interracial Contact and Black Racial Attitudes: The Contact Hypothesis and Selectivity Bias. *Social Forces 74*(1), 205–226.

Priest, N., Slopen, N., Woolford, S., Philip, J. T., Singer, D., Kauffman, A. D., . . . & Williams, D. (2018). Correction: Stereotyping across Intersections of Race and Age: Racial Stereotyping among White Adults Working with Children. *PLoS ONE 13*(10), e0205614. https://doi.org/10.1371/journal.pone.0205614

Pronczuk, M., & Specia, M. (2020, June 30). Belgium's King Sends Letter of Regret over Colonial Past in Congo. *New York Times*, p. 1.

Putnam, R. D. (2015). *Our Kids: The American Dream in Crisis.* New York, NY: Simon and Schuster.

Quashie, K. (2012). *The Sovereignty of Quiet: Beyond Resistance in Black Culture.* New Brunswick, NJ: Rutgers University Press.

Rabaka, R. (2011). *Hip Hop's Inheritance: From the Harlem Renaissance to the Hip Hop Feminist Movement.* Lanham, MD: Lexington Books.

Rabaka, R. (2015). *The Negritude Movement: W.E.B. Du Bois, Leon Damas, Aime Césaire, Leopold Senghor, Frantz Fanon, and the Evolution of an Insurgent Idea.* Lanham, MD: Lexington Books.

Rainwater, L. (1966). Crucible of Identity: The Negro Lower-Class Family. *Daedalus, 95*(1), 172–216.

Reding, N. (2010). *Methland: The Death and Life of an American Small Town*. London, UK: Bloomsbury.

Rempson, J. L. (2016). *The African American Male School Adaptability Crisis*. Bloomington, IN: AuthorHouse.

Richardson, D., & Eltis, D. (2015). *Atlas of the Transatlantic Slave Trade*. New Haven, CT: Yale University Press.

Rosenberg, M., & Simmons, R. G. (1971). *Black and White Self-Esteem: The Urban School Child*. Washington, DC: American Sociological Association.

Ryan, W. (1965, October). Savage Discovery: The Moynihan Report. *The Crisis, Magazine of the NAACP*, 220–232.

Ryff, C. D., & Keyes, C.L.M. (1995). The Structure of Psychological Well-Being Revisited. *Journal of Personality and Social Psychology, 69*(4), 719–727.

Schifrin, N. (2020). Outrage over George Floyd Catalyzes Movements for Racial Justice Abroad. *PBS NewsHour*. Retrieved from https://www.pbs.org/newshour/show/outrage-over-george-floyd-catalyzes-movements-for-racial-justice-abroad

Schmidt, C. K., Piontkowski, S., Raque-Bogdan, T. L., & Ziemer, K. S. (2014). Relational Health, Ethnic Identity, and Well-Being of College Students of Color: A Strengths-Based Perspective. *The Counseling Psychologist, 42*(4), 473–496.

Sellers, R. M., Smith, M. A., Shelton, J. N., Rowley, S. A., & Chavous, T. M. (1998). Multidimensional Model of Racial Identity: A Reconceptualization of African American Racial Identity. *Personality and Social Psychology Review, 2*(1), 18–39.

Seth, P., Scholl, L., Rudd, R. A., & Bacon, S. (2018). Overdose Deaths Involving Opioids, Cocaine, and Psychostimulants—United States, 2015–2016. *MMWR: Morbidity and Mortality Weekly Report, 67*(12), 349–358.

Shailor, J. (2010). *Performing New Lives: Prison Théâtre*. London, UK: Jessica Kingsley.

Sheets, H. M. (2019, September 22). Incarcerated Artists Draw to Be Free. *New York Times*, Art Section, p. 20.

Shetterly, M. L. (2016). *Hidden Figures: The American Dream and the Untold Story of the Black Women Mathematicians Who Helped Win the Space Race*. New York, NY: HarperCollins.

Shockley, K. G., & Hilliard, A. G. (2008). *The Miseducation of Black Children*. Chicago, IL: African American Images, division of Independent Publishing Group (IPG).

Sides, J. (2006). *LA City Limits: African American Los Angeles from the Great Depression to the Present*. Berkeley: University of California Press.

Singleton, G. H. (1982). Birth, Rebirth, and the "New Negro" of the 1920s. *Phylon (1960–), 43*(1), 29–45.

Smith, J. D. (1980). Symbolic Antagonist of the Progressive Era. *The Centennial Review, 24*(1), 88–102.

Smith, T. B., & Silva, L. (2011). Ethnic Identity and Personal Well-Being of People of Color: A Meta-Analysis. *Journal of Counseling Psychology, 58*(1), 42.

Spencer, M. B. (1995). Old Issues and New Theorizing about African American Youth: A Phenomenological Variant of Ecological Systems Theory. In R. Taylor (Ed.), *Black Youth: Perspectives on Their Status in the United States* (pp. 37–70). Westport, CT: Praeger.

Spencer, M. B., Cross, W., Harpalani, V., & Goss, T. (2003). Historical and Developmental Perspectives on Black Academic Achievement. In C. Yeakey & R. Henderson (Eds.), *Surmounting All Odds: Education, Opportunity, and Society in the New Millennium* (pp. 273–304). Greenwich, CT: Information Age Publishing.

Stapleton, K. R. (1998). From the Margins to Mainstream: The Political Power of Hip-Hop. *Media, Culture & Society, 20*(2), 219–234.

Stevenson, H. C., & Arrington, E. G. (2009). Racial/Ethnic Socialization Mediates Perceived Racism and the Racial Identity of African American Adolescents. *Cultural Diversity and Ethnic Minority Psychology, 15*(2), 125–136. doi:10.1037/a0015500

Stone, A. (1992, February 28). We Are the U.S. in Microcosm. *USA Today*, pp. A1, A6.

Stone, S., Saucer, C., Bailey, M., Garba, R., Hurst, A., Jackson, S. M., . . . & Cokley, K. (2018). Learning while Black: A Culturally Informed Model of the Impostor Phenomenon for Black Graduate Students. *Journal of Black Psychology, 44*(6), 491–531.

Strauss, L., & Cross, W. E., Jr. (2005). Transacting Black Identity: A Two-Week Daily-Diary Study. In G. Downey, J. S. Eccles, & C. M. Chatman (Eds.), *Navigating the Future: Social Identity, Coping, and Life Tasks* (pp. 67–95). New York, NY: Russell Sage Foundation.

Sue, D. W., Capodilupo, C. M., Torino, G. C., Bucceri, J. M., Holder, A., Nadal, K. L., & Esquilin, M. (2007). Racial Microaggressions in Everyday Life: Implications for Clinical Practice. *American Psychologist, 62*(4), 271–286.

Tatum, B. D. (2003). *"Why Are All the Black Kids Sitting Together in the Cafeteria?": And Other Conversations about Race.* New York, NY: Basic Books. (Original work published 1997)

Thomas, C. W. (1971). *Boys No More: A Black Psychologist's View of Community.* Glencoe, IL: Glencoe Press.

Toner, R. (1992, July 5). New Politics of Welfare Focuses on Its Flaws. *New York Times*, p. A1.

Turner, S., & Bound, J. (2003). Closing the Gap or Widening the Divide: The Effects of the GI Bill and World War II on the Educational Outcomes of Black Americans. *The Journal of Economic History, 63*(1), 145–177.

Umaña-Taylor, A. J., O'Donnell, M., Knight, G. P., Roosa, M. W., Berkel, C., & Nair, R. (2014). Mexican-Origin Early Adolescents' Ethnic Socialization,

Ethnic Identity, and Psychosocial Functioning. *The Counseling Psychologist,* 42(2), 170–200.

Vandiver, B. J., Cross, W. E., Jr., Worrell, F. C., & Fhagen-Smith, P. E. (2002). Validating the Cross Racial Identity Scale. *Journal of Counseling Psychology,* 49(1), 71–85.

Wald, J., & Losen, D. J. (2003). Defining and Redirecting a School-to-Prison Pipeline. *New Directions for Youth Development,* 2003(99), 9–15.

Wallace, M. (1978). *Black Macho and the Myth of the Superwoman.* New York, NY: Dial Press.

Watson, D. (2018, May 20). Once a Maintenance Worker at Colonial Williamsburg, Leroy Graves Is among the World's Top Upholstery Conservators. *The Virginia Pilot.* Retrieved from https://pilotonline.com/entertainment/arts/exhibits/article_b04da7f6-58ad-11e8-9447-f75c7f4b1eaa.html

White, W. (2001). *Rope and Faggot: A Biography of Judge Lynch.* Notre Dame, IN: University of Notre Dame Press. (Original work published 1929, New York, NY: Alfred K. Knopf)

Wolgemuth, K. L. (1959). Woodrow Wilson and Federal Segregation. *Journal of Negro History,* 44(2), 158–173.

Worrell, F. C. (2012). Forty Years of Cross's Nigrescence Theory: From Stages to Profiles, from African Americans to all Americans. In J. M. Sullivan & A. M. Esmail (Eds.), *African American Identity: Racial and Cultural Dimensions of the Black Experience* (pp. 3–38). Lanham, MD: Lexington Books.

Worrell, F. C., Mendoza-Denton, R., & Wang, A. (2019). Introducing a New Assessment Tool for Measuring Ethnic-Racial Identity: The Cross Ethnic-Racial Identity Scale–Adult (CERIS-A). *Assessment,* 26(3), 404–418.

Worrell, F. C., Vandiver, B. J., Cross, W. E., Jr., & Fhagen, P. E. (2016). *The Cross Ethnic Racial Identity Scale—Adult.* (Unpublished Scale). The University of California, Berkeley.

Worrell, F. C., Vandiver, B. J., Schaefer, B. A., Cross, W. E., Jr., & Fhagen-Smith, P. E. (2006). Generalizing Nigrescence Profiles: Cluster Analyses of Cross Racial Identity Scale (CRIS) Scores in Three Independent Samples. *The Counseling Psychologist,* 34(4), 519–547.

Wuthnow, R. (2019). *The Left Behind: Decline and Rage in Small-Town America.* Princeton, NJ: Princeton University Press.

Yip, T., & Cross, W. E., Jr. (2004). A Daily Diary Study of Mental Health and Community Involvement Outcomes for Three Chinese American Social Identities. *Cultural Diversity and Ethnic Minority Psychology,* 10(4), 394–408.

Zimmermann, C. R. (2018). The Penalty of Being a Young Black Girl: Kindergarten Teachers' Perceptions of Children's Problem Behaviors and Student–Teacher Conflict by the Intersection of Race and Gender. *The Journal of Negro Education,* 87(2), 154–168.

Index

Page numbers followed by the letter t refer to tables.
Page numbers followed by the letter f refer to figures.

ABPsi (Association of Black Psychologists), 3, 23, 51–52, 57–58, 72
absolutism, 54
Acharya, Avidit, 130
Active Resistance stage, 26t
Act Prohibiting the Importation of Slaves (1807), 142
Adams, Anne, 49
Adams, Maurianne, 46
Adams, Sam, 7
addiction, 124, 127
adjustment, theory of Negro, 106–107, 109
Africana Center (Cornell University), 2–3, 7
African aesthetic, 21
African identity, 50–52
African independence movements, 21
African psychology (AP), 3, 50–52
African Psychology in Historical Perspective and Related Commentary (Azibo), 50

AfriCOBRA aesthetics movement, 70–71
Afrocentricity, 15; and African psychology, 50–52; and Association of Black Psychologists, 57–58; and blacker-than-thou attitudes, 56–58; and black identity, 72; challenge of, 50; and critique of Nigrescence, 50–58, 61, 75–76; as cultural phenomenon, 52–53; and empirical approaches, 3; and Optimal Psychology, 54–56; and white nationalism and eugenics, 23
"Afrocentricity and African Psychology" (Cokley), 53
Afrocentricity and the Academy (Conyers), 53
agency, black, 99, 108, 136, 137–138, 145–147
"aha!" moment, 24, 93
Aid to Families with Dependent Children, 126–127
"All lives matter," 48
alternate identity options, 64

Always Another Country (Msimang), 44
Amutah-Onukagha, Ndidiamaka, 86, 89
Anderson, James, 148
Angelou, Maya, 37, 79, 88, 94, 154
anger, 27
AP (African psychology), 3, 50–52
Arendt, Hannah, 22
Armstrong, Louis, 98
assimilation, 107, 109, 110–111, 113–114
Assimilation subscale, 66
Association of Black Psychologists (ABPsi), 3, 23, 51–52, 57–58, 72
attachment-bonding, 82, 88–89, 92–96
Atwater, Lee, 121
authentic story, 42
Awad, Germine, 3, 53
Azibo, Daudi, 50

Bailey, Pearl, 96, 98
Bakari Project: A Lifeline for African American Adolescent Development and Success (Caldwell-Gunes & Parham), 52–53
Baldwin, James, 79, 153
Baldwin, Joseph A., 50
Banks, Nathaniel P., 146
Banks, W. Curtis, 8
"barbershop bias," 6–8, 16
belonging, 70
benevolent societies, 145
Berry, John, 64
Best, Steven, 28
bicultural competence, 89
biculturalism, 8–9
Biko, Steve, 44
Biles, Simone, 96
binary hypothesis, 69–70
biogenetic inferiority, 113
biogenetic-melanin hypothesis, 51, 52, 53
biometrics, 97
birthing, breeding *vs.*, 140–141
The Birth of a Nation (film), 10, 114, 121
black aesthetic, 40
black agency, 99, 108, 136, 137–138, 145–147
black artists, 40–41, 102–103
Black Bourgeoisie (Frazier), 12, 110, 122
black consciousness: and being "woke," 41; death of Martin Luther King Jr. and, 14, 19, 21–22; deindustrialization and, 15; and identity-change models, 24–31, 25t, 26t, 29t, 30t; and social mobility, 49–50
black culture: accessibility to, 93–94; belief in inferiority of, 112–113
black diversity, 103
blacker-than-thou attitudes, 27, 56–58
black family. *See* family structures and dynamics
black feminism, 14, 27, 31, 37, 44–46, 57
blackfishing, 91–92
black GIs, 27–28, 132–133
black identity: defining, 71–73; and eudaimonia and meaning in life, 67–71; individuality and, 98; as normative, 69
Black Inventors in the Age of Segregation (Fouché), 149
black juvenile delinquency, 10, 117–121, 124–130
Black Lives Matter (BLM) movement, 31, 33, 36–37, 47, 48, 102
Black Macho and the Myth of the Superwoman (Wallace), 123
black migrants, 116
black militancy, 27
black music, 94–95, 96
black nationalism, 51
Black Nation of Islam, 51, 84
blackness: expressions of, 94; how to define, 46
Black Panthers, 44
black people, as normal, 145–147
black perspective, 9
black poverty, 12, 101, 112–113, 121, 124–130
black power, 21, 22; and accessibility to black culture, 93
black protests, 102
Black Reconstruction (Du Bois), 99, 100, 108, 109, 136, 137–138
Black Skins, White Masks (Fanon), 21
black social movements, 21, 40, 69
black studies, 5–7, 13, 49
"black style," 72–73
black underclass, 105, 112, 113, 122, 132
black uplift: W.E.B. Du Bois on, 99–100, 106, 108–109, 113–115, 119–120; one-generation, 108–109, 114, 116, 147–150
Blackwell, Matthew, 130

black women: as feminists, 27, 31, 37, 44–46, 57; and legacy of slavery, 120–121; racism and gender discrimination against, 90–91
Black World (periodical), 2
Blasingame, John, 139
BLM (Black Lives Matter) movement, 31, 33, 36–37, 47, 48, 102
Bluefield Colored Institute, 151–152
Bluefield State College, 152
Bluestone, Barry, 125, 126
Bonanno, George, 144
Boyd-Franklin, Nancy, 82
Boykin, A. Wade, 3, 58, 81
Boys into Men: Raising Our African American Teenage Sons (Boyd-Franklin & Franklin), 82
Boys No More (Thomas), 23–24
Bracey, John, 84–85
Bradley, Thomas, 116, 150, 153
Breathe: Letters to My Son (Perry), 88
breeding, *vs.* birthing, 140–141
bridging, 82, 92, 102, 103–104
broken family, 11, 107–108
Bronfenbrenner, Urie, 8
Brooklyn, Illinois, 146, 152
Brooks, Gwendolyn, 70
Brown-Duckett, Thasunda, 92
Brubeck, Dave, 94
Bryant, Kobe, 50
Buchanan, Lucile, 136, 146–147, 150, 152
buffering, 82, 83–92; and bridging, 92; and code-switching, 89–92; cost of, 88; and dance of twoness, 103; as endurance and survival, 83–85; and everyday living while black, 85–87; and psychology of black functioning in open spaces, 88–92
buffering stance, 91
Bullard, Eugene, 136
Bunche, Ralph, 116
Bush, George H. W., 121

Caldwell, A. B., 151
Caldwell-Gunes, Roslyn M., 52–53
California, black sharecroppers in, 115–116
Calverton, V. F., 110
Cambage, Liz, 50

Carmichael, Stokely, 22, 44
Carter, Betty, 98
Carter, Robert, 5, 32
caste system, 100, 108, 117
castration, 27, 28, 123
categorical "either/or" thinking, 27
centrality, in evolution of identity, 39
Central Park Five, 122
CERIS (Cross Ethnic-Racial Identity Scale), 38
Césaire, Aimé, 21
Cha-Jua, Sundiata Keita, 146
character traits, 138–139, 149–150, 152
Charlottesville, Virginia, Unite the Right march in, 131
Chicago: school segregation and inequity in, 117–119; South Side of, 2, 6, 152–153, 155
Chicago P.D. (television show), 155
Chicago race riot, 119
Chicago School, 105, 106–107, 109, 111
Chicago School Board, 118–120, 132
Chicago Urban League (CUL), 119
child development, 13, 139, 142–144, 152
child socialization. *See* socialization
civilization: W.E.B. Du Bois on, 107; and eugenics, 109; E. Franklin Frazier on, 109, 111–115, 137, 153–154; legacy of slavery and lack of, 127, 137; Booker T. Washington on, 138–139
civil rights movement: and accessibility to black culture, 93; racism after, 90–91
Clark, Kenneth B., 4, 5, 7–8, 114, 122
Clark, Mamie, 4, 5, 7–8, 114
class differentiation, 110
Clear service, 97
Clinton, Bill, 67, 128
closed ecologies, social identity in, 83
Coates, Ta-Nehisi, 86
Cochran, Phil, 2
code-switching, 89–92; as bicultural competence, 89; and blackfishing, 91–92; buffering and, 89, 91; and creativity, 94–96; examples of, 78, 89; and imposter syndrome, 78, 91–92, 102; process of, 89–90; racism and, 90–91; reverse, 91–92; and self-esteem, 101; and socialization, 82

Cokley, Kevin, 3, 38, 52, 58, 91
Cole, Nat King, 89, 98
Colonial Williamsburg, 95
The Colonizer and the Colonized (Memmi), 21
colorism, 35
"color line," 108
Coltrane, John, 3, 96
Combahee River Collective, 45–46, 47
Confrontation Stage, 26t
consciousness development, 21–22, 23
consciousness raising, 32, 41
Conyers, James, 53
Coontz, Stephanie, 126
counternarratives: by black studies, 13; to collectivism, 98; to deficit perspective, 14; for deindustrialization, 15, 153; of W.E.B. Du Bois, 120; to GI bill, 132; on identity, 75; inclusion of LGBTQIA as, 75; to miseducation, 41; in Optimal Psychology, 54
COVID-19 pandemic, 133–134
creativity, attachment-bonding, code-switching and, 94–96, 102–103
crime and criminality: black, 117, 135; deindustrialization and, 67, 127–128
CRIS. *See* Cross Racial Identity Scale (CRIS)
Crisis (journal), 147
Critical Race Theory, 3, 30, 53
Cross, Charlene, 6
Cross, Dawn, 1
Cross, Dee, 7
Cross, Margaret Carter, 1
Cross, Sarah Hatter, 150–151
Cross, Tuere Binta, 1, 37, 94
Cross, William E., Jr.: birth and early life of, 6–7; black uplift in relative of, 150–154
Cross Ethnic-Racial Identity Scale (CERIS), 38
Cross Nigrescence Model, 19, 24–31, 25t, 26t, 29t, 30t, 44
Cross Nigrescence Theory. *See* Nigrescence Theory
Cross Racial Identity Scale (CRIS), 19–20; Assimilation, Miseducation, and Racial Self-Hatred subscales of, 66–67;

development of, 33, 38; and group *vs.* self-identity, 39, 41; and identity matrix concept, 47; and positive black identity, 72–73
CUL (Chicago Urban League), 119
Cultural Diversity and Ethnic Minority Psychology (journal), 32
cultural identity, 82, 88–89, 92–96
culture-based Afrocentricity, 52–53
culture of poverty trope, 114, 115
Curry, Stephen, 49–50
Curry, Tommy J., 40, 122–123
Curwood, Anastasia, 123

Damas, Léon, 21
Dark Ghetto (Clark), 122
Davis, Miles, 3, 37, 95, 96, 153
de Beauvoir, Simone, 22
deficit perspective: and black uplift, 99–100, 108–109, 113–116, 119–120; deindustrialization and, 128; and delinquency rates, 117–121; W.E.B. Du Bois and, 13, 106–109, 111–114, 116, 119–120, 135, 136; E. Franklin Frazier and, 10–14, 16, 105–115; and gender, 121–123; *vs.* real legacy of slavery, 130–134; *vs.* socioeconomic status and poverty, 124–130; summary of, 134–136; and superpredator trope, 121–123
DeGruy, Joy, 12, 105
deindustrialization, 16; and black consciousness, 15; effect on blacks of, 67, 126–128, 135, 153; effect on whites of, 65–66, 124–130, 135, 136; and Nigrescence, 48–50; and poverty, 124–130, 135; and self-esteem, 65–66
delinquency, 10, 117–121, 124–130
development, psychosocial stages of, 80–83
Developmental Inventory of Black Consciousness (DIBC), 23
dissonance theory, 25–26, 58, 74
divergent viewpoints, 60–61
diversity training, 31, 76
Division 35 (APA), 32
Division 45 (APA), 32
doll studies, racial preference, 4, 5, 8–10, 114

Donaldson, Jeff, 2, 70
Dorsey, George, 27–28
double-consciousness, 105; attachment-bonding and, 92; and black functioning in open spaces, 88; W.E.B. Du Bois on, 9, 77–78, 79, 100, 105; Erik Erikson and, 15, 81, 101; and self-esteem, 100–101; and signifying, 9–10; and vigilance, 101–102
double shifting, 118–120, 132
Douglass, Frederick, 13, 37, 136, 138, 152
Dow, Dawn Marie, 86
drug addiction, 124, 127
drug trade, deindustrialization and, 97
Du Bois, W.E.B.: on agency, vision, and motivation of ex-slaves, 108, 136, 137–138, 145–146; on black family, 108, 111–112; on black people as normal, 145–146; black stories used by, 111–112; on black uplift, 99–100, 106, 108–109, 113–114, 116, 119–120, 147, 149; and civilization-assimilation trope, 107, 111, 112; decoupling of intent from consequence by, 137–138; and deficit perspective, 13, 106–109, 111–114, 116, 119–120, 135, 136; on double-consciousness, 9, 77–78, 79, 92, 100, 105; on education of ex-slaves, 100, 114, 136, 145; first Department of Sociology founded by, 105; and E. Franklin Frazier, 7–8, 104–109, 113–114, 135, 137–138, 153–154; on legacy of slavery, 7–8, 108, 114; on poverty, 108; on self behind veil, 78–79, 155
Dukakis, Michael, 121
Duncan, Tim, 50
DuSable High School (Chicago), 117–118
dysfunctionality, trauma and, 144

Early Seating Upholstery: Reading the Evidence (Graves), 96
Ebonics, 14, 149–150
Eckstine, Billy, 96, 98
ecological settings, and social identity, 83, 93
ecology of human development, 8–9, 13, 141, 143, 144
education: access to, 113; and attachment-bonding, 93–94; of blacks in South, 147–148, 151–152; of ex-slaves, 145, 146–150, 151; inequities in, 117–120, 132; and miseducation, 35, 39, 41–42, 66–67; as protection against oppression, 122; and school segregation, 5, 10, 117–120; and uplift, 100, 114, 130–131, 136, 147–148
Education of Blacks in the South (Anderson), 148
ego identity status, 62
Egyptian Mystery System, 51, 55, 56, 61, 72
"either/or" thinking, 27
Ellington, Duke, 96, 153
emergent fascism, 51
Eminem, 135
empathy, 51
empirical black psychology, 3, 57–58
Encounter stage, 24, 25, 26, 26t, 42, 74
endurance, buffering as, 83–85
entrapment ecologies, social identity in, 83
epiphany, 20, 25, 59, 145
ERI (Ethnic Racial Identity), 62
Erikson, Erik: developmental theory of, 61; and double-consciousness, 15, 81, 101; on history and personality, 22; on identity development, 80; on meaning in life, 65; on social identity, 15, 82, 93
essentialism, 11, 12, 50, 52
ethnic identity, 61–67
Ethnic Racial Identity (ERI), 62
eudaimonia, 55, 65, 66, 67–71, 89
eugenics: and African psychology, 51, 52; and Afrocentric models, 23, 53; and Chicago School, 107; E. Franklin Frazier and, 109, 110, 112
European colonization, 48
Evans, Bill, 94
Evans, Gil, 95
Evanston West Side Service Center, 2
everyday buffering, 85–87
everyday living while black, 85–87, 99
exceptionalism, 13
existentialism, 22
existential psychology, 14, 22, 84
existential self, 58–61, 60f, 68, 70

Falling from Grace (Newman), 124
family structures and dynamics: broken family as, 11, 107–108; "damaged" black, 10, 11, 12, 106; and delinquency rates, 117; W.E.B. Du Bois on, 107, 111–112; female-headed families as, 123; E. Franklin Frazier on, 106, 107–108, 113, 114, 143; Daniel Patrick Moynihan on, 107–108, 112; poverty and, 124–130
Fanon, Frantz, 21, 74
farmers, black, 133
fascism, emergent, 51, 131
fatalism, 109, 111, 112
Fauset, Jessie, 153
Faustian Dilemmas, 83
Federal Housing Administration home loans, 132–133
feminism, black, 14, 27, 31, 37, 44–46, 57
feminization, 123
Ferguson, Ann, 123
Festinger, Leon, 25–26
Fhagen-Smith, Peony, 33, 34f, 36, 37
fictive kin, 143
Fine, Michelle, 123
Fitzgerald, Ella, 3, 98
Floyd, George, 47, 48
forgiveness, 87, 88
Fouché, Rayvon, 149
Frankl, Viktor, 22
Franklin, Anderson, 3, 82
Frazier, E. Franklin: *Black Bourgeoisie* by, 122; and black delinquency, 117–121; on black poverty, 112–113, 129; on black uplift, 147, 149; on civilization and assimilation, 110, 111, 113–114, 137, 146; on class differentiation among Negroes, 110–111; and code-switching, 101; culture of poverty trope of, 114, 115; and decoupling of intent from effects, 137–140; deficit perspective of, 10–12, 111–115, 155; and deindustrialization, 16–17, 153; dissertation of, 107, 109–111; and W.E.B. Du Bois, 7–8, 104–109, 113–114, 135, 137–138, 153–154; on ecologically distinct "zones," 110–111; and eugenics, 109, 110, 112; on family structure and dynamics, 106, 107–108, 113, 114, 143; on female-headed families, 123; flaws in theory of, 115–117, 134–136; on legacy of slavery, 105, 118, 120–121, 127, 137; Moynihan Report and, 127–128, 129; *The Negro Family in the United States* by, 111–115; on pathology of racism, 110; on progress and hope, 110–111; sexism of, 123; weaponization of black stories by, 111
Freedmen's Bureau, 145
free Negroes, 113
Fuller, Hoyt, 2

Galileo, 56
gangsterism, 127–128, 135
Gardner, J. Ann E., 44
Gates, Henry Louis, Jr., 49, 94, 153
Gelles, David, 92
gender: and deficit perspective, 121–123; and Nigrescence, 44–48
GI(s), black, 27–28, 132–133
GI benefits, 132–133
The Gift of Black Folk (Du Bois), 114, 116
Giovanni, Nikki, 70
"giving back," 50
Gladwell, Malcolm, 22, 47
globalization, 49, 65, 124–130
Goffman, Erving, 77, 82–83
Graves, Leroy, 94–95
Graves Method, 95–96
Gray, Joyceann, 151
Groth, Emily, 124
group identity, 15; defined, 80; as multidimensional construct, 39, 81–82; vs. self-identity, 39–41. See also social identity (SI)
guilt, 29t
Gurdjieff, George Ivanovitch, 55
Gutman, Herbert, 135, 139

Hamilton (musical), 95
The Handbook of Multicultural Counseling (Casas), 32
Hansberry, Lorraine, 7
Harlem Renaissance, 21, 50
Harris, Abril, 86, 89
Harris, Robert, 49, 153
Harrison, Bennett, 125, 126

Harrison, Kathy, 81–82
Hartman, Saidiya, 94, 106
Hatter, Hamilton, 13, 150–154, 155
Hawes, Jennifer Berry, 87
HBCU (Historically Black College or University), 58
Helms, Janet, 19, 31, 32–33, 45
Henderson, Bill, 98
Hendrix, Jimi, 94
Henson, Josiah, 20
hidden self, 40, 78
hierarchy of needs, 23, 25
high blood pressure, 88
High Race Salience (HRS), 33–35, 34f
hip-hop culture, 15, 28, 49
Historically Black College or University (HBCU), 58
Hitler, Adolf, 100, 131
Homel, Michael W., 117–118, 119, 132
home ownership, 115–116, 132–133
homophobia, 52
hooks, bell, 45, 79
Horton, Willie, 121, 124, 154
House of Blackness, 2
housing segregation, 115
HRS (High Race Salience), 33–35, 34f
Hughes, Langston, 50, 101, 153
human development, ecology of, 8–9, 13, 141, 143, 144
humanism, 31, 51, 57, 70, 80–81, 98, 99, 110
human plasticity, 93, 98
Hurston, Zora Neale, 7, 101, 153
hypersexuality, 121
hypertension, 88

identity: and eudaimonia and meaning in life, 67–71; evolution of, 39
identity-change models, 14, 19–31, 25t, 26t, 29t, 30t, 74–75
identity classifications, 64
identity complexity model, 31
identity development, generic notions of, 31, 32–33
identity enactments, 78–79, 98
identity focus, 70
identity matrix, 31, 33, 45, 47
identity measure, 23

identity models, 32
identity status perspective, 38
identity variation, 50, 62
identity work, 81, 88–89
ideology, in evolution of identity, 39–40
Immersion-Emersion stage, 26, 29t, 52
imposter syndrome, 78, 91–92, 102
"in-betweenness," 26
incarceration: mass, 121, 144–145; and social identity, 83–85, 99
incarceration buffering, 83–85
"In Defense of Quantitative Methods: Using the 'Master's tools' to Promote Social Justice" (Cokley & Awad), 53
individuality, 15, 97–98
individuation, 97–98
infant-mother attachment, 13
innovation, attachment-bonding, code-switching and, 94–96, 102–103
In Search of Being: The Fourth Way of Consciousness (Gurdjieff), 55
Integration Stage, 30t
interior self, 79
Internalization-Integration Stage, 30t
Internalization stage, 28–29, 29t, 30–31, 30t, 46
Internalized Racism (IR), 33–35, 34f
interpretation of results, 3
intersectionality, 31, 32–33, 37
intragroup buffering, 97
IR (Internalized Racism), 33–35, 34f

Jackson, Bailey: and gender, 44, 46–47; and generic notions of identity development, 31, 32; identity-change model of, 19, 23, 25t, 26t, 31; on identity matrix, 31
Jackson, Mary, 96
James, LeBron, 49
Jamila, Shani, 45, 90
jazz, 94–95, 96
Johnson, Charles S., 119
Johnson, Guy Benton, 108, 114
Johnson, Jack, 136, 153
Johnson, Katherine, 96
Jones, James, 81
Jordan, Michael, 96

"just being myself," 98, 103
juvenile delinquency, 10, 117–121, 124–130

Kambon, Kobi Kazembe, 50
Kant, Immanuel, 147
Kardiner, Abram, 4–5, 12
Kellner, Douglas, 28
Kennedy, Randall, 122
kin, fictive, 143
King, Martin Luther, Jr., 14, 19, 21–24, 45, 74, 156
King, Wilma, 139, 142–144
kinship, in slavery, 142–143
Kranish, Michael, 20–21
Ku Klux Klan (KKK), 10, 129

Lane, Frazier T., 119
law enforcement, shootings by, 47–48, 85
laws "targeting" black people, 67
Lebron, Chris, 87
Lee, Don L., 2, 70
The Left Behind: Decline and Rage in Small-Town America (Wuthnow), 130
legacy of slavery: black juvenile delinquency and, 118; black poverty as, 127; decoupling intent from effects in, 137–140; W.E.B. Du Bois and, 108, 114; E. Franklin Frazier on, 105, 118, 120–121, 127, 137; ineffective socialization as, 10; lynchings as, 130; and "must be" hypothesis, 11–12; political, 130; as race war and Southern white fascism, 130–134; and sexuality, 120, 121; *vs.* systemic racism, 48
Leopold II (King of Belgium), 48
Lewin, Kurt, 22
Lewis, Ramsey, 7
Lewis, Virgil A., 151
LGBTQIA community, 37, 45, 51, 52, 73
lifespan perspective, Nigrescence and, 19, 33–37, 34f
literacy, and uplift, 114, 130–131, 136
living while black, 85–87, 99
Lorde, Audre, 45
Low Race Salience (LRS), 33–35, 34f
lumpenproletariat, 11, 145
lynchings, 27, 28, 124, 130, 131

Madhubuti, Haki R., 2
Majors, M. A., 149
Makari, George, 134
Malcolm, Roger, 27
Malcolm X: and Black Nation of Islam, 84; and black power, 22; and black women, 44, 45; identity change of, 21, 99; and lifespan perspective, 37; and "Negro" stage, 24
male-centric narrative, 27, 31
Mandela, Nelson, 156
Marcia, James, 61–67
The Mark of Oppression (Kardiner & Ovesey), 4–5, 10, 12
marriage, in slavery, 142
mask, self behind, 40, 78, 92–98, 100
Maslow, Abraham, 22, 23, 25, 74
mass incarceration, 121, 144–145
materialism, 54
Mathis, Johnny, 98
Mays, Willie, 96
McClain, Dani, 87
meaning making, 15, 67–71
MEIM (Multigroup Ethnic Identity Measure), 41, 62–64, 66
melanin, 51, 52, 53
Memmi, Albert, 21, 74
Mendenhall, Ruby, 153
Me Too movement, 33, 36–37, 91
Mettler, Suzanne, 132
MIBI (Multidimensional Inventory of Black Identity), 39, 41
migrants, black, 115
Miller, T. C., 151
Milliones, Jake: and gender, 44; identity-change model of, 19, 23, 25t, 26t, 29t, 30t, 31; and male rage, 27
miseducation, 35, 39, 41–42, 66–67
Miseducation subscale, 66–67
Misty Monroe: Unapologetically Black, 41
MMRI (Multidimensional Model of Racial Identity), 39
Modern Jazz Quartet, 95
Monk, Thelonious, 3; 96
Monroe, Misty, 41
Moore, Maya, 50
Morley, Robert, 125–126
Morrill Act (1890), 152

Morrison, Toni, 153
Moynihan, Daniel Patrick ("Pat"), 16, 49, 107–108, 112, 127, 129
Moynihan Report, 12, 49, 124, 127, 128
Msimang, Sisonke, 44, 45, 60–61
mulattoes, 113
Multicultural Inclusive subscale, 47, 73
"multicultural stance," 38
multidimensional group identity, 39, 81–82
Multidimensional Inventory of Black Identity (MIBI), 39, 41
Multidimensional Model of Racial Identity (MMRI), 39
Multigroup Ethnic Identity Measure (MEIM), 41, 62–64, 66
music, 94–95, 96
"must be" hypothesis, 11–14
Myers, Linda James, 52, 54–56

NAACP (National Association for the Advancement of Colored People), 5, 89, 147
Nadanolitization, 25t
National Association for the Advancement of Colored People (NAACP), 5, 89, 147
Nation of Islam, 51, 84
needs, hierarchy of, 23, 25
Negritude social movement, 21, 74
The Negro Family: The Case for National Action (Moynihan Report), 12, 49
"Negro" identity, 24, 25t, 43, 60, 75–76
The Negro in Chicago: A Study of Race Relations and a Race Riot (report), 118–119
Negromachy, 24, 25t
Negro psychopathology, 5, 61
Negro-to-black conversion experience, 59
"The Negro-to-Black-Conversion Experience" (Cross), 2
Nelms, Charles, 147–150, 153
Neville, Helen, 49, 153
Newkirk, Vann R., 133
Newman, Katherine, 124
"New Negro," 21
New Negro Movement, 21
Nigrescence: and being "woke," 41–42; defined, 73–74; and deindustrialization, 48–50; and existential self, 58–61, 60f; gender and, 44–48; male-centric understanding of, 27; origin of term, 21, 74; and personality, 75; scales that measure, 33, 37–39; and social mobility, 48–50
Nigrescence Encounter, 36
Nigrescence lifespan model, 19, 33–37, 34f
Nigrescence models, 14, 19–31, 25t, 26t, 29t, 30t, 74–75
Nigrescence Theory: *vs.* African-centered perspective, 50–58, 61, 75–76; extension of, 32–33, 45; and group- *vs.* self-identity, 39–41; and history, 20–21; and identity-change models, 24–31, 25t, 26t, 29t, 30t; and miseducation, 41–42; and reference group change, 59
normal, black people as, 145–147
normative perspective, 61–67, 69
Noted Negro Women: Their Triumphs and Activities (Majors), 149
nurseries, on plantations, 143

OBAC (Organization of Black American Culture), 2
Obama, Barack, 37, 87, 102
Obama, Michelle, 37
objectification, 40
open but constrained ecologies, social identity in, 83
open, expansive ecologies, social identity in, 83
open spaces, psychology of black functioning in, 88–92
Optimal Psychology, 54–56
Organization of Black American Culture (OBAC), 2
other-group orientation, 62–64
Our Kids: The American Dream in Crisis (Putnam), 124
overcrowding, in schools, 117–118, 119
overdose deaths, 124
Ovesey, Lionel, 4–5, 12
Oyserman, Daphna, 81–82

parental identity frames, 33–35, 34f
Parham, Thomas, 19, 32, 33, 52–53

Park, Robert Ezra: and Chicago School, 105, 107, 110, 111; on culture, assimilation, and civilization, 107, 110, 139; on family structure, 143; E. Franklin Frazier and, 11, 111, 119
Passive Acceptance stage, 25t
pathology, 60
Payne, Yasser, 65, 123, 153, 154
performance of self, 78–79
Perry, Imani, 86, 88, 143
personal identity (PI), 58–59, 80
personality, Nigrescence and, 75
personality characteristics, 138–139, 149–150, 152
personal responsibility, and poverty, 128–129
"personal space," 40
The Philadelphia Negro (Du Bois), 100, 108, 111, 113–114, 116
Philippe (King of Belgium), 48
Phillips, Richard, 84
Phillips, Ulrich Bonnell, 112
Phillips High School (Chicago), 118
Phinney, Jean, 61–67
phrenology, 134
PI (personal/private identity), 58–59, 80
Picasso, Pablo, 95
Pickens, William, 146–147, 150, 152
plasticity, 93, 98
Platt, Anthony M., 11, 119
police shootings, 47–48, 85
"The Political Legacy of American Slavery" (article), 130
portable psychological strengths, 12
portals, in schools, 118, 132
postnatal care, inadequate, 86
post traumatic slave syndrome, 12
Post Traumatic Slave Syndrome (DeGruy), 105
poverty: black *vs.* white, 124–130; and code-switching, 101; culture of, 114, 115; and deficit perspective, 12; deindustrialization and, 124–130, 135; W.E.B. Du Bois on, 108; E. Franklin Frazier on, 112–113; and personal responsibility, 128–129
Pre-conscious Stage, 25t
predator trope, 121–123

Pre-encounter Stage, 25t, 73, 75–76
prefrontal cortex, 80, 93–94, 98
prenatal care, inadequate, 86
pride, 29t
Prince, Biannca, 94
private identity (PI), 58–59, 80
proactive socialization, 82, 103
profile analysis, 38
Project 10, 46
prostitution, 120, 135
protective socialization, 82, 103
Provident Hospital, 6
psychological blackness, 38
psychological fragmentation, 55
psychological independence, 23
psychological strengths, portable, 12
Psychology of Women, 32
psychopathology, 5, 61
psychosocial stages of development, 80–83
public education, 93–94
Putnam, Robert D., 124

Quashie, Kevin, 31, 40, 78
"the quiet self," 40, 79

Rabaka, Reiland, 49, 71, 94, 153
race, and intersectionality, 30–31
race-related stress, 88
race riot, 118–119
race war, 131
racial essentialism, 50, 52
racial identity, 15
racialization, 32, 40
racial preference doll studies, 4, 5, 8–10, 114
racial segregation, 5, 10
racial self-hatred, 35, 39, 66, 71–72
Racial Self-Hatred subscale, 66, 72
racism: after civil rights movement, 90–91; and intragroup buffering, 97; systemic, 12, 48, 101
rage, 27, 28, 29, 29t, 57
Rainwater, Lee, 117
rapprochement, 29
Reconstruction, black uplift during, 106–109, 130–131, 135–136, 152
recycling, 33, 36–37

Redirection Stage, 29t
re-engagement, 29–30
Reese, Pee Wee, 103
reference group orientation (RGO), 58–59
regard, in evolution of identity, 39
Rempson, Joe L., 5, 12, 105, 115, 122
research designs, 3
resilience, 81, 84, 88, 99, 144
RGO (reference group orientation), 58–59
Rickey, Branch, 104
Robinson, Jack Roosevelt (Jackie), 88, 103–104, 116, 150, 153
Roof, Dylann, 87
Rope and Faggot: A Biography of Judge Lynch (White), 91
Rosenberg, Morris, 100, 101
Rushton, J. Philippe, 53
Russell, Bill, 88
"Rust Belt," 124

Saint Valentine's Day Massacre, 10, 135
salience: of ascription, 76; and being "woke," 36; code-switching and, 103; in Cross Racial Identity Scale, 72; in Multidimensional Inventory of Black Identity, 39; in Multigroup Ethnic Identity Measure, 63–66, 68; in Nigrescence lifespan model, 19, 33, 35; in Nigrescence Theory, 39; in social identity, 15, 59; in socialization of children, 96
Sartre, Jean-Paul, 22
school segregation, 5, 10, 117–120
school-to-prison pipeline, 67, 97, 133
SCLC (Southern Christian Leadership Conference), 89
second-generation success stories, 146–147
segregation, 5, 10
self-actualization, 82, 101
self behind the veil, 78, 92–98, 100
self-centeredness, 98
self-concept, 58–59, 68, 79
self-consciousness, 15
self-determination, 99
self-esteem: double-consciousness and, 100–101; ethnicity and, 63–65; measure of collective, 64; in racial preference doll studies, 4–5; socialization and, 36
self-esteem scale, 64
self-hatred, 35, 39, 66, 71–72, 114
self-identity, group identity *vs.*, 39–41
self-reflection, 15
Sellers, Robert, 39
Sen, Maya, 130
Senghor, Léopold Sédar, 21
SES (socioeconomic status), 11, 12, 16–17, 99, 124–130
sexism, 123
sexual behavior, Negro, 120, 121
sexual immorality, 11
Shades of Black (Cross), 3, 21, 61
Shakur, Tupac, 96
shamanism, 54, 55
Shambhala organization, 55
sharecroppers, black, 115–116
Short, Ted, 94
Sides, Josh, 115–116
signifying, 9–10
Simmons, Roberta G., 100, 101
Simone, Nina, 94
skin-bleaching products, 20
slavery: breeding *vs.* birthing in, 140–141; child development in, 13, 139, 142–144, 152; decoupling intent from effects of, 137–140; 100% evil trope of, 13; and social identity, 83–85, 99; and trauma, 144–145; youth experience of, 139, 142–144. *See also* legacy of slavery
Smalls, Biggie, 96
Smith, Bessie, 153
social adjustment theories, 106–107, 109
social change. *See* black uplift
social class, 114
social identity (SI), 77–104; and attachment-bonding, 82, 88–89, 92–96; and bridging, 82, 92, 102, 103–104; and buffering, 82, 83–92, 97; and code-switching, 78, 79, 82, 89–92, 94–96, 101, 102; and creativity/innovation, 94–96, 102–103; and cultural identity, 82, 88–89, 92–96; defined, 80; and double-consciousness, 15, 77–78, 81, 88, 92, 100–102; and ecological settings, 83, 93; and imposter syndrome,

social identity (SI) *(continued)*
78, 91–92, 102; and individuation and individuality, 97–99; and Nigrescence, 58–59; overview of, 78–81; and private/personal identity, 80; and psychosocial stages of development, 80–83; range of, 93; and self-actualization, 82, 101; and self behind the veil, 78, 92–98, 100; and self-concept, 68, 79; and self-esteem, 100–101; summary and conclusions about, 99–104; and vigilance, 82, 87, 88, 89, 101–102
social identity stances, 15
socialization: "damaged" black family structures and, 10; and delinquency, 117, 121, 123; protective *vs.* proactive, 82, 103; and self-esteem, 36; and slavery, 13–14, 140–141
Social Justice Education Program, 46, 47
social mobility: blockage of, 133; and Nigrescence, 48–50
social movements, 145
social pathologies, 136
social stigma, 81
Society for the Psychological Study of Culture, Ethnicity and Race, 32
socioeconomic status (SES), 11, 12, 16–17, 99, 124–130
sociopathy, 51, 130, 131
Soul Machine (Makari), 134
The Souls of Black Folk (Du Bois), 40, 108
Southern Christian Leadership Conference (SCLC), 89
Southern Redeemers, 112, 135–136
The Sovereignty of Quiet: Beyond Resistance in Black Culture (Quashie), 40
Spencer, Margaret B., 58, 82, 98, 155
steady Eddies, 37
stereotypes: and "blacker-than-thou" mindset, 27; about black family, 11; in Cross Racial Identity Scale, 66; and deficit perspective, 114, 120–123; and double-consciousness, 81; and everyday living while black, 85–86; in identity-change models, 25t; and miseducation, 67
Stevenson, Howard, 82

stigma management, 81, 88, 103
Stolen Childhood: Slave Youth in Nineteenth-Century America (King), 139
Storer College, 151
Strauss, Linda Clark, 38, 98, 103
street-level drug trade, deindustrialization and, 97
street life, 49, 127, 135, 153
stress, race-related, 88
Strode, Woody, 116
superpredator trope, 121–123
survival, buffering as, 83–85
Swim, Janet, 71
systemic racism, 12, 48, 101

Tatum, Beverly D., 33, 96
Taylor, Cecil, 3
Taylor, Jerome, 23
Taylor, Major, 20–21, 153
Teaching for Diversity and Social Justice (Adams, Bell, and Griffin), 46
"Tenderly" (song), 98
Tenement Housing Law, 120
Tharpe, Keith, 122
Thomas, Charles: on existentialism, 22; on gender, 44; identity-change model of, 19, 23–24, 25t, 26t, 29t, 30t, 31; on transcendental capacity, 29–30, 47
Till, Emmett, 6, 27, 28, 130
Toomer, Jean, 153
trait analysis, 39
transcendental capacity, 30, 31
transcendental perspective, 24, 25, 55
transpersonal psychology, 14, 22, 55, 74, 75
trauma: slavery and, 144–145; and transpersonal psychology, 55
triggering event, 24, 25
TRIOS, 81, 88
Triple Quandary thesis, 81
Trump, Donald, 61
Tubman, Harriet, 37, 152
Tucker, Robert L., 153
Turner, James, 1–3, 7, 49, 94, 153
twoness, 77–78, 103
Tynes, Brendesha, 49, 153

underground economy, 127
unemployment, 126–127, 128
uniqueness, 97–98, 103
Unite the Right march, 131
uplift: W.E.B. Du Bois on, 99–100, 106, 108–109, 113–115, 119–120; one-generation, 114, 116, 147–150

vagrancy, 120
VA (Veterans Administration) home loans, 132–133
Vandiver, Beverly, 37, 38, 153
Vaughan, Dorothy, 96
Vaughan, Sarah, 96, 98
veil, self behind, 40, 78, 92–98, 100, 155
Veterans Administration (VA) home loans, 132–133
victim-blame analysis, 12
victimization process, 117
vigilance, 82, 87, 88, 89, 101–102
voting rights, 133
vulnerability thesis, 122–123

Walker, Madame C. J., 153
Wallace, Michele, 123
Wall of Respect mural, 2
Washington, Booker T., 11, 13, 138–139, 152

Washington, Kenny, 116
White, Walter, 91
white nationalism, 23
"white privilege," 130, 133
whites, effect of deindustrialization on, 65–66, 124–130
white supremacy, 115, 132
Wilson, Amos, 7
Wilson, Woodrow, 10
Withers, Bill, 98
Without Sanctuary: Lynching Photography in America (Allen), 131
"woke" state, 20, 21, 26, 32, 36, 41, 150
Woodard, Isaac, 27
World War II, returning black GIs after, 27–28
Worrell, Frank, 37
"worthy poor," 128–129
Wretched of the Earth (Fanon), 21
Wuthnow, Robert, 130

Yates, Frank, 3
Yip, Tiffany, 64, 71
youth, experience of slavery by, 139, 142–144

zones, ecologically distinct, 110–111, 113

WILLIAM E. CROSS JR. is Professor Emeritus of Higher Education and Counseling Psychology at the University of Denver and the author of *Shades of Black: Diversity in African American Identity* (Temple), coeditor of *Meaning-Making, Internalized Racism, and African American Identity*, and coauthor of *Dimensions of Blackness: Racial Identity and Political Beliefs*. He is the recipient of the 2020 Gold Medal Award for Life Achievement in the Applications of Psychology from the American Psychological Association.

www.ingramcontent.com/pod-product-compliance
Lightning Source LLC
Chambersburg PA
CBHW032025230426
43671CB00005B/202